THE SPECTACULAR GENERIC

CRITICAL GLOBAL HEALTH:
EVIDENCE, EFFICACY, ETHNOGRAPHY
A series edited by Vincanne Adams and João Biehl

THE SPECTACULAR GENERIC

CORI HAYDEN

Pharmaceuticals and the Simipolitical in Mexico

Duke University Press *Durham and London* 2023

© 2023 DUKE UNIVERSITY PRESS
All rights reserved
Printed in the United States of America on acid-free paper ∞
Designed by Aimee C. Harrison
Typeset in Untitled Serif and Helvetica Neue LT Std
by Westchester Publishing Services

Library of Congress Cataloging-in-Publication Data
Names: Hayden, Cori, [date] author.
Title: The spectacular generic : pharmaceuticals and the Simipolitical in Mexico / Cori Hayden.
Other titles: Critical global health.
Description: Durham : Duke University Press, 2023. | Series: Critical global health | Includes bibliographical references and index.
Identifiers: LCCN 2022033185 (print)
LCCN 2022033186 (ebook)
ISBN 9781478019046 (paperback)
ISBN 9781478016403 (hardcover)
ISBN 9781478023678 (ebook)
Subjects: LCSH: Medical policy—Mexico. | Generic drugs—Mexico. | Pharmaceutical industry—Political aspects—Mexico. | Public health—Economic aspects—Mexico. | Medical policy—Latin America.
Classification: LCC RA395.M6 H39 2023 (print) | LCC RA395.M6 (ebook) | DDC 362.10972—dc23/eng/20220802
LC record available at https://lccn.loc.gov/2022033185
LC ebook record available at https://lccn.loc.gov/2022033186

Cover art: Photograph by Gerardo Emmanuel García Rojas.

Contents

vii   PREFACE
ix   ACKNOWLEDGMENTS

1   INTRODUCTION. R_x for MX: Dr. Simi's Mexican Revolution

29   **1**   Same and Not the Same

71   **2**   Simipolitics: State and Not the State

106   **3**   No Patent, No Generic

144   **4**   Access, Excess

178   **5**   Supergeneric vs. Mere Commodity

197   CODA
201   NOTES
217   REFERENCES
237   INDEX

Preface

Whenever I say that I am writing a book about generic medicines, I get stories, affirmations, questions, and dispatches; friends, colleagues, strangers, and new acquaintances share their own pharmaceutical deliberations, experiences, and economic and bodily stresses. On the one hand, generic drugs can seem mundane, even banal; they are more notable for what they are not than for what they are. They are the "no-name" or unpronounceable versions of the ridiculously expensive Mucinex on the CVS pharmacy shelf. Perhaps a generic bupropion is the only version of the Wellbutrin your insurance company will cover, if you are lucky enough to have health insurance; perhaps you've recently bought a vat of generic ibuprofen at Costco. But of course even in these very middle-class, US-rooted registers, they are not so mundane. Their price, their sameness (or not?), and the routes through which they become available (or not) to you, to me, to a family member, to a population at large sit at the crucible of some very big matters, simultaneously intimate, political, and economic. Monopoly pricing on insulin due to a lack of generic competition in the United States is devastating people's lives. A friend tells me she would never take a generic version of her epilepsy medicine; the stakes are too high. Another wonders why US Americans are so weird: Why on earth would you line the pockets of a multinational pharmaceutical company when you could take generics instead? They're the same, but better! And certainly in the political economies of pharmaceutical access and inequality, generics play a key role: they have been at the center of storied histories of HIV/AIDS activism, global movements for access to essential medicines, and health justice. Perhaps, in fact, you are wondering what it will take for governments to convince Pfizer to waive its patent on the COVID-19 vaccine and allow other labs to make generic versions of it.

Generic medicines thus raise some very big, intimately lived questions—what I have just pointed to is already quite a lot. But the "we" and "you" in the sentences above also sit uneasily, for there is no generic experience of the consumption of drugs, nor is there anything undifferentiated about the (mal)distribution of medicines and health (which are, in turn, resolutely not the same thing) in this world. There is also, I have come to understand in the course of conducting the research underlying this book, nothing "generic" about what generic medicines are, the questions that they raise, and the ways they can come to reorganize or configure politics, markets, even "commodities" themselves. Generics are more than they seem.

I began thinking about and seeing generic medicines utterly anew around 2004, when they suddenly started flooding commercial pharmacies in Mexico City, where I had been working on other aspects of pharmaceutical politics for a number of years. As I quickly came to understand, generic drugs were not the same—not the same as I was used to assuming, not the same as each other, and not the same political-pharmaceutical objects everywhere. What has happened in Mexico over the last two decades, as this book will reveal, is important on its own terms. But it is also important because it is part of something larger; it expands our vocabularies and our understanding of what can happen when, as is the case in so many ways and in so many places, the elements that have underpinned an imagination of health care as social solidarity, however embattled and imperfect, come undone and are put together again, in ever-new arrangements. This book provides a deep dive into the way generics have exploded as a spectacular market and have rearranged pharmaceutical politics in Mexico. It is thus about the ways that pharmaceutical production and generic substitution can ground ever-shifting iterations of nationalism, populism, and a twenty-first-century politics of the copy. It is about the ways that cheap private consumption can both displace and reorganize the public provision of medicines and health care. For better and for worse, this deep dive might just help us see a future.

Acknowledgments

This book is the result of an extended period of research that began inchoately in 2004 in Mexico City, Mexico, and that ended in 2015, though I have continued to follow the trajectory of the people, events, and politics that grounded this work in the intervening years as I have put this book together. For reasons I'll explain below, I also took this investigation to Argentina in 2006. In Mexico, I worked primarily in Mexico City and Guadalajara, the latter a hub for the Mexican pharmaceutical industry and hence home to major generics laboratories as well as government-authorized, third-party laboratories that evaluate generic bioequivalence. Over summers and winters, on research trips lasting from two weeks to two months, I spent time with and interviewed a wide range of people with varying relationships to and with medicines and generics. Of course, the potency of this topic is that it is not a specialist concern. In my prior research, the qualities of medicinal plants was a topic that could easily generate hours of incidental conversation, and many of the people I met or whom I already knew ("there" as well as "here") have multiple relations to, feelings about, and experiences with the questions of health and illness, doctors, clinics, and medicines and their potency. Those conversations, both formal and informal, profoundly influenced my thinking and have dictated the shape of this research. Layered on top of and around those conversations, I spent time in generics laboratories in Mexico City and Guadalajara and in third-party testing labs. The pharmacy chain Farmacias Similares (Similar Pharmacies) became a major focal point of this book, and thus I spent a good deal of time in its pharmacies and in the company's Mexico City corporate headquarters. With the generous help of colleagues, friends, and long-standing interlocutors, I sought out pharmacists and physicians; the directors, pharmacologists, and chemists working for some of Mexico's major generics laboratories; pharmaceutical (name-brand and generic) trade association members and leaders in Mexico; academic research pharmacologists; regulators and consultants for the government; Farmacias Similares franchise owners and people who had opened their own smaller generics pharmacies; people who bought generics and those who refused to consider taking them; the "simi" (similar)-loyal and the simi-skeptical alike; the generics-friendly and the generics-curious.

The operations of Farmacias Similares were, in all of this, a key orienting device, though never my sole focus. They were certainly a crucial vector for taking this inquiry out of Mexico. Similares has (or has had) a presence across Latin America. But perhaps nowhere were the company's exploits more intriguing to me than in Argentina, home to an infamously powerful domestic drug industry which has held an important but not often discussed relationship to the changing global politics of protectionism and pharmaceutical globalization (Andrew Lakoff's work is a notable exception). While in Buenos Aires I interviewed pharmacists, government figures and researchers, pharmaceutical executives, public- and private-sector physicians, and would-be consumers of generic medicines, weighing their new options in a rather differently configured landscape of national and populist commitments to the domestic copy.

Throughout, I have accrued more debts to, and learned more from, far more people than I can adequately thank here. Throughout the book, I have given pseudonyms to most of my interlocutors; the primary exceptions are public officials and those whose published work I am citing. Further, given the sensitive nature of many of my conversations with pharmaceutical industry insiders and government officials, there are many people to whom I am indebted who have asked that I not print their names. Of those I can publicly thank, let me start by noting my deepest gratitude to the *incomparables* Laura Cházaro García, María Carranza Maxera, Alejandra Castañeda, Casey Walsh, Emiko Saldivar, and Carolina Sánchez Vázquez, whose friendship, brilliance, generosity, and knowledge helped me get this project started and who kept me thinking—and often, housed—throughout this project's many lives and in its many locales. Similarly, for the insights, support, orientations, and invitations to think together, I thank Carlos López Beltrán, Teresa Rójas Rabiela, Raquel Pêgo, Eduardo Quintanar, Vivette García, Eduardo Menéndez, Miruna Achim, Nuria Valverde, and Sandra Rosental. To generous colleagues at Maver, Kener, and the Cinasi labs in Guadalajara, thank you. For the gift of their time and thoughts on all manner of things generic and similar, I especially thank Beatriz Castañeda, Francisco Rosas, Juán Martín M., Juán

Pedro M., Sylvia, Jorge, Laura Trujillo, Hector Bolaños, Gustavo Zamora, Patricia Facci, María del Carmen Gutiérrez, and Jaime Tortoriello, as well as Jorge, Eulalia, Eva, Fabrice, Cármen, Tábatha, Hernan, Marú, Rodrigo, Ana María, Lalo, Diana, Gude, and Emma. For their generous introductions to and insights on pharmaceutical matters in Argentina, I am especially grateful to Andrew Lakoff, Daniel Maceira, Federico Tobar, Horacio Sívori, Carlos Forment, Sylvia Hersch, Patricia Saidón, Martín Nemirovsky, Graciela Jacob, and Mireille Abelín.

For the inspiration of their work, their insights on pieces of this project, and the pleasure of shared forums, I thank the members of the Oxidate collective (Lochlain Jain, Jake Kosek, Diane Nelson, Joe Dumit, Joe Masco, M. Murphy, Jackie Orr, Miriam Ticktin, Liz Roberts, and Jonathan Metzl), and Mario Biagioli, Maurice Cassier, Carlo Caduff, Lawrence Cohen, Ivan da Costa Marques, Tim Choy, Susan Craddock, Sophie Day, Zé de Abreu, Stefan Ecks, Jean-Paul Gaudillière, Cathy Gere, Julia Hornberger, Lilly Irani, Galen Joseph, Amy Kapczynski, James Leach, Lawrence Liang, Hélène Mialet, Celia Lury, Kenneth Shadlen, Kris Peterson, Mahdavi Sunder, Kaushik Sunder Rajan, Dominique Tobbell, and Nina Wakeford. Among the many forums where I have been fortunate to present the ever-developing elements of this book, I note with particular thanks the engagement of students and faculty in Mexico City at the Universidad Autónoma Metropolitana, at Cinvestav's Departments of Pharmacology and Scientific Theory and Method, and at UNAM's Instituto de Investigaciones Filosóficas. I thank faculty and graduate students at the Departments of Anthropology at the University of Aarhus, Chicago, Columbia, Edinburgh, California–Santa Cruz, and Harvard; the STS and science studies programs at UC Davis, UC San Diego, and Chicago, and the Workshop on Theory and History at the University of Toronto. For their research assistance and their insights, I thank Zahra Hayat, Valerie Black, Mondee Lu, Ksenia Korobkova, Chris Hebdon, and Mila Djordjevic. Thank you to Tom for keeping me sane and to Marc Stears for the encouragement and inspiration. For sending me down the rabbit hole and keeping me company there, my deepest thanks to Tim Choy and Jake Kosek. I am grateful to Ken Wissoker for his patience and encouragement, to Josh Tranen and Ryan Kendall for their help, and to the copyeditors and designers at Duke University Press for their hard work and thoughtful attention. For their close and indispensable readings of versions of this manuscript and for the encouragement to let it go, I thank the exceptionally thoughtful anonymous readers for Duke University Press, as well as Vincanne Adams, M. Murphy, Mark Essig,

Joseph Dumit, Donald Moore, and the magical, brilliant, and deeply missed Diane Nelson, who took me on a walk in the woods some years ago and showed me how to let this book go. Thank you, Diane.

And finally, to the utterly singular Lisa Conrad, wise and wonderful: you have known this book as long as you have known me. Thank you for sticking with us both.

Introduction

R_X FOR MX: DR. SIMI'S MEXICAN REVOLUTION

Everywhere one goes in Mexico today, it seems, the phrase "Lo mismo, pero más barato!" (The same, but cheaper!) calls out from the billboards and storefronts of the pharmacy chain Farmacias Similares (Similar Pharmacies). Ever since its debut in 1997, Similares has had an outsize presence in Mexico's public sphere. It debuted with great fanfare and no shortage of controversy precisely at the moment when the federal government began to allow generic medicines to be sold commercially for the first time. The enterprise's avuncular, cartoonish mascot Dr. Simi—an identity that its founder, Víctor González Torres, still assumes as his own—invited the popular classes and, certainly, middle-class consumers too into the pharmacy's first storefronts with the compelling promise of medicines that were "up to 75% cheaper!" than name-brand "original" drugs (see figures I.1 and I.2). It was a powerful claim in a context in which transnational drug firms, the proprietors of those leading-brand drugs, had dominion over more than 80 percent of Mexico's pharmaceutical market (Cruz 2002a; Cruz 2002b; González Amador 1997; Secretaría de Salud 2005, 24, 32). In fact, counter to many US Americans' long-standing experience of Mexico as a destination for buying cheap medicine, pharmaceuticals were not cheap at all for those living in Mexico and earning Mexican pesos in the 1990s. While nonbranded generic medicines were distributed within the public health system, one could not simply walk into a commercial pharmacy and pick an ibuprofen off the shelf instead of Advil, nor could a

I.1 Farmacias Similares' flagship pharmacy, Mexico City, 2005. PHOTO BY AUTHOR.

doctor send someone to the corner pharmacy with a prescription for a generic version of their hypertension medicine. For the tens of millions of Mexicans who were excluded from the public health system in the late 1990s, the licit option for buying medications was to purchase expensive brand-name drugs. The high cost of these drugs had, not surprisingly, become central to a looming, widespread "crisis" in access to medicines at the end of Mexico's twentieth century.

It was in this context that González Torres/Dr. Simi issued his generic rallying cry, "Defend your domestic economy!" Dr. Simi's early promise was indeed "liberation" of household and nation: the liberation of Mexicans from the chokehold of foreign drug companies and their high prices, and the liberation of off-patent generics (i.e., medicines no longer under exclusive patent protection) into a low-cost consumer market. Simi's inaugural challenge to Big Pharma generated plenty of attention, not least from those same transnational labs whose representatives in Mexico immediately—and with short-lived success—demanded the closure of González Torres's first eight outlets (Cruz 2002a). Transnational industry resistance proved futile, however. Generics quickly became a hyper-visible feature of popular commerce in Mexico, far beyond Simi's own virally expanding franchises.

I.2
Dr. Simi mascot,
Buenos Aires,
Argentina, 2006.
PHOTO BY
C. SHAYLOR.

As the first eight outlets quickly multiplied to thirty-five hundred throughout the country (Chu and García-Cuellar 2007), thousands more generics pharmacies sprouted up in Mexico alongside and in competition with Similares. The rapid rise of generics and their pharmacies has radically transformed the pharmaceutical itineraries of millions of people, making possible the novel prospect of consuming "health" in the form of cheap(er) copied medicines.

But this transformation has had implications far beyond the consumption of medicines. In the decade and a half following his debut in the generics market, González Torres/Dr. Simi became a force not only in the world of pharmaceuticals but also in politics. In fact, his operations have so thoroughly entangled these domains that I will call them *pharmapolitical* from here on.

A run for president of Mexico in 2006 (Dr. Simi, *candidato*, was a composite of man and mascot) was the least of it: the Similares enterprise has set in motion, and made dramatically visible, a number of unexpected turns in the pharmaceutical politics of access. Its operations have vividly shown how generic substitution becomes much more than a matter of simply replacing one drug with another (see also Gomart 2001; Lovell 2006).[1] Karl Marx, one of our most prominent theorists of the magical violence of "equivalence" under capitalism, would surely lead us to expect that the substitution of equivalents could generate some remarkable excess.

Some of that excess is categorical. From the start, Mexican consumers found themselves navigating a surfeit of equivalent generic copies as "generics," "interchangeables," and Dr. Simi's "similars" all tumbled into pharmacies at once. Competing not just with patented "originals" but with each other, these different kinds of generic drugs became, in the eyes and practices of consumers, doctors, entrepreneurs, and regulators, potent sites of distinction, enchantment, and stratification. And that wasn't all. Pharmaceuticals—the drugs, themselves—were only one locus of substitution and its excesses. In Dr. Simi's hands, the generic formula, "the same but . . . ," provided a syntax for some (un)canny simulations of deeply familiar, even cartoonishly recognizable, populist politics and tactics, from the attempted run for president to the mural adorning a central stairway in Similares' corporate headquarters (a Simi version of Diego Rivera's famous nationalist mural in Mexico's Palacio Nacional), and so much more. Dr. Simi's explicitly political imitations and interventions gave tangible shape, in turn, to a much larger pharmapolitical transformation in Mexico and beyond. Well past Dr. Simi, the rise of *los genéricos* has created an almost infrastructural market force in which generics and their similars do not solely compete with drugs made by "the transnationals." Rather, the commerce in generics has come to *copy*, and *compete with*, the Mexican state in delivering primary care and medication to millions of people.

Far from signaling the end of the question of access, then, the "liberation" of generics into Mexico's consumer market has generated new openings and some potent contradictions. This book asks how something as presumably prosaic as generic medicines could become such a spectacular site of commercial-pharmaceutical proliferation and political pageantry. It examines the implications of these proliferations for how we think about access to health care and medicines, the shape-shifting relationship between populism and the domestic copy, the tensions between private consumption and a public politics of health, and the precarious promise of generics as "mere" commodity drugs.

Though firmly rooted in the specificities of Mexico's contemporary pharmaceutical politics, the processes I track in this book are not, in any way, simply about Mexico. Dr. Simi, fittingly and vexingly enough, makes the point himself. With his commercial incursions across Latin America, including in Chile, Venezuela, Peru, Guatemala (aided by a short-lived association with Rigoberta Menchú), Costa Rica, and Argentina, Víctor González Torres has supplemented his Mexican pharma-populism with appeals to a Pan–Latin American struggle for affordable medicines, calling for a "Bolivarian revolution" in pharmaceuticals, with decidedly mixed success. One of the more intriguing targets of Simi's attempted expansion has been Argentina, home to a famously powerful domestic pharmaceutical industry, a distinctively nationalist and antipatent politics, and a complex history of populist commitments to the pharmaceutical copy. Thus, beginning with a story that unfolds in Mexico, the analysis to come travels briefly to Buenos Aires, where Dr. Simi's efforts to bring his brand of pharmaceutical liberation ran up against a radically different configuration of generic pharmapolitics. Building from Dr. Simi's trajectories in Mexico and Argentina, this book brings into view the many relations—from medicines, to "state" and "market," to equivalence itself—that are activated, doubled, and troubled through the politics of generic substitution.

Points of Departure

A Problem of Access: From Scarcity to Peculiar Abundance

To lay out the coordinates underpinning this analysis, let me first provide a brief account of the particular problem of access to which generic drugs became an answer in Mexico. The question of price is a driving force in this story of scarcity and its complex remedies. Farmacias Similares' claims ("up to 75% cheaper!") of course made the point explicit. But as decades of activism and critical work on public health and pharmaceutical politics have shown, a drug's price is always about more than itself (see Cassier and Correa 2007; Krikorian and Kapczynski 2010; Peterson 2014). As so many examples have made vividly clear—we need think only of current mobilizations around the prohibitively high price of insulin in the United States versus Canada—the tangled knot of access, affordability, and price is fundamentally a question of social contracts or, more specifically, of the institutional, political, and economic arrangements through which medicines and health care are allocated, sold, and otherwise distributed or kept out of reach (Rauhala 2019).

Mexico's late twentieth-century "crisis in access to medicines" was the result of serious transformations in the arrangements for mass health care that had prevailed for almost fifty years. Since the 1940s and 1950s, the dominant guarantors of health care and social security have been venerable public health institutions, the largest of which are the Instituto Mexicano del Seguro Social (IMSS; Mexican Institute of Social Security) and its counterpart for state employees, the Instituto de Seguridad y Servicios Sociales de los Trabajadores del Estado (ISSSTE; Institute for Social Security and Services for State Workers). There are also counterparts for members of the military and the state petroleum company Pemex. As is common in many guild-based social security arrangements the world over, these institutions imagine the citizen-beneficiary as holder of the "proper job" (Ferguson and Li 2018): they cover *only* the formally employed and their dependents. Though embattled and at times the targets of serious critique and discontent (Schwegler 2004), IMSS and ISSSTE remain central pillars in the landscape of health and social security in Mexico.[2]

But tying access to health and medicines to formal employment is a precarious bargain. Such an arrangement is especially poorly suited to the mass informalization of labor. By the end of Mexico's twentieth century, the category of the "formally employed" excluded roughly 55 to 59 percent of the population (Knaul et al. 2012). We are talking, then, about an estimated fifty to sixty million people who had no access to IMSS, ISSSTE, or its sibling programs (Knaul et al. 2012). And without access to medications in the public sector's pharmacies, many uninsured people had to turn to commercial pharmacies (for licit alternatives, at least), where drugs were exceedingly expensive for the "simple" reason that the transnational industry virtually owned the commercial market. In other words, there were only leading-brand patented drugs for purchase in private pharmacies.[3] Studies of the situation in the late 1990s and early 2000s showed the disproportionate amount of household spending swallowed up by out-of-pocket pharmaceutical costs for Mexico's poorest people, making pharmaceutical consumption one of many key threads in the story of late twentieth-century inequality in Mexico (Wirtz et al. 2012). To make matters worse, the already high prices on drugs for sale in pharmacies had increased dramatically between 1994 and 1997, the period marking Mexico's rocky entry into the North American Free Trade Agreement (NAFTA) and, not unrelated, the devastating peso devaluation of 1994. Given these conditions, many things started to unravel in the late 1990s—not least, the existing arrangement of pharmaceutical and health-care provision.

This crisis of access was thus a crisis of both state and market. And the approaches that have unfolded in Mexico over the first two decades of the twenty-first century have been *expansions* of both. This point is crucial to the emergence of Dr. Simi and to the recompositions that he has made spectacularly visible. It also makes the story of generic drugs in Mexico (and Argentina) an intriguing part of a broader conversation about the politics of neoliberalism and responses in Latin America in the first decades of the 2000s. As feminist theorist Verónica Gago (2014) has argued so eloquently, neither a strict notion of neoliberalism nor its presumed opposite, a populist "return of the state," adequately describes the forms of governance that emerged in much of Latin America immediately following the "immiserations" of the neoliberal 1990s. Gago argues that what characterized the notably left-leaning administrations of, for example, Lula in Brazil and the Kirchners in Argentina was a complex formation in which the state's "return" and expansion often took the financialized form of the market (1–28).[4] As I'll argue in chapter 3, indeed, the emergence of a generics market in Argentina in the early 2000s was seen by some on the left in nearly analogous terms: turning to the market principle of generic substitution (the same, but cheaper!), for some critics, did not amount to a progressive move to enhance access to medicines but rather belied the state's embrace of the free market to solve a major social problem.

In Mexico, the late twentieth-century Partido Nacional Revolucionario (PRI; Institutional Revolutionary Party) was (in)famous for its commitment to neoliberal market "openings" and "reforms." And unlike in Brazil and Argentina, Mexico's government in the early 2000s remained oriented to the right rather than to the left. Nonetheless, following the tenor of Gago's analysis, we can raise similar questions about what Tara Schwegler has so astutely chronicled as the hybrid, multivalent forms of neoliberal governance and economic rationalities that marked late 1990s and early 2000s Mexican governance (2008, 684; 2011, 133).[5] Here, I will argue that the emergence of the market for generic medicines, together with a spectacularly massive and rapid expansion of the health-care state, has raised some pointed questions about what might be considered state, what is market, and how we might tell them apart. It also gives us a view onto one of the many domains in which the scarcities of the late 1990s and early 2000s have redounded into peculiar, provisional, contradictory "abundances" (see also Garcia 2015).[6]

Let me start, then, with a note on what I mean by the expansion of a market in this context. The federal government's initial intervention into Mexico's problem of access was to double down on low-cost consumption as a key delivery mechanism for getting (licit) drugs into bodies. In 1997 and 1998, the administration of President Ernesto Zedillo set in motion two major interventions meant to clear the path for generic drugs to circulate in the commercial sphere. A prescription decree, effective January 1, 1998, required physicians to prescribe medicines by their active ingredient and not exclusively by brand name (e.g., "enalapril" rather than "Renitec"). This requirement is the very *condition of possibility for generic substitution*; it creates a demand for generics. The stakes in this simple act of renaming are incredibly high, not just in Mexico but in many contexts across the globe, including in the United States where the "right to substitute" has been the locus of hard-fought battles among regulators, physicians, insurance companies, pharmacists, and the innovator industry since the mid-twentieth century (Tobbell 2012; Greene 2014). In a 2004 interview in his offices at Universidad Autónoma Metropolitana (UAM; the Metropolitan Autonomous University) Unidad Iztapalapa, pharmacoeconomist Raúl Molina Salazar pointedly described the prescription decree's consequences: "When you get doctors to stop prescribing by brand name, you have already broken monopolies." In an ancillary move, Zedillo's secretary of health sought to guarantee a quality supply of generics by establishing new regulations that manufacturers long accustomed to selling their drugs to the public sector would have to meet to sell generic medicines in the commercial market. Generics were thus required to satisfy both the long-reigning standards of stability, safety, and good manufacturing practice *and* a new threshold of (bio)equivalence to the drug for which they would be a substitute.

During the following administration, a second expansion took place: that of the state. The administration of Vicente Fox, whose election in 2000 displaced the PRI from its seventy-one-year hold on the postrevolution institution of the presidency, undertook a major intervention in extending the reach of the state in matters of health. In 2003, Julio Frenk, Fox's secretary of health, launched the Seguro Popular, a now-famous experiment in providing "social insurance" for those who were otherwise excluded from the state's health apparatus (Frenk, Gómez-Dantés, and Knaul 2009). Just as generic drugs emerged as doubles (and trebles) of leading-brand medicines, this program was in many ways a double of IMSS—a modified version of the Seguro Social for those who did not have formal work. As I'll discuss in chapters 2 and 4, the Seguro Popular enrolled over fifty million people by 2012; it became a touchstone in the annals of global health, heralded, at least briefly, as a major success story in international efforts to convert mass lack of health insurance into universal coverage (Wirtz et al. 2012; Pueblita 2013; Bonilla-Chacín and Aguilera 2013; Martínez, Aguilera, and Chernichovsky 2009).

At stake in both of these developments—the creation of a generics market and the creation of the Seguro Popular—was the constitution of, and a scramble for, the uninsured (and the insured but underserved) as a market, population, and political constituency all at once. The results of these moves have been powerful, unsettled, and unsettling not only in political and pharmaceutical terms but also in epistemological terms. The elegant simplicity of the very principle of generic substitution—the same, but cheaper!—contains multitudes and has unleashed some confounding, potent multiplicities.

A Postpatent Recomposition

A meditation on generic multiplicity was not what I expected to write when I first began this project. As an anthropologist of science, technology, and medicine, I had been working in Mexico since the mid-1990s on some rather different dimensions of contemporary pharmaceutical politics—in particular, novel "sourcing" arrangements seeking to turn Indigenous and folk knowledge and medicinal plants into profitable pharmaceuticals (Hayden 2003). In the summers of 2004 and 2005, as I continued to spend time in Mexico City, I became intrigued by the rapid emergence and proliferation of generics and generics pharmacies; they were new and important and a growing topic of conversation everywhere I went. This project's roots thus lie partly in conversations I found myself having with just about everyone I knew (friends, colleagues) and quite a lot of people I didn't know (largely strangers with whom I was squashed into a *pesero* in Mexico City, lurching past yet another Farmacias Similares or a Farmacias de equivalentes) about these new drugs. Everyone, it seemed, was talking about them, trying them, refusing to try them, and weighing in on them, and so was I. What are they? Are they really the same? Aren't they? Such questions were not, so to speak, generic: they very quickly became impossible to disentangle from a widespread polarization or at least ambivalence about González Torres-as-Dr. Simi in particular. Are Similares really *lo mismo* (the same)? Is Simi for real? "He's doing something important for us!" Simi fans would tell me. "He's taking advantage of the poor!" skeptics charged.

But it would be disingenuous to say that generics simply demanded my attention, out of the blue. I was already looking for them, in a sense, and I was looking for them through a particular lens, guided by my abiding interest in how the expansion of intellectual property regimes in Latin America and beyond were changing how medicines, among many other things, could circulate. Did the sudden emergence of generic drugs in Mexico signal a resurgent politics of the public—the public domain, the public interest, public health, even a reassertion of the state—in the face of the expansion of patent regimes and the power of the multinational pharmaceutical industry (Hayden 2007)?

That my initial attention should be drawn in that direction, configured in such language, was a direct reflection of how the circuits of health, global pharmaceuticals, and intellectual property (IP) regimes were powerfully reorganized in the 1990s (Abbott 2005; Peterson 2014; Petryna, Lakoff, and Kleinman 2006; Sunder Rajan 2006). Liberalized trade agreements such as the North American Free Trade Agreement (NAFTA) and the World Trade Organization (WTO), and its Agreement on Trade-Related Aspects of Intellectual Property Rights (TRIPS), demanded ever-stronger pharmaceutical patent enforcement across the Global South, upending decades of protectionist and public health–oriented approaches to manufacturing and selling drugs in many countries (Shadlen 2007; Shadlen and Guennif 2011; van der Geest and Whyte 1998). Before the TRIPS provisions came into effect in the mid-1990s, many nations in the Global South claimed the "sovereign right" to exempt pharmaceuticals from patentability and thus to produce (or buy) copied versions of drugs still under patent elsewhere (Cassier and Correa 2013, 1).[7] The assertion of this "right to imitate," as Argentine trade negotiator Carlos Correa described it in the late 1990s, was based on the argument that medicines are central to public health (Correa 2000). In Argentina, for example, a dominant, self-described *copista* (copycat) drug industry has thrived since the 1960s, buttressed by the state's embrace of the principle that pharmaceuticals are a public good and thus should not be subject to patents in the first place (Katz and Burachik 2007).[8] The trade-driven expansion of patent regimes was explicitly meant to curtail this right to imitate by requiring that countries across the Global South grant twenty years of monopoly protection for new drugs before other (and usually cheaper) versions could be legally produced. These new patent regimes, meant to "open" and hence protect more markets for the transnational pharmaceutical industry, coincided with the emergence of the global HIV/AIDS epidemic, raising the stakes even further—drug patents and monopoly pricing vividly and urgently became matters of life and death (Biehl 2009; Nguyen 2010).[9]

The expansion of patent regimes and attendant structures of regulation and governance gave shape to one key understanding of the liberatory potential of generics on a globalized stage. That is, generic drugs—a materialization of the demand to the right to copy—became a site for complex reassertions of state sovereignty (including demands for public-health exceptions to patents) in the face of the multinational industry and trade-driven demands noted previously.[10] This scenario triggered my initial interest in generics as public politics. When the Mexican government set the conditions for millions of people to gain wider access to cheaper generic medicines, it did so in the thick of a range of high-profile, state-based, and treatment-activist-driven efforts to resist, seek exception to, or otherwise bend these new intellectual property regimes ever so slightly back in the favor of public health—from South Africa's struggle to stand against the Clinton-Gore administration over patents on frontline HIV/AIDS medicines, to India's success in delaying the implementation of TRIPS until 2005 (thus becoming a major provider of antiretrovirals to the Global South), to Brazil's vaunted (though not uncomplicated) program initiated in 1996 to guarantee universal access to HIV treatment.[11] In Mexico, HIV/AIDS activists were certainly making their own demands for treatment access but without much success beyond the left-leaning government of Mexico City, which was able to offer provisional programs for free and low-cost antiretrovirals in the early 2000s. But overall, as explained by Jaime Martínez, the director of an HIV/AIDS advocacy organization, HIV activists in Mexico had found themselves relying for the most part on compassionate access programs brokered directly with multinational firms themselves.[12] Mexico's generic politics were not going to be of much help where gaining access to frontline (still-patented) HIV/AIDS treatment was concerned.

Instead, those hoping for more accessible medicines in Mexico saw a much more prosaic copy politics take shape in their name—one premised simply on generic substitution for a wide range of medicines (analgesics, antibiotics, cough syrups, erectile dysfunction medicines) that had already gone off-patent. That move is, in turn, nothing more than a recognition of the bargain that is built into patent regimes in the first place: once a patent expires, the molecule in question reverts to the public domain, and the drug can legally be manufactured by other laboratories. Nevertheless, as I quickly came to understand, there was nothing remotely prosaic about what happened next. The pharmapolitical interventions, popular engagements, and explosions of commercial and entrepreneurial possibilities unfolding through this new market in the generic, the same, and the similar profoundly upended my vocabularies and assumptions about what a politics of generic substitution might be and what it might do. Thus, I have come to ask: What happens when generics are "liberated" not just from patents but into newly invented consumer markets? What are the coordinates and the analytics that might be adequate to address *this* pharmapolitics?

Mexico's commerce in generic medicines drops us right into what we might call a postpatent nexus[13]—that is, a successor problem space that has taken shape in the decades following the initial rollout of the TRIPS agreements, with their (and our) focus on IP regimes. We get some sense of what a postpatent analytic looks like in the work of my fellow travelers in the anthropology of pharmaceuticals, who have so astutely charted how the structure and tactics of the transnational industry have changed along with the expansion of patent regimes from the mid-1990s—changes that demand, perhaps, a change in analytics as well.[14] Thus, for example, the "financialization" of the industry and, with it, the imperative to increase shareholder value and returns on investment have worked hand in hand with those new IP regimes, sparking what some have called new forms of capital (Sunder Rajan 2006), value (Ecks 2021), and, in Joseph Dumit's (2012) analysis of the United States, new definitions of health itself. The centrality of clinical trials to companies' ability to continue to bring new drugs to high-cost and treatment-saturated markets like those of the United States has sparked the globalization of a clinical trial industry promising to deliver experimental subjects (Petryna 2009; Sunder Rajan 2017).[15] Adriana Petryna and Kaushik Sunder Rajan have in turn shown how this demand for experimental subjects (and, in Sunder Rajan's work, the demands of pharmaceutical capital more broadly) has profoundly molded regimes of state governance in India, central Europe, Latin America, and elsewhere. These observations give us one way to conceptualize a pharmapolitics, or what Sunder Rajan calls in his work in India *pharmocracy* (2017).

And we can certainly get a feel for what a postpatent problem space looks like in the range of tactics multinational laboratories use to protect their markets well beyond the use of patents. Many free-trade agreements now include "TRIPS-plus" provisions that extend data exclusivity protections, making it harder for generics companies to gain access to the information needed to copy an off-patent drug. Or we might consider the seemingly perverse calculus at work in drug companies' decisions to withdraw a particular medicine, or even all of their medicines, from specific countries or markets altogether rather than run the risk of having their medicines counterfeited, pirated, or reimported back into higher-priced markets (Banerjee 2017; Ecks

2008; Kapczynski 2009; Sunder Rajan 2011). Kristin Peterson (2014) calls such tactics efforts to secure "permanent monopoly" well beyond the deployment of patents per se.

What has happened in Mexico provides a very different view into pharmaceutical markets and their expansions after the patent. *This* postpatent nexus is one in which it is generic medicines (in their multiplicity) that are on the rise, globally, as major drivers of pharmaceutical market expansions in many countries, including Mexico and Brazil (Bourne Partners 2012). It is a nexus in which off-patent market exuberance and excess configure access and its many contradictions. It is a nexus in which pharmacies, often more than drug laboratories, articulate new kinds of distinction as value (see Ecks and Basu 2009). And it is one in which "potency"—economic, political, and pharmaceutical—lies not in the singular brand name but in the multiplier effects of copying. In Mexico, all this leads to a story in which generic medicines and their proliferations are neither an example of "state capture" by pharmaceutical interests nor a simple or rarefied return of the state or defense of the public interest. Rather, Mexico's generics nexus is a complex restaging of the promises of a state in the form of a consumer market.

What kind of pharmapolitics is this then? It is one, I will argue, in which the spectacular proliferations of generic medicines—the peculiar fecundity of this commercial, regulatory, and popular pharmaceutical field—reverberate in and as politics. Generic substitution is "political" here not just in the biopolitical sense that it concerns the state's management of the health of its population or in the sense that the governance of pharmaceutical markets and the provision of medicine and health care are produced in the maw of capital's demands. Rather, as I'll elaborate throughout this book, it is Simipolitical: it provides an entrée for engaging the spectacular excesses of generic substitution in simultaneously pharmacological and political form. In the remainder of this introduction, I will lay out the key elements of this argument, explaining what I mean by the spectacularly generic, first in pharmaceutical terms and then in closely related political terms.

Spectacularly Generic

A Generic Market Exuberance

The rise of *los genéricos* provides a window, first, into the peculiarly pharmaceutical proliferations that have been the hallmark of Mexico's approach to access—one that has sought to resolve the problem of mass lack, or scarcity, with a turn to the consumption of mass commodities. If, prior to 1998, there was nary a generic medicine in sight in Mexican commercial pharmacies, by the mid-2000s, the commercial sphere seemed nearly saturated with them. I do not mean *saturated* in the way that economists or even chemists use the term (i.e., to signal that maximum concentration has been reached—whether of a compound in a solution or a product in a market niche). To the contrary, I want to evoke a kind of brimming over that utterly defies this sense of limit. Generics pharmacies have brought people and pharmaceutical copies into ever-intensifying contact with each other as licensed, approved generic medications have exuberantly entered the circuits, practices, and price structures of everyday, street-level popular commerce, where they resolutely did not circulate before. While name-brand drugs for hypertension, for example, can (still) cost up to $300 pesos (US$30) for a month's supply, generic versions were suddenly available for the cost of a pirated DVD ($25 pesos, or roughly $2.50) or a lime popsicle or two ($10 pesos, or US$1), often in the same routes of popular commerce: on busy thoroughfares, in metro stations, and in *barrios populares* or working-class neighborhoods. If generics registered no measurable impact on the private market in 1998, by 2005 they had captured close to 12 percent, and they have continued to constitute the fastest-growing segment of the Mexican pharmaceutical market (Bourne Partners 2012).

Intimately entangled with this rapid growth have been the vivid excesses that new consumer markets seem so adept at generating (F. Schwartz 1996, 171). The brimmings over to which I refer are not just about numbers and market expansions. Another kind of copiousness—a confounding and generative categorical abundance—immediately captured my attention and that of just about everyone I know in Mexico. This scenario has become the driving force for one of the major interventions of this book, which takes seriously the pharmaceutical configuration of equivalence as a relation that is, we might say, *more than*. From 1998 to the present, Mexican consumers have been navigating a crowded field of copied, generic medicines, including chemically equivalent generics, bioequivalent interchangeable generics (popularly called *equivalentes* or sometimes *intercambiables*), and the perpetually vexing similars. Though not an official regulatory term in Mexico, similars have emerged as a durable popular classification, a designation associated with the medicines sold in Farmacias Similares: "I'm going to Simi, to buy a similar!" say the Simi loyal.

There will be much to say about, and through, this multiplication of generic kinds in the next chapters. Here, by way of introduction, I will simply note that this crowded catalog of generic kinds and their equivalencies is in part a reflection of how liberalized trade agreements help configure postpatent markets in generic medicines. That is, NAFTA and the WTO not only set the scope of patent protection, thus determining when other labs may legally start manufacturing an initially patented medicine. Demands by NAFTA and the WTO for "regulatory harmonization" have also required new thresholds for what will count as a good enough copy once drug patents have expired.[16] Thus, even when generics are produced legally in IP terms, their licitness can remain a major site of political, regulatory, and technical contest, registered in the highly charged idiom of quality as "equivalence."

As we will see in chapter 1, Mexico's particular jumble of generic kinds was partly an effect of these regulatory contests. In turn, for all of its peculiarities, Mexico is not unique. Over the last twenty years, commercial and popular idioms, shifting regulatory regimes, and trade-driven harmonizations have collided in countries across the Global South, generating myriad scenarios in which lo mismo (the [pharmaceutical] same) is nothing if not a field of proliferating difference. Consider what anthropologists Núria Homedes and Antonio Ugalde found in 2005 when they set out simply to compare new generic regulatory regimes across ten Latin American countries, including Peru, Ecuador, Argentina, Mexico, Chile, and Brazil. Their exercise was stymied by an utter lack of fungibility: the terms for sanctioned copied, equivalent drugs operating in these countries varied widely (*genéricos*, *copias*, *intercambiables*, and *similares*), and each term had different parameters or definitions. Eventually waving a flag of near-surrender, Homedes and Ugalde (2005, 66–67) noted the "high levels of confusion" among their expert informants: not only did the term *generic* have different meanings from country to country, but it also kept changing, "depending on the context."

Confusion certainly seems a reasonable term to use here. But I consider this riot of incommensurability an opening, an invitation to inquire into the generative pharmapolitics of "the same," from a fecund commercial field to a politics waged in the name and in the form of proliferating generic equivalencies. In other words, I am interested in far more than the familiar argument that "equivalence" is itself contingent, or that it is an illusory abstraction beneath which hides concrete variations, or that it is "made up" (as in, constructed) in the classic science studies sense. Rather, I am interested in the explicit mobilization of equivalence's variations and the ways that these proliferations are set in motion in Mexico as loci of distinction and, certainly, of value: an exuberance of the samenesses that matters.

Dr. Simi's own idioms (a colleague here in the United States insists I call them Simi-semiotics) set this more expansive opening in motion. Mexico's generics market teems with proliferating samenesss and similarities that are lo mismo—always with a difference. Commercial claims, riffs, and names in Mexico have brought Simi's copious formulas to life in dizzying ways. In the early 2000s, generics pharmacies began to reproduce fissiparously across Mexico City and the rest of the country, hiving off versions of themselves (as franchises, always same and different); versions of each other (such as the twin pharmacies, side by side near the Zona de Hospitales in Tlalpan, with identical signs and slogans: "Similares y Genéricos, Up to 75% Cheaper!"); and, most notably, versions of Similares. In the first decade of the 2000s, many pharmacy owners trying their hands in this new market cheerfully copied Simi's Farmacias Similares, calling their shops Farmacias de Genéricos y Similares, or Simylares, to such an extent that Víctor González Torres took to complaining about the "pirates" who plagued him. Competitors and imitators did not just borrow the *Similar* name; they also adorned their pharmacies with similar slogans, riffing off the original, "The same, but cheaper!" with slight isomeric modifications: "La misma sustancia pero más barato!" (The same substance but cheaper!), or "Es igual pero más económico!" (It's equal but more economical!). A Chinese medicine dispensary took things a bold quarter-turn further: "Lo mismo pero más poderoso!" (The same but more powerful!).

There is an extravagance to these idioms as they simultaneously animate and interrupt the market and pharmacological promise of equivalence itself. Generic sameness has become so heterogenous that, for most people I know who are navigating this commercial landscape, *interchangeables*, *generics*, *equivalents*, and *similars* have nearly become proper nouns—sites and sources of distinction in and for themselves.

The Pharmaceutical's Commodity Form

Such categorical extravagance is one of the reasons why I have invoked the idea of the spectacular in the title of this book. Genericness of course commonly points to the opposite of that which is spectacular or distinctive, excessive, hypervisible. That which is generic should, on the contrary, have little to do with such vivid excess; more to the point, genericness often serves as the undifferentiated ground against which such distinctions shine (see Hayden 2013). But post-Marxist theorists of capitalism and its excesses offer some useful insight here. For Guy Debord, Jean Baudrillard, and many others, the spectacular points to the overwhelming dominance of the modern (twentieth-century) world by commodification and its stratifications. More specifically, it refers to the saturation of the social with images, surface, signs, and brands (Debord 1994) and, further, as if calling forth an actor named Dr. Simi and his similar copycats, to a world thoroughly saturated by "copies without originals," in Baudrillard's well-known terms (Baudrillard 1994).[17] In this light, perhaps spectacular genericness is not so discordant. After all, generic drugs, in the contexts I am addressing here, are commodities in the common sense of "things" (i.e., relations) that circulate in the sphere of privatized exchange, mediated by the equivalencies of exchange. But even more importantly, as I'll explain, generic medicines are literally the *pharmaceutical's commodity form*—a relationship on which rests, no less, the promise of access to mass health in the specific and provisional form of market-mediated consumption of cheap(er) copied drugs. The generic proliferations and excesses that drive much of this book, from Dr. Simi and beyond, are anything but examples of specifically Mexican excess, or Latin American confusions, or Argentine unharmonious irregularities. Rather, they point to the constitutive peculiarities and precarious promise of generics as commodity drugs.

What does it mean to say, then, that generics are the pharmaceutical's commodity form? We often invoke the notion of commodification to signal that something of concrete use has become marketized (as in concerns over the commodification of life, or water, or knowledge) and hence brought into the sphere of generalized and privatized exchange, profit, and exploitation. But that is not quite what I mean here; after all, in the contexts in which I am immersed, arguing that pharmaceuticals are commodities in that sense is hardly an argument at all. Rather, the explosion of generics has brought my attention to the closely related, ancillary definition in which capitalist markets treat commodities as always potentially equivalent and interchangeable with each other, no matter what laboratory, factory, or farmer may have produced them.[18] We might think of terms like *commodity pork* (Blanchette 2020) or products in bulk. However improbably and however violently this idea erases the labor that produces commodities, a commodity is meant to materialize the very idea of interchangeability, or fungibility, regardless of its source of production.

This understanding of a commodity is essentially the World Health Organization's definition of generic drugs. The WHO defines a generic medicine as "a multisource pharmaceutical product [one that can be made by multiple laboratories] that is intended to be interchangeable with the comparator product"

(World Health Organization 2005). Like energy commodities (e.g., petroleum), generic multisource drugs are meant to circulate without reference to their specific context of production: it does not or should not matter which laboratory has produced them. When I say, with this point in view, that generics are the pharmaceutical's commodity form, I am not making an esoteric argument. The formulation is commonplace in industry circles, as when a biotechnology company executive notes offhandedly that, after a pharmaceutical's patent expires, "the product becomes a commodity" (Charles 2005) or when the United States is described as a "commodity generics market" in which "generic makers" are largely considered interchangeable with each other (Singer 2010).

Patent-holding pharmaceutical labs thus see the "becoming-commodity" of their products as a kind of minor abjection, a fall from branded uniqueness into the world of mere interchangeability (and generic competition). And as we'll see in chapter 5, this fall into mere commodification is something leading-brand producers often try to stave off for as long as possible, in ever more "inventive" ways. But I am suggesting here that the fact that generics are supposed to be interchangeable commodities in the first place is precisely why they might be spectacular in the sense that I have just described. There is nothing mere about them: commodities are nothing if not relations of excess, surplus, value, and hence stratification and inequality. In Mexico's generics market, and quite explicitly in Dr. Simi's hands, this broader argument has vividly and explicitly *become pharmaceutical*.

Gathering-To

The excesses of the pharmaceutical copy as commodity—the similar, the generic, that which is same and not the same, "simylar" pharmacies that copy Dr. Simi's Similares, a surfeit of generic incommensurability across Latin America—are certainly copious, and even confounding. If one of my interventions in this book is to take these proliferations seriously in their own right, I am, at the same time, also determined not to propel us off the copy-commodity cliff. Equivalents, copias, and similares do not go on and on of their own accord, as if driven by an autonomous logic of the commodity, much less as if we are living in a fully spectacularized world auto-populated by "copies without originals."

Rather, as I'll discuss in the following section, these many iterations of the equivalent generic are gathered to and through particular political histories, conditions of possibility, and even "aesthetics," cartoonish though they may be in some actors' hands. Hence a second reason for opening this book with an invocation of the spectacular: I am particularly intrigued by the ways that generic copied drugs, in Dr. Simi's hands, have been delivery vehicles for a vivid fusion of political and market forces; for some fascinating mass-mediated, as-if populist political pageantry; and for the simulation, we might say, of a "state," itself hardly a stable "original" in the first place. If I am interested in how pharmaceutical equivalencies multiply, becoming sites and sources of distinction themselves, Dr. Simi's spectacular political projects spark another follow-on question: How is a particular iteration of the political configured in and through this fecund pharmaceutical field of equivalents, interchangeability, and similarity?

For readers steeped in the histories and theories of populism and governance in Latin America, that question has likely posed itself already, at least in the form of an inescapable resonance. The concepts of interchangeability and equivalence, on the one hand, and their constitutive undoing or excess, on the other, have long been part of the fabric of conversations on postcolonial political formations in Latin America. Specifically, the questions I have just broached in pharmaceutical form are the questions scholars have long asked about the elusive promises of liberal citizenship—based on abstract principles of equivalence and interchangeability—emerging from the racialized caste orders of colonial Spanish rule (Sánchez 2016). The essayist and public intellectual Carlos Monsiváis wrote of early twentieth-century attempts in Mexico to represent and constitute a new "public" as *la ronda de seres intercambiables* (a series of interchangeable beings) (2000, 21).[19] Anthropologist Rafael Sánchez (2016) examines, in Venezuela, the Bolivarian postindependence project of eliciting a new political field, constituted in one of its forms as "a horizontal domain of abstract exchangeability among potentially autonomous, interchangeable individuals" (6). Just like the equivalence of the interchangeable generic drug, political idioms of formal equivalence have always anticipated, and even precipitated, their own vulnerability, queering, undoing, and excess. Sánchez in particular gives this excess a *similar* turn, tracing in gorgeous detail the oscillations in Venezuela between ruling elites' imaginations of a polity made of interchangeability and equivalence (as in the equality of citizens) and the potent crowd dynamics and populist politics that continually swamp formal equivalence with relentless "dispersions," manifold similarities, and "mimetic excess" (6).[20] In other words, steeped in theories of populism and the crowd, Sánchez paints a portrait of two hundred years of alternation and entanglement between ruling elites' appeals to the "same" and populist, crowded excesses of the "similar."

The resonance of these political idioms with Dr. Simi's commerce in interchangeables and their similars is one on which many colleagues with whom I've discussed this project have long remarked. It is not coincidental, of course. *Equivalence* and *interchangeability* are the defining terms of modern liberalism and individualism, nationalism (postcolonial and otherwise), and capitalism writ large; and the tensions between equivalence and difference, interchangeability and similarity's mimetic excess, lie at the heart of vast archives of work in postcolonial and anticolonial theory, crowd theory, philosophy and political theory, Black studies, anthropology, linguistics, psychoanalysis, and feminist and queer theory (among others). Here, I am trying to dwell in this tension *pharmaceutically* (Stengers 2009).[21] There is something (almost comically) overdetermined and yet singularly intriguing about Dr. Simi's interventions and the ways that they enliven these political-theoretical tensions between equivalence and similarity, interchangeability and mimetic excess. Dr. Simi activates this dynamic—he names it, potentializes it—in pharmapolitical form.

This is not transcendent philosophical territory: in the next section, I will preview some of the ways that Dr. Simi, under the banner of the same *and* the similar, uses the market in manifold equivalent medicines to *crowd*—to gather and elicit multitudes. The role of the copy here is central: copying belongs to the domain of generic pharmaceutical production certainly, and its excesses help animate the story to come, but it also belongs to theorizations and practices of populist politics. Indeed, in Dr. Simi's hands, the commerce in generics has become the engine of, and a mimetic model for, his Simiversion of a bygone populist state. In his pharmaceuticalized efforts to elicit "the Mexican people" as a market and a constituency, Víctor González Torres/Dr. Simi has made himself into a domestic copy of Mexican politics itself.

From Import Substitution Industrialization to Simi:
The Domestic Copy, Redux

The multifaceted Simi enterprise, which provides the scaffolding for the pharmapolitical projects undertaken by Víctor González Torres, points to several intimately related ways of considering the crowding of generic copies, well beyond their categorical proliferation. When González Torres first emerged in the commercial sphere in Mexico, his appeal to would-be consumers drew quite specifically on a storied and not-too-distant history of nationalist and popular invocations of the domestic copy, including his pointed pharmaceuticalized appeals to national sovereignty in the 1970s ("Defend your domestic economy!"). Across Latin America, notions of the similar, the substitute, the alternative, or the same with an important difference have long held as idioms of politics and as ways to hail "a people." They have worked this way in the broader scope of theories of populism, as I'll discuss in chapter 2, but also more concretely in the idioms of politics and mass access to commodities that defined the era of import substitution industrialization (ISI), the hallmark national development strategy that defined many Latin American states' economic policies from the 1930s to the 1960s (see Medina, da Costa Marques, and Holmes 2014). In Mexico, as in Argentina and Brazil (among other countries), ISI worked through targeted industrialization, protectionism, and efforts to encourage the consumption of domestically produced goods that would substitute for expensive foreign imports. These domestic substitutes ranged from manufactured goods (Argentine *electrodomésticos* ["home appliances"]), to natural-refined resources (Mexican petroleum), to "authentic" national-popular cultural forms (rancheras in Mexico or samba in Brazil). As a political ideology, ISI was meant to encourage popular buy-in or incorporation into the project of the nation-state through the consumption of that which is authentically *lo nuestro* (ours) (da Costa Marques 2004; García Canclini 1995, 2001; Yúdice 2001; Lomnitz 2001).

Much critical work on lo nuestro has focused on "culture" and the folkloric, but pharmaceutical production and drug costs have long been in the thick of these national(ist)-populist formations. In fact, there may be no more vivid instantiation of ISI's nexus of populism, nationalism, and the politics of the domestic substitute than the brief surge of state-driven pharmaceutical nationalism that unfolded under Mexican president Luis Echeverría from 1970 to 1976 (Soto Laveaga 2009, 2010; on Echeverría more broadly, see Kiddle and Muñoz 2010). At that time, 80 percent of the pharmaceutical market was held by foreign companies, as it was again in the late 1990s when Dr. Simi and generic drugs entered the scene. Echeverría's pharmaceutical interventions included all the hallmarks of corporatist national populism, including protectionist moves to jump-start a long-faltering domestic industry. He rescinded an existing pharmaceutical patent law and effectively nationalized the pharmaceutical industry, mandating that all companies within the country be at least 51 percent Mexican-owned (Sherwood 1991, 168–69). These moves were far from a triumph for, say, left-leaning anti-imperialism. As Gabriela Soto Laveaga (2010) has shown, Echeverría's appeals to pharmaceutical sovereignty were part of a pacification strategy—a tool in the Mexican state's own dirty war against left-leaning students, campesinos, and other "militants" in the early 1970s—as he specifically mobilized the domestic production of pharmaceuticals as a way to bring potentially disaffected "popular actors" into a national(ist) project and onto the side of the state.

If Echeverría's efforts to nationalize pharmaceutical production were deeply complex, they were also short lived; they were immediately reversed by the succeeding administration in 1980. Indeed, by the time Dr. Simi appeared in Mexico, state appeals to lo nuestro across Latin America were largely considered obsolete, felled by the trade regimes and neoliberal shifts that, by the late 1990s, had dismantled the protectionism undergirding the productive and consumptive infrastructures of import substitution (Lomnitz 1992). These moves—including the deregulation of the flow of capital, the privatization of state industries, and various forms of austerity—began well before NAFTA came into effect. Mexico underwent a brutal process of structural adjustment following the international debt crisis of 1982, and in the Southern Cone, many neoliberal and market-oriented openings were set in motion by the dictatorships of the 1970s and 1980s.

But in the wake of many decades of *aperturas* in Mexico led by the PRI, we might still ask to what extent the domestic copy or domestic production has fully ceased to organize formations of national-"ish" politics. Certainly the promise of nationalist domestic production writ large is alive again in Mexico today, under the presidency of Andrés Manuel López Obrador, who was elected in 2018 by promising a "transformation" of Mexican society. His pledge has been to return to the people that which is theirs and to reverse the damage that decades of neoliberalism and economic globalization has inflicted on the poor—a turn I will address at the end of this book.

From the moment of Farmacias Similares' emergence at the turn of the twenty-first century, Dr. Simi, too, was claiming to deliver on the broken promises of the PRI's one-party state, at precisely the moment when it—like the national popular—was thought to have run aground. Víctor González Torres was, indeed, busily using the commerce in copied pharmaceuticals to animate his own similar version of a populist state that would again care for "those who have the least." Much as early twenty-first-century political formations in Latin America have scrambled the coordinates of state-led populism, neoliberalized market interventions, and domestic production, Dr. Simi specifically and the generics market more broadly have been central to a recomposition of the elements of state and market, forged in and through a new politics of substitution.

Aperturas

The story of generic medicines has thus been thoroughly entangled in the better-known political trajectories of post ISI-contemporary Mexico, from NAFTA'S market liberalizations or *aperturas* (openings, a decidedly ambivalent term), to the short-lived fall (in 2000) of the long-ruling PRI, to the intensification of the devastating drug war that, since 2006, has killed over two hundred thousand people and has been responsible for nearly seventy thousand disappearances. It is common and not unwarranted to call contemporary Mexico a "drug state" (see Castañeda and Campos Garza 2009). While I do not want to trade in facile stereotypes, it is crucial to note that the generics market and the rise of *el narco* share some very concrete conditions of possibility.[22] Together they raise important questions about how the state can be simultaneously doubled, undercut, and recomposed by the force of contemporary drug markets and consumption (Garcia 2015).[23]

The rise of Dr. Simi took root precisely in a moment when the PRI had just lost its monopoly on power. This outcome was long in coming, but most proximately, it was the fallout of the Salinas de Gortari years, which ended on a brutal combined note: with Mexico's entry into NAFTA in 1994 came a debilitating peso devaluation (quite central to the inaccessibility and unaffordability of medicines prior to 1999), the violent suppression of the Zapatista rebellion in Chiapas, and Salinas's rapid departure from the country with a fortune in public funds. The "reforms" of Ernesto Zedillo's administration (1994–2000)—among them the effort to address high drug prices by ushering cheaper medicines into the commercial marketplace—were not enough to keep the PRI in power. With the election of Vicente Fox (the former CEO of Coca-Cola México), of the Right-leaning, Catholic-forward, business-friendly Partido Acción Nacional (PAN), the year 2000 marked the first time since the Mexican Revolution that a political party other than the PRI had held the presidency. Fox's term saw, among many other things, the rapid expansion of the generics market and the advent of the Seguro Popular.[24]

The events of the early 2000s raised the key question of who, or what, would "fill the space[s]" left by the PRI's exit, the opening of specific market sectors to private capital, and the changing scope and modalities of the corporatist state. In the early to mid-2000s, as Farmacias Similares and myriad other generics enterprises expanded across the country, Dr. Simi/González Torres made some rather spectacular claims to this opening by gathering to his name and to the sale of copied medicines just about every conceivable element of a recognizable Mexican political machine—its insides and its outsides ("civil society") as well.

As we'll see in detail in chapter 2, Víctor González Torres deployed a vast array of familiar performances of the Mexican state, from establishing "social assistance programs" for the marginalized to giving out basic goods at popular fiestas hosted in city squares. In 2003, Similares introduced its own short-lived health insurance program (the Sistema de Salud del Dr. Simi, or Simi Seguro for short) at precisely the same time that the federal government launched its new program, the Seguro Popular. By 2005, Dr. Simi was leading "anti-corruption" marches on the storied Paseo de la Reforma in Mexico City under the banner of his National Movement against Corruption (Movimiento Nacional contra la Corrupción; MNA). No longer targeting the "transnationals," González Torres managed to gather thousands of people in the streets of the capital as he declared an all-out "war" on corruption in the Seguro Social (IMSS)—precisely at a moment when the drug cartels were declaring war on the state. All of this, which I will discuss at greater length in chapter 2, constituted the buildup to Dr. Simi's attempted presidential run in 2006.

But the most significant of these Simipolitical formations emerged from González Torres's move to establish low-cost medical clinics adjacent to Similares pharmacy outlets. The effects of this model have been tremendously powerful, far exceeding the Simi enterprise itself. Generics pharmacies across the country, from major chains to tiny shops the size of a closet, now feature this clinic-pharmacy combination, offering low-cost walk-in primary-care consultations (usually twenty to thirty pesos, or US$2 to US$3) in working- and middle-class neighborhoods, on quiet streets and busy thoroughfares alike. The rise of generics in Mexico has thus not only brought low-cost copied drugs into the circuits of popular commerce; it has brought low-cost primary care into these circuits as well. An article in *El Economista* commented on the intensity of Simi's health-care presence: "In many locations, the saturation is such that [Similares] has managed to open two or three *consultorios* for each pharmacy; there are locales that have up to eight physicians attending patients simultaneously" (Coronel 2012). Indeed, by 2012, Dr. Simi's consultorios in particular had become the *second-leading providers of primary-care visits in Mexico*, behind only IMSS itself (Coronel 2012).

But what, precisely, is the relationship between these generics clinics and the public sector? Generics clinic-pharmacy combinations have certainly come to serve as an important resource for those who do not have access to IMSS and ISSSTE. But just as important, they have become a compelling substitute for many disaffected beneficiaries of IMSS and ISSSTE, unhappy with the state institutions' wait times, difficult-to-access physical locations, or their want of "care" in an affective sense. They are also, not incidentally, pulling business away from pricey private *consultas* (many public-sector physicians compensate for poor pay by opening their own private clinics where they work in the afternoons and evenings, charging anywhere from three hundred to one thousand pesos or more, per visit). In a (de)regulatory context in which just about anyone can open a pharmacy-clinic anywhere, the proliferation of generics pharmacies as founts of cheap medical attention has changed the calculus of access in multiple ways.

Thus medicines, private primary care, *and* the state all are becoming loci of substitution, sites for the proliferation of that which is the same but cheaper, the same and not the same. It is this activation that constitutes *Simipolitics*, a term that invites some creative thinking about how generic pharmaceutical multiplicities might help us conceptualize the shape and content of the political, specifically but not only where the provision of health and medicines is concerned (see Hayden 2013). In the new commerce in generics, the spectacularly pharmaceutical and the spectacularly political are intimately entwined. This book offers an analytic sensibility for understanding how the one redounds in the other.

Chapters

The following chapters start by dropping us directly into the proliferations that felt so distinctive, and so befuddling, to me and to so many of my interlocutors—consumers, regulators, physicians, commercial and political actors—as generic medicines became available in Mexico in the early 2000s. Chapter 1, "Same and Not the Same," tackles head-on the question of generic equivalence and its vivid multiplications in Mexico and beyond. Here, I take seriously the ways in which popular and commercial idioms, regulatory and trade demands, manufacturing practices, and pharmaceutical chemistry and pharmacology all multiply the ways that drugs are, in chemist Roald Hoffmann's felicitous phrase, simultaneously "same and not the same." This distinctly chemical formulation provides a conceptual architecture for rethinking the puzzle of generic equivalence and hence the pharmaceutical's commodity form, and it sets the terms for much of the analysis to follow.

Chapter 2, "Simipolitics: State and Not the State," explores how that which is same and not the same reverberates in Mexico's politics of health care and pharmaceutical provision as well as in theories and practices of populism more broadly. Introducing us more thoroughly to Víctor González Torres and his commercial avatar/identity Dr. Simi, this chapter elaborates two key Simipolitical dynamics. First, the chapter argues that the low-cost consumer market for generics doesn't just work as an atomizing force, set against the state as a locus of solidarity or care. In Dr. Simi's hands, the market in generics crowds; it gathers in the name of and with the similar, in the name of and *as if* the state. Second, and by extension, Simipolitics will help us understand how state and market are not stable, preexisting entities, locked in battle. Rather, just as the landscape of health care was being rearranged in Mexico, so, too, were the elements of state and market themselves rearranged or recomposed.

Chapter 3, "No Patent, No Generic," follows González Torres in his bumpy efforts to expand to Argentina shortly after the 2001 to 2002 economic crisis there. Exploring the ways that the powerful Argentine copycat drug industry has simultaneously pushed back against patents, dominated the domestic drug market, and aligned itself *against* a politics of generic substitution, this chapter traces the distinctive coordinates of the problem to which generics have been proposed as a solution. As such, it also questions the very meaning of a "generics market" as something that might be repeated across borders and nations. What room could there be for a Dr. Simi if, as I was told over and over again, generics actually do not exist in Argentina? Contemplating these differences generates another set of analytic recalibrations and hence a reorganized vocabulary for thinking about the relationship between originals and copies, the proper copy and its improper counterparts, the domestic copy and access, the state and the market.

Chapter 4, "Access, Excess," returns to Mexico and works as a companion or double to chapter 2. If "access is the magic word," as the head of Mexico's pharmaceutical regulatory agency announced in 2012, then a key question follows: To what, exactly, are people being granted access? Here, I ask how the commercial sphere of generics itself comes to multiply a range of recognizable state functions beyond the provision of medicines and primary care, including the discernment of drug quality, the clientelist distribution of employment, jobs and training for newly graduated doctors who cannot find work in the overtaxed Seguro Social, and the provision of "social security" in the form of work and modest doses of pharmaceutical capital for people opening generics pharmacies and for those who work in them. This chapter, then, traces the politics of Mexico's generics market beyond the question of consumption, placing these developments in broader dialogue within global health about the expanding role of low-cost, private pharmacies as an answer to overwhelming health burdens on individuals and on public health sectors.

Chapter 5, "Supergeneric vs. Mere Commodity," addresses the question posed to me by a frustrated interlocutor musing on a decade of generic complexity in Mexico: "Who's winning?" This chapter explores the prospect that the generic proliferations, multiplications, and uncertainties or confusions discussed in prior chapters are being treated by multinational drug labs as an opportunity to assert themselves in the very generics markets that were supposed to challenge their dominance in the first place. From the resurgence of "company-branded generics" (as in a generic escitalopram made by the Swiss multinational lab Sandoz) to the emergence of new categories of copied *biological* pharmaceuticals ("biosimilars," "biobetters," and more) in Mexico and globally, this chapter explores how genericness is both being undermined and mined for its auratic possibilities—not just by Dr. Simi (for example) but by leading-brand drug laboratories as well. The developments discussed in this chapter deliver us to a formation of postpatent generic exuberance that simultaneously repeats and flips on its head much of what we have seen throughout this book, as multinational companies, too, are turning generics into a site and source of distinction.

To understand what is happening today in multiple generic spheres—the global emergence of biosimilars, the rise of cheap consumption as a key pillar of "universal access" internationally, or the peculiar shape(s) of a twenty-first-century populist politics of the copy—we need to start with Simipolitical first principles. The next chapter sets us on that task, with a fundamental, though not foundational, question: *Serán lo mismo?* (Are they/aren't they the same?).

Same and Not the Same 1

The Puzzle of Equivalence

When generic medicines emerged in Mexican pharmacies for the first time in 1999 and 2000, the secretary of health tried to address, with some urgency, the question that so many people immediately attached to these drugs: *Serán lo mismo?* Are they really the same? *Aren't they? How can they be the same and be so much cheaper?* As sympathetic physicians described the challenge to me in the early 2000s, the success of the government's politics of pharmaceutical access, premised on creating a market for cheaper generic substitutes for leading-brand drugs, would rest firmly on the cultivation of a widespread "culture" of *genéricos*. In turn, that project would depend on convincing the consuming public, not to mention prescribing physicians, that generics were equivalent to their leading-brand counterparts. But how might a government agency do this in the face of enormous pressure from the transnational industry, members of which loudly denied the possibility of these new generics' equivalence while decrying a proliferation of *parecidos* (lookalikes) and "quack brands" (Salazar 2000)? In the face of resistance from many Mexican physicians who were not (yet) at all convinced? In light of the utter unfamiliarity of the generic as a kind of pharmaceutical?

In an initial attempt to counter these obstacles, the Office of the Secretary of Health launched a poster campaign that threaded the vital question

1.1 "What cures," lime popsicle public service poster campaign, secretary of health, Mexico City, 2005. PHOTO BY AUTHOR.

of generic equivalence through a reassuringly familiar object of popular consumption: the much-loved lime popsicle (*la paleta de limón*) (see figure 1.1).

In the now-infamous posters, three green popsicles were lined up next to each other, varying subtly in shape. Below the three popsicles were three unnamed pharmaceuticals, varying subtly in form (oblong pill, capsule, round tablet). The accompanying text offered an evocative rendering of the mechanisms of substitution, organized around the matter of like substance:

> y recuerda . . .
> Las tres saben bien, es por el limón.

> Las tres curan,
> es por la Substancia Activa
>
> And remember...
> The three [popsicles] taste good because of the lime.
> The three [pills] cure,
> because of the Active Substance.

At the bottom of the poster was a picture of a pyramid of powder. It was the chemical substance: *lo que cura* (that which cures) and that which makes substitution through equivalence possible.

Three outward forms, one single substance: the proposition was simple (even a bit overdetermined in a largely Catholic country), and it was powerful. The lime popsicle campaign asked would-be consumers to disregard the superficial trappings of look and feel, the aura of the brand, and instead *to remember* something they presumably already knew: the essence of a drug lies inside. Chemical matter—the substance that cures—offered the evocatively concrete promise of things made the same across the confounding forces of economic and class inequality, North-South axes of difference, the asymmetries produced by intellectual property regimes, and the seemingly endless marketing budgets of multinational "innovator" firms. The promise of equivalence makes generic medicines a locus for "postcolonial dreams of equity in an unequal world," to borrow Kris Peterson's evocative phrase (2014, 154).

That is a hefty burden for chemical compounds, and lime popsicles, to bear. And lo, the lime popsicle campaign did not exactly triumph as the last word on what generic equivalence is and how it works. Meant to clear up or counter early confusion and doubts about *that which cures*, the poster campaign instead became firmly part of the terrain of contest in Mexico's epic, early twenty-first-century pharmaceutical "war" over the definitions and potency of the same (Salazar 2000). Is it the "active substance" that cures? Is it the brand name? As the question was posed to me by a number of people who identified themselves with the demographic of *los que menos tienen* (those who have the least): Can "rich people's medicines" (leading-brand drugs) and "poor people's medicines" (cheaper generics) really be the same? Who can claim equivalence and on what grounds? Far from settling these matters, the lime popsicles, and the entire roiling market of generics to which they referred, fully activated the tensions and excesses at the heart of equivalence as a pharmaceutical relationship. There would be no easy reductions or materialities here.

Of course, far beyond the pharmacological questions at stake, we should not expect the matter of equivalence to be easily resolved. As Karl Marx argued—from his ruminations on linen and coats to his comparison of commodities to chemical compounds that may have the same constituent elements but different formulations (Marx 1978, 315)—the equivalence of things of a "like substance" (his phrase) cannot be as straightforward as we might, in these circumstances, dare hope. Aptly enough, in fact, Marx found in chemicals and in chemistry a wellspring of fruitful idioms and materials for thinking about the questions at the heart of capitalism's potent abstractions (Leslie 2005).[1] Even or especially in the form of chemical substance, that white powder piled at the bottom of the lime popsicle poster—the stuff of equivalence—is not intrinsic to "things-in-themselves." Marx reminded us that equivalence is what animates exchange value and thus enables the thingification of human labor—it is what lies at the heart of the violence and peculiarities of capitalism (see also Nelson 2015).[2] Of the many abstractions animating our contemporary lives, indeed, equivalence might just be the mother of them all (Stengers and Pignarre 2011, 53–54).

For these reasons, among many, I have found that it is difficult to pose questions about, or in the idiom of, equivalence without feeling unmoored or fearing that I am leaving my readers to "swim in abstractions" (Choy 2018). Such effects run counter to the very reasons I am interested in the question: from the moment generic medicines and the infamous Dr. Simi stepped into Mexico's pharmaceutical landscape, the promise and the puzzle of "lo mismo!," the *generic*, the *equivalent*, and the *interchangeable* became tangibly, vividly, and intimately enlivened, opened up for reflection, consumed and refused, and made tactile, even spectacularly so. I cannot get out of my head, for example, the ways that Dr. Simi (or, rather, versions of him) became a target of more than just the transnationals. In the early to mid-2000s, teenage boys took to filming their friends running down the street, tackling one of the legions of dancing, costumed Dr. Simi mascots gyrating in front of Farmacias Similares storefronts, and posting the footage on YouTube under their newly created genre "Tumbando Dr. Simi" ("Taking out Dr. Simi").[3] In so many ways, lo mismo was not a far-off technical matter, nor one left to regulators in the cordoned-off halls of government. It was within reach; it was sticky, like a lime popsicle. But equivalence wasn't just tactile, specific, or concrete. It was, as we'll see, multiple and meaningfully, materially so. The story to come, then, is not a matter of equivalence's (de-)mystification but of its multiplication.

To explore how generic equivalence has multiplied, in some nonreductively pharmaceutical, even "chemical," ways, I am going to launch headlong into the specifically generic question: Are they really the same? I am taking this question on in part because it matters, for nonarbitrary reasons, to just about everyone (including consumers, regulators, pharmaceutical chemists, generics manufacturers, and physicians) with whom I engaged in the course of my research. I have my own experiences and hunches about this drug or that one, this generic or that brand name; you probably do as well. But there is another reason to tackle this question, beyond wanting and even needing to know the answer. All that has happened in Mexico with the rise of generic medicines suggests to me that we might just need to *recompose* that question, and with it the puzzle of equivalence.

As I noted in the introduction, *equivalence* is the operative relation in the regulation, definition, and quality of generic medicines in Mexico, in the United States, and in many spheres of production and circulation. It is this fact that leads me to argue that generics are, in a particular sense, the pharmaceutical's commodity form: they are meant to be fungible, or interchangeable. They are not unique because they are not distinguishable by their source. But if generics are "commodity drugs" in that sense, we must also note that medicines—so closely tied to matters of health, and life, and illness, and death—are not just any commodity. The stakes are particularly high for ensuring their quality: If generics' equivalence (to the drug for which they will be substituted) is a proxy for generics' quality, how could we *not* insist that regulators and manufacturers demonstrate their sameness? The specter of the diminished copy hovers directly over this question, its burden of proof, and the force of the *really* in "are they really the same?"[4]

When generics were introduced in Mexico, the transnational pharmaceutical industry's trade association in Mexico (CANIFARMA) wasted no time eliciting exactly such fears of the diminished copy. The group sponsored a cheeky ad campaign in the early 2000s that directly targeted the earliest and loudest entrants into this new market, the pharmacy chain Farmacias Similares, asking, "Do you feel better? Or do you feel *Similar*?"[5] From exposés in the US press over the poor quality of generic medicines made in China or India to the problem of substandard or adulterated medicines circulating in Nigeria (Peterson 2014), such concerns routinely constitute generic equivalence, in its transnational iterations, as a particular kind of regulatory and epistemological question.[6] Either a generic is the same as the original and thus it is good—equivalent, adequate—or it is not the same, and so it is less than, a diminished copy, inadequate.[7] Not surprisingly, given all that is at stake in generic substitution, dueling claims about generics' equivalence (or lack thereof) have long been a global battleground and even a geopolitics.

But, what if, in engaging the question and its platonic burden this way, we are trying to solve the wrong puzzle? While the debates over generics in Mexico have persistently raised the question of sameness, they have also substantially transformed it. From Dr. Simi's capacious rhetorical moves, to the regulatory categories allowing different kinds of generics to circulate side by side, to consumers' everyday commensurations, lo mismo (the same) has become far more than an either/or proposition. It has emerged as a both/and multiplication: a proliferation of relations that are, to borrow a phrase from chemist Roald Hoffmann (1995), simultaneously *same and not the same*. Hoffmann's formula captures the spirit of a broader set of interventions by chemists, philosophers, feminist theorists, and science studies scholars for whom chemistry and chemicals are anything but the reductive ground that could, for example, anchor or resolve ambiguities, not to mention questions of equivalence (see Agard-Jones 2013; Barry 2005; Bensaude-Vincent and Stengers 1996; Murphy 2017).[8] As so much of this work shows, chemical compounds are not even *self*-identical. They, themselves, are abstractions, moments in time; they shape-shift and take on different forms depending on the context. A water molecule is one of eighteen different isotopic forms of H_2O. A therapeutic compound—say, a fluoxetine, a thalidomide, or an enalapril—can take "handed," or "chiral," forms in the way that your left hand and right hand are the same but not interchangeable. As was the case with thalidomide, this chirality can matter significantly and even catastrophically to a drug's biological effects in bodies (Hoffmann 1995, 26–43). Versions of the same antiretroviral compound synthesized using different pathways can end up configured differently, such that they bind differently to target receptors (Cassier and Correa 2007). The "substances that cure," in other words, are always already versions of themselves.

Confounding the idioms that might plausibly organize questions about generic medicines (original versus copy; sameness versus difference), "same and not the same" produces another itinerary through the question of equivalencies, plural. Same and not the same vividly evokes for me the ways that regulators, would-be consumers, generics merchants, entrepreneurs, and chemists working in Mexican generics labs have all articulated and set in motion the proliferating possibilities opened up by the substitution of pharmaceutical equivalents. These dynamics are at work in the multiplier effects of marketing and commercial idioms and the way "consumers"—people who buy and take these medicines—make their own samenesses that matter. They are also at work within the very domains we might expect to stabilize the meaning of pharmaceutical equivalence, including the government ministries charged with pharmaceutical regulation, the scientific practices involved in such regulation, and the manufacturing protocols that purport to ensure some version of equivalence. Together, these practices are busily recomposing equivalence as a relation and, with it, the pharmaceutical's commodity form.

In this chapter, I begin my analysis of Mexico's twenty-first-century pharmaceutical politics by immersing us in the questions that so vividly defined the generics market in its early days and that captured so many people's imaginations, doubts, and hopes. The first section describes how federal regulations effective in 1998 created this new pharmaceutical playing field—setting the terms of contest for the next decade and half at least—and tracks how the equivalencies set in motion in the regulatory domain reverberated and further multiplied in commercial and popular practices. In the second section, I will loop back, briefly, to locate this regulatory story in a broader, international trajectory. The heterogeneities that make "the generics question" so complex in Mexico are not at all specific or internal to Mexico. Rather, they point to the multiplier effects of harmonization more broadly. Third, and finally, we will see that these generic multiplicities are, in turn, far more than the effects of commercial exuberance or regulatory unharmony. A closer look at the practices of manufacturing, equivalence testing, and quality control in mass production shows how sameness—even the sameness of originals to themselves—continues to multiply with distinction and meaningful difference.

Section 1: Mexico's Generic Multiplicities—
Regulation and Commerce

As we saw in the introduction, the mere fact of being able to walk into a commercial pharmacy to buy a generic hypertension medicine (for example) was an altogether novel prospect at the turn of Mexico's twenty-first century. From the late 1940s to 1998, licit pharmaceuticals in Mexico had circulated in two largely disconnected spheres. Generic medicines (that is, off-patent copies of "original" medicines) were among the drugs distributed in the public sector as part of the approved formulary. But in private pharmacies, expensive, leading-brand drugs were the only medicines available for sale. When that arrangement began to fall short as a means of providing mass access to medicines, particularly in light of the widespread informalization of labor, the federal government turned to generics as a new force of market competition. President Ernesto Zedillo's efforts to create a private market for generic medicines beginning in 1998 thus meant, in the first instance, creating the conditions for the medicines that Mexican generics labs had long produced for the public sector (colloquially known not as "generics" but rather as the "drugs the *Seguro* gives you") to be placed into circulation in private pharmacies across the country. This redirection—same drugs, different channels of distribution—is our first key to understanding the puzzle of equivalence and its recompositions.

The novel legislative changes ushering generic drugs into commercial pharmacies effectively made room for two competing kinds of generic copies: generics and "interchangeable generics." The difference between them resided (and still resides) in the thresholds of equivalence that they were and are meant to meet. "Regular" *genéricos* in Mexico referred to those drugs whose sameness was based on chemical equivalence: the premise that two hundred milligrams of ibuprofen equal two hundred milligrams of ibuprofen, whether the tablet claims a brand name or simply the name of the active compound, and whether it is made in Mexico or India or Switzerland or the United States. Paired with the basic requirements of good manufacturing practice (GMP), chemical equivalence had been the standard required for copied drugs distributed through Mexico's public-sector health institutions from the 1950s to the late 1990s (see Dirección General de Normas 1998a). These public-sector institutions were, in turn, the primary buyers for domestically made copied pharmaceuticals until 1998. The lime popsicle campaign was a vivid articulation of this regime of equivalence, with its focus on the active compound—the chemical substance—as the coin of equivalence, the substance that cures.

Simultaneously, the emergence of the private-sector generics market in Mexico in the late 1990s saw the introduction of a second and arguably higher threshold, *bioequivalence* (Dirección General de Normas 1998b). This threshold has been required for generics approved in the United States, Europe, and Canada since the 1970s, though its parameters have not always been the same across this Global North. Since the mid-1990s, bioequivalence has been ascendant, globally, through the politics of regulatory and trade harmonization; it has thus been bundled into multilateral and bilateral trade agreements, including NAFTA and the agreements overseen by the WTO (Zahl 2016; Steinijans and Hauschke 1993). The bioequivalent generic is now a new kind of copy in Mexico as well as in Argentina, Brazil, India, and other circuits of liberalized trade and pharmaceutical regulation. For the moment, we can just say that bioequivalence indicates that the drugs being compared are absorbed into the bloodstream of human subjects at a similar rate and at similar concentrations. Under a regime of bioequivalence, chemical equivalence is not (good) enough: the sameness of two drugs must also be triangulated through a brief encounter with biological bodies.

Effectively acknowledging the coexistence of these two thresholds of equivalence, the Mexican regulatory state invented the insignia GI, for *genérico intercambiable* (interchangeable generic), to adorn the packaging of drugs approved as bioequivalent. There was a complex set of naming conventions that emerged with generics then. Leading-brand "originals" had brand names (e.g., Advil), but so did "regular" generics—those approved for sale as chemical equivalents, such as "Bestafen" (Laboratorios Best's own-brand ibuprofen). But a bioequivalent, interchangeable generic was marketed only with the name of the active substance, coupled with the GI insignia, as in "ibuprofeno GI." The designation GI is unique to Mexico, and it is meant to signal that the medicine is a "true" generic, a true commodity drug. These GIs often were and remain more expensive than medicines approved as (merely) chemically equivalent—closer to 30 percent lower than the prices commanded by leading-brand drugs.

From the beginning, then, Mexican consumers were introduced to a new category of medicine—the generic—that was already multiple. Two different kinds of generics corresponding to different kinds of equivalence circulated alongside each other, same and not the same. Generics had emerged in the market not just as doubles of original drugs but as doubled themselves.

Meanwhile, the federal government was not the only entity helping make and proliferate generic copied kinds. As if the state's generics and interchangeable generics were not confounding enough, there was Dr. Simi and there were his "similars." Víctor González Torres, proprietor of Farmacias Similares, leapt into this new market precisely by activating the many promises, tensions, and excesses at the heart of equivalence. He did so as a pharmacy entrepreneur but also, not incidentally, as owner of the González Torres family's generics laboratory Laboratorios Best. Like most other established generics labs in Mexico, Laboratorios Best had, until 1998, sold its medicines primarily to the Seguro Social and thus had long produced chemically equivalent copies, the sameness of which was so nicely illustrated by the secretary of health's lime popsicles. While Similares' slogan "The same but cheaper!" laid unambiguous claim to the new promise of generic substitution, their Simi-semiotics—from the pharmacy name, to Dr. Simi himself, to the drugs they initially called *similares*—reminded us of something else that we might already suspect: perhaps equivalence is a difference machine.

If *genéricos* are copies that have been approved as chemically equivalent, and GIs are copies that have been approved as bioequivalent, what then are similares? To the Simi-loyal and to Simi-critics alike, not to mention countless domestic industry experts and transnational business intelligence analysts, similars are an important but slippery pharmaceutical kind in Mexico. Elsewhere—including in Brazil, one of Latin America's pharmaceutical powerhouses—the *similar* has occupied its own official regulatory niche amid copied pharmaceuticals (see Sanabria 2014).[9] In Mexico, the term has a different biography. It is not an official regulatory term, but it exists nonetheless, having become uniquely and enduringly associated with drugs sold by the chain bearing the Similares name: *the* Farmacias Similares, not to be confused with legions of copycat pharmacies calling themselves similares or *simylares*. Thus, even though one could argue (following Simi's own arguments) that the chain mostly sells regular and interchangeable generics, just like other pharmacies selling licensed copied drugs in Mexico, many people—critics and the Simi-loyal alike—insist that what you buy in Simi's pharmacies are actually similares—as in, "I'm going to Simi to buy a similar." Such a declaration stands in pointed contrast to what many of my interlocutors would tell me about going to any other kind of generics pharmacy: "I'm going to the *genéricos* to buy a *genérico*."

There is nothing necessarily "mere" about the *similar* designation, nor is it a vernacular mistake. The Simi enterprise invested in exactly this popular kind-making from the start, with early publicity enjoining potential customers: "Ask your doctor to prescribe the less expensive brand, known popularly as *similares*." The auratic magnetism of Similares (the subject of the following chapter) proved compelling enough that the term in fact became firmly attached to the drugs the chain sells.

But this magnetic attachment quickly became a force that the enterprise tried to disavow, a twist that only adds to the classificatory thicket here. Faced with a growing sense of a possible gap between the "truly [bio]equivalent" and the "merely similar," the company's associates turned around and began to try, without much success, to delink the Similares franchise brand from

1.2 "We sell Generics. We are called Similares," banner in Farmacias Similares, Mexico City, 2013. PHOTO BY AUTHOR.

the drugs they sell. Hence, Simi's own employees, from cashiers to vice presidents, began to remind us as often and loudly as possible that there is actually no such thing in Mexican regulation as a similar. The young people working the counters still try, over and over again, to retrain their dedicated clientele: "No, no, no. We don't sell similars! Similars don't exist! They're generic medicines!" Meanwhile, a Similares franchisee whom I know and with whom I discussed this scenario at length in 2008 stood by the concept of similars as something different than generics, by which she meant interchangeable generics. "They *are* similars," she countered. "It's not true that they aren't!"[10]

This more-than-confusing scenario led one physician I interviewed early on to conclude triumphantly (and prematurely, it turned out) that Similares had "hung themselves with their own rope!"[11] A year prior, doctor Mónica Aguirre, the chief chemist of González Torres's own Laboratorios Best, conveyed to me in a lengthy conversation at the enterprise's headquarters her exasperation with the situation and with "everyone's" misrecognitions: "Todos dicen que vendemos medicamentos similares. No es cierto! Son medicamentos de marca, fabricados por laboratorios nacionales!" (Now everyone says we sell *medicamentos similares*. It's not true! They're branded medicines [chemically equivalent generics, adorned with the pharmacy's own-brand names], made by national [Mexican] laboratories!)."[12] A poster hanging in a Farmacias Similares in the south of Mexico City almost a decade later, in 2013, was still gamely trying to make the point: "We sell Generics. We are called Similares" (see figure 1.2).

SAME AND NOT THE SAME   39

One slightly flummoxed industry analyst in these early days tried to parse the situation for the US Department of Commerce: "Particular to Mexico is a third market of generic pharmaceuticals (in addition to "nonbioequivalent" generics and GIs).... SIMILARES are neither lawful nor unlawful, [*sic*] they somehow pertain to an ambiguous area in the Mexican legislation. The quality of SIMILARES is subject to compliance with the good manufacturing practices applicable to any pharmaceutical industry, but their interchangeability and dissolution profile are not. This situation has created confusion not only among consumers but also among producers."[13] Similares' seeming unclassifiability is captured beautifully here. The term—like the enterprise itself, as we will see in the next chapter—has a potency and a capacity to be everything and no-thing, "neither lawful nor unlawful," tremendously popular (and *popular*) yet nonexistent, something that bewilders drug consumers and drug producers alike. What this analyst did not say is that his description of similares lines up rather nicely with the characteristics of ("regular") generics and hence with the drugs long produced for, and distributed by, the public sector—that is, approved drugs that simply have not been subject to bioequivalence testing (the threshold indicated by his reference to interchangeability and dissolution). With this omission, he quietly confirmed the power of commerce and distribution outlets to exceed the official categories of pharmaceutical regulation, such that Similares are credited/blamed with the creation of their own "third market."

Dr. Simi's capacity to simultaneously inhabit, extend, and confound Mexico's regulatory and official categories brings to light just how important the commercial sphere has been to the proliferation of generic equivalencies in Mexico. This lively relationship between regulatory and commercial multiplicity lies at the heart of generics' spectacular exuberance as I am proposing it in this book: it shows us how generics can become potent sites and sources of distinction, of marketing coups, and of proliferations of names, signs, and kinds. In this relationship, we start to see the multiplication of genericness as a more-than-mere-commodity form.

Distinctively Similar

The commercial sphere—the street-level, hypervisibility of pharmacies selling these many kinds of copies—was a crucial engine for equivalencies' multiplications and stratifications. To make sense of this point, it is worth noting how and where consumers began to encounter generics, interchangeables, and similars. It is not the case that these drugs primarily began to show up in existing pharmacies, sitting on shelves right next to leading-brand, over-the-counter drugs. To the contrary, many already existing, smaller private pharmacies—the kinds that sell perfume, stationery, and *medicinas de patente* (patented, leading-brand drugs)—as well as tony chains such as Sanborn's, did not (and still do not) stock generics. Instead, Mexico's rather capacious regulatory and zoning regime (see chapters 2 and 4) enabled a new species of pharmacy to proliferate specifically as a delivery vehicle for these new medicines. Thus emerged, at the beginning of the twenty-first century, thousands of new pharmacies dedicated to selling generics and their similars. Among them were chains such as Farmacias Similares; its chief competitor Farmacias del Ahorro (Discount Pharmacies), run by Víctor Gonzalez Torres's brother; and other powerhouses such as Farmacias San Pablo and Farmacias el Fénix. So, too, emerged a vast number of smaller, one-off kiosks started by retirees, taxi drivers, and first-time shop owners, also selling only generics, interchangeables, similar, or a combination. The consumer practice of choosing a generic over a leading-brand drug, and even of opting for an interchangeable rather than a similar, was often made simply by the act of walking into *this* pharmacy rather than *that* one.

Thus, if Mexican regulatory categories had produced a substrate of generic multiplicity, it was pharmacy chains, pharmacy names, and pharmacy claims that brought this multiplicity and its stratifications to life. They did so through a potent commercial idiom that turned pharmaceutical sameness, equivalence, and interchangeability into almost-proper nouns. These terms were not "different" names for the same thing; rather, they announced and helped materialize specific, distinctive equivalencies. From the emergence of a new pharmacy chain called, quite simply (and boldly), Genéricos Intercambiables to a host of smaller kiosks calling themselves Farmaciás de genericos, the regulatory fecundity of equivalent kinds found a potent match in the ways that consumer markets themselves can be such effective engines for producing equivalence as a relation that is more than.

Dr. Simi's own formulations quite powerfully activated such multiplicities, as rivals tried to match the success of Simi's Farmacias Similares by opening copycat stores (called, for example, *Simylares* or *similares*) (see figure 1.3) and by working variations on the "same but cheaper" theme, from "It's equal but more economical!" to "The same substance but much cheaper!" The iterations continued to spin, as we might expect of such a perfectly "generic" slogan. Simi's idiom quickly traveled outside of the terrain of medicines altogether; for example, in 2008, a construction company outside of Cuernavaca,

1.3 A non-"Similares" generics pharmacy, Mexico City, 2008. PHOTO BY AUTHOR.

roughly 50 kilometers (30 miles) south of Mexico City, claimed to be the "Similares de construcción: lo mismo pero más barato!" ("The Similars of construction: the same but cheaper!"). The Spanish filmmaker Jota Izquierdo, who has made an intriguing documentary about Tepito (Mexico City's famous black market), focusing on Mexican vendors' relationships with, and travels to, China, has his own business cards adorned with the slogan "Lo mismo pero más barato."[14] The Bank IXE ran a billboard in 2014 with this provocation: "Discover why we say IXE is the same [*lo mismo*], but it's not equal."[15] Make no mistake: Dr. Simi is the reference point for these iterations, within and beyond the sphere of pharmaceuticals. They point and wink and nod at him, demonstrating, with every repetition, just how powerfully González Torres has magnetized himself both to the generic principle of market competition and to the generative potential of slippage, difference, and excess therein.

Of course, mass marketing has been built precisely on the challenge of creating and maintaining distinction within a field of overwhelming likeness (Coombe 1998; Mazzarella 2003, 254). But the "semiotic explosions" that Frederic Schwartz (1996) invokes to describe what can happen in consumer

1.4 Twinned Farmacias de Similares y Genéricos, same and not the same, Colonia Doctores, Mexico City, 2006. PHOTO BY AUTHOR.

markets for new kinds of things are doubly intensified here, as "similarity" and "sameness" are themselves the "things"—the material-semiotic things—that are proliferating and differentiating. In this sense, I cannot help but think about the work of another Schwartz—cultural studies scholar Hillel Schwartz (1996, 39)—and his argument that mid- to late twentieth-century marketing in the United States explicitly celebrated doubleness, or the repetition of the same ("Doublemint gum!"; "Which twin has the Toni?"), not just as a way to sell particular goods but to sell the pleasures and wonders of mass consumption and production itself (see figure 1.4).

There is certainly pleasure in Mexico's generic and similar repetitions: the ever-expanding catalog of repeating, similar-to-Simi slogans are playful, mocking, smart, ironic, funny, and, given the vast success of Dr. Simi's pharmacies in particular, a decent business move for those seeking to borrow some of his distinctive magnetism. But these generic and similar commercial practices have also firmly upended the relationship between sameness and distinction—mere copy and charismatic original—that the very ideas of branding and commercial aura are supposed to shore up (Hayden 2013; Lury 2004; see also Taussig 1993).[16] If doubleness can enchant, it does so in a particularly pointed way in the post-NAFTA, North-South dynamic of Mexico's market for generic medicines.

Here is how a US-based physician characterized the marketing dilemma faced by generics, compared with leading-brand drugs, in the United States: "It's hard to sell something that's 'as good but less expensive.' It does not have the same sexiness" (Mishori 2011). The sentiment certainly captures something important about how price and brand names can work as differentiators in many contexts, especially in the United States where strong intellectual property protection, coupled with direct-to-consumer advertising, tilts the sexiness factor very heavily in favor of the major manufacturers and their major marketing budgets ("Ask your doctor about Humira"). But this formulation misses something important: it cannot contemplate the possibility that generics might in themselves, and for themselves, become fecund sites of reenchantment (as Farmacias Similares enjoined, "Ask your doctor to prescribe the affordable brand, known as similars!").[17] If Mexico's pharmaceutical landscape is any indication, *the same but cheaper* is plenty sexy, to the point where the phrase itself has become a potent commercial meme, a meta-generic marketing slogan. The saturation of the commercial public sphere with pharmacies and pharmaceuticals, and with a complex kind of Simi-semiotics (proper to Dr. Simi and exceeding his reach), was in many ways the most visible and consequential aspect of Mexico's spectacular generics landscape.

Serán? *Can* They Be?

Consumers, a loaded term to which we will attend more carefully in chapter 2, were not left passively navigating the various and possibly confusing equivalencies churned up by initial regulatory multiplicity and ever-inventive pharmacy owners. Tempted by price differentials of up to 75 percent, as Simi and his counterparts so boldly declare, many people who opted to try these new generic medicines in the early to mid-2000s, or who were considering trying them, and even those who declared in no uncertain terms that they would *never* try them, actively posed to others and to themselves the very question to which the government's lime popsicle poster was addressed: Where should we anchor pharmaceutical efficacy and substantive sameness?

Certainly, as the types of generics multiplied, so did questions about them. In my interviews and in the extensive time I spent in pharmacies and talking with people about these new drugs, the question of equivalence was often posed to me, aloud, in the future conditional: *Serán lo mismo?* (Can they be the same?). The question in this form was a speculation, not an empirical yes or no matter. It held a great deal of room—there was room for hope, and possibility, and doubt. Could they be the same? Aren't they? They're not really, are they? For many of the people with whom I mulled over such questions in those early days, the puzzle of these medicines and their equivalence turned the critical spotlight directly on expensive leading-brand drugs. In Mexico City, Jaime Martínez, an enthusiastic convert to Dr. Simi's pharmacies, put the point to me defiantly in 2004, as he zeroed in on the superficial deceptions of the expensive brand-name drug: "What are we paying for when we pay so much more? Nothing! Just packaging, just the name! But it's the same! [*Es lo mismo!*]." Others posed the key question aloud to me, open to the possibility but not yet sure of the answer: "But how can generics be so much cheaper and still be the same?" Hovering over the whole question was the visible presence of the transnational drug industry, whose de facto monopoly on Mexico's private market was very much under threat. If the industry's representatives in Mexico dismissed many of these new generics as being of dubious quality, public-sector physicians, for their part, argued with each other in published forums, calling each other out on misplaced allegiances: "Be careful who you are in bed with when you declare the 'lack of quality' of generic copies!" (Quijano 2006, 79). Meanwhile, many of those who declared themselves loyal to Farmacias Similares roundly defended Simi's drugs against the enterprise's attackers: as Martín Ramírez, a building manager in Mexico City, told me when we talked at length about Simi's medicines in 2004, "Of course they're the same. The transnationals want us to think they're not, but they are!"[18] There seemed to be little possibility of a neutral stance on the matter of originals, generics, similars, and their equivalencies. Sameness—lo mismo!—was not a metaphysical property or a pharmacological certainty but an argument and a declaration of allegiance: *be careful who you're in bed with!*

Many of these deliberations directly pitted generics of varying kinds against leading-brand drugs. But others organized the matter of sameness and difference, and hence presumptions of quality and doubt, along different axes, suggesting the many points where chains of pharmaceutical equivalency might be made or broken. The horizons for generic commensuration often exceeded the bounds of the hemmed-in dichotomy between brand-name originals and generic copies, not to mention the leveling force of lime popsicles. Sometimes the distinctions that mattered were between classes of drugs: a friend declared that, at the insistence of her physician, she would never risk taking a generic version of her antiepilepsy medicine, though generic analgesics would be fine. Sometimes differential risks were assumed for oneself but not one's cherished others: "I'll buy generics for myself, but I would never give them to my children," a middle-class woman in her mid-thirties explained to me in 2004.[19] In Mexico's famously "plural" popular medical landscape, medicinal plants, traditional medicine, *naturismo*, and homeopathy, especially Flores Bach (Bach homeopathic remedies), also provide key points of comparison (see Napolitano 2002). In an interview in 2004, when generics were still relatively new objects on the pharmaceutical scene, Jorge Ramos, an importer of medicinal plants from Central America who lives in Mexico City, explained to me that "the generic" is like "the medicinal plant"—it is stripped down to its essence, rid of all the "extraneous packaging, hype, and modification." For him, *lo genérico* offers a kind of purity. "Pura sustancia," he told me: nothing but substance.[20] An academic colleague of mine, meanwhile, told me that her husband was taking generics in the way that he takes homeopathic medicines, that is, as a kind of "alternative medicine."[21]

Notably, as consumers multiplied the axes of comparative relations, they also started to articulate hierarchies between and among generics, interchangeables, and similars. Often, as I noted previously, the choice of pharmacies was one of the ways that people put these stratifications to work, with not-subtle class implications. For many of my middle-class interlocutors, the chain Farmacias San Pablo, which started to distinguish itself in the mid- to late 2000s by largely selling "interchangeable" generics, or GIs often emerged at the top of a hierarchy of trusted pharmacies associated with trusted medicines. Farmacias de Ahorro was very often next on the list, a bit cheaper and *probably* just as good. For those who could afford to spend a little more and who did not, for many reasons (see chapter 2) trust Dr. Simi or his medicines, Farmacias Similares came in resolutely, without question, at the very bottom. One of the articulations of this distrust was the widespread, but by no means universally shared, suspicion or accusation that Dr. Simi's similares were, in fact, less than—less than equivalent and hence less than good.

And here, the lime popsicles return, though presumably not in the way that the secretary of health had intended; they became intimately embroiled in the polemics about Simi and in fact they became stuck to him/it/them. It was

Farmacias Similares and Víctor González Torres in particular whose drugs were immediately singled out, as early as 2000, by transnational industry critics decrying the prospect of a market awash in diminished copies (Salazar 2000). Reflecting on the confusing classificatory abundance characterizing Mexico's generics market in the early to mid-2000s, and the persistence of similars in particular as a suspect or not properly generic kind, the director of a German pharmaceutical lab in Mexico pointed straight to the *paletas de limón*: "The origin of all of this mess? The little ad with the lime popsicles, which was later withdrawn, that said that they are all the same. . . . The only ones who believed in that message were a few clever ones [*vivos*] who took advantage of the idea to launch a ton of quack brands" (Salazar 2000). The argument has persisted in the form of accusations that similares—the drugs sold in Similares—not only did not meet the bioequivalence standard but were not even chemically equivalent.

To be clear, that accusation was not an endorsement of antireductionist philosophies of chemistry; rather, the Similares enterprise was accused of practicing what Kris Peterson (2014) has called, in the context of her work in Nigeria, "chemical arbitrage." That is, as Peterson shows in that context, one way for manufacturers to compete on price is, obviously, to doctor the kind or amount of chemical substance in the medicine (11–12). In 2010, lamenting the still-unsettled state of Mexico's pharmaceutical market and its peculiar abundance of offerings, a cranky Mexican blogger reupped the persistent injunction *to remember*: "Let's remember the lime popsicle ads. . . . The same ingredient but at a much lower cost. In that moment people questioned the quantity of lime that those 'cheaper' ['*más barato*'] popsicles had, and that was the beginning of the legal needle-threading, and the birth of a franchise that is still successful today: 'Farmacias Similares' and its similar medicines" (*Las historias de un ente mexicano* 2010).[22] As if confirming the close affinity between these two enduring but contested images of lo mismo, the only time I saw an exemplar of the infamous lime popsicle poster out in the world was in a franchise of Farmacias Similares in Coyoacan, Mexico City, in 2005, long after the federal government had suspended the campaign. (The rather terrible photo of that poster, which appeared in the opening pages of this chapter, was one I managed to take in that pharmacy.) And the first time I had heard of it was a year earlier, at Similares' corporate headquarters, when, in the course of a long interview, the chief public relations officer who had received me made wry note of a government ad campaign that "hadn't worked particularly well." "The famous lime popsicles," she said, her eyes narrowing into something between a smirk and a twinkle. And then she declared, triumphantly, "'The same but cheaper' has worked much better."[23]

Perhaps Simi's slogan had worked much better. Accusations that Simi was undertaking a kind of chemical arbitrage did not in fact lead to inevitable conclusions about the quality of Simi's medicines, especially in the eyes of those who identified themselves explicitly as the beneficiaries of Simi's interventions. For Martín Xavier, a doorman who lives with his family on the ground floor (i.e., in an apartment in the parking garage) of an apartment building in the center of Mexico City, the proposition for those with "few resources," like him and his family, was simple: "We couldn't afford medicines before. Now we can."[24] Responding to physicians' and transnational labs' articulations of doubt about Similares' drugs in particular, Simi's staunch defenders, including Martín, offered some pointed rejoinders.

That is, Martín did not completely refuse the critiques of Similares' inequivalence. Rather, he absorbed them, and then he recomposed them. "Of course they're the same!" he insisted in the midst of our expansive discussion in which he reflected on the many ways that Simi is "doing something important" for families like his. Then he added, "It's possible that they can take longer to work, but they're the same!"[25] Yolanda Machado, a sixty-year-old woman and longtime (off and on) Seguro Social beneficiary who now buys many of her drugs in both los genéricos (various generics pharmacies) and in Similares, told me the following, with a laugh and a wink: "Maybe they come *rebajados* [watered down], so you have to take two, but they're the same!"[26]

The oft-noticed fact that Simi's standard presentation of ibuprofen, for example, was an enormous 800-milligram pill (it looked to be the size of a horsefly or perhaps a horse pill) helped fuel these kinds of observations: maybe a Simi drug's active substance is "weaker," so either *they* have to double or even quadruple it, or *you* do. But for all these caveats about possible differences, Simi's defenders and customers insisted that the drugs are nevertheless the same. Equal parts defiant and playful, these formulations worked as a deft redirection of the supercharged politics of generic equivalence, turning accusations of Simi's lack into something else: a confidence in the distinct possibility that generics, similares, and leading-brand originals *can be* the same, even when they are not.

Simi's claims to both sameness and similarity had in some ways already named and made space for such a capacious possibility. But so had the state's own regulatory idioms. After all, what Martín and Yolanda articulated, in part, was the possibility that differences in time and absorption ("Maybe it takes longer to work" is the very thing that bioequivalence testing can reveal) might sit very comfortably alongside the fact of chemical equivalence ("It's still the same compound"). Their insistence on the simultaneity of these two possibilities—same and not the same—spoke aloud the state's categories and their amplifications in the commercial sphere. But it also refused the presumed hierarchical relation between them. After all, while the state's chemically equivalent generics and bioequivalent interchangeable generics were introduced side by side, same and not the same, they were not in fact meant to be equal. And their simultaneity was not meant to endure.

Section 2: Harmonizations

So, *are* they really the same? In the first five years of Mexico's generics market, consumers, physicians, patients, pundits, entrepreneurs, and capacious commercial idioms persistently invoked and offered their own answers to this constitutive question of generic equivalence. Far from resolving the matter, Mexico's federal regulatory agencies had only proliferated the possibilities. One can certainly start to imagine, then, why there might have been calls to "regularize" Mexico's generics landscape: to clarify categories and equivalencies, to stamp out the confusions, to streamline definitions, to weed out the confusing duplicates and improper copies—to harmonize, as the language of international trade agreements put it.

Since the late 1990s, regulators in successive administrations have indeed tried to assert some control over these proliferations and hence over this market. One of the most important salvos on this front came in 2005, late in President Vicente Fox's term, when the federal government issued a future-looking reform to the Ley General de la Salud (General Health Law). This reform amended Article 376, which governs the processes for renewing drug registrations: the new declaration attempted to call into being a world in which, by 2010, all drugs sold as generics in Mexico would meet the bioequivalence standard that had been first introduced in 1998.[27] The government's stated aspiration was to phase out chemically equivalent generics or what became, in negative terms, "nonbioequivalent copies." That soon-to-be-banished category included, by implication, the not-really-real similars. In fact, the press often described the 2005 decree as if the secretary of health had specifically "declared war" on Víctor González Torres/Dr. Simi. The state's 2005 move was meant to produce a regulatory near future in which only the bioequivalent GI would count as the off-patent drug's *proper copy*.[28]

The aspiration of that 2005 decree—to reduce several kinds of copies to one—in turn did not arise from strictly domestic concerns. The bioequivalence requirement introduced in 1998, and reaffirmed in 2005, was in many ways a direct response to NAFTA's requirements that Mexico harmonize its regulation on generic approvals to US standards. The language (and asymmetrical geopolitical muscle) of harmonization promises to tamp down or control regulatory multiplicity. But here I'd like to suggest the opposite: harmonization created the very generic multiplicities to which we have just been introduced. That is, bioequivalent generics in Mexico were introduced alongside—but also hierarchically set against—the chemically equivalent medicines that had long been produced in Mexico, sold to IMSS and ISSSTE, and consumed by millions of people over a period of roughly fifty years.

Thus let me broach another constitutive question, one that was posed to me (not entirely rhetorically) by more than a few generics manufacturers with whom I have worked: Why *did* bioequivalence emerge as a new threshold in Mexico after fifty years in which chemically equivalent copies of once-patented drugs had been considered of quality in Mexico's public health sector?

Such a question has been part of the terrain of contest ever since bioequivalence first emerged as a proposed regulatory threshold in the United States in the late 1960s. Scholars of the history of medicine and drug regulation in the United States, including Dominique Tobbell, Daniel Carpenter, and Jeremy Greene, have shown that there were many reasons why this new threshold gained traction beginning in the late 1960s and 1970s, eventually supplanting chemical equivalence as the required form of equivalence for generic drug approvals (Carpenter and Tobbell 2011; Tobbell 2012, 163–92; Greene 2014). Those late 1960s debates took place in the midst of concerted multiyear attempts to pave the way for generic substitution in order to control medication costs in the United States. As these scholars have shown, and as I'll discuss in greater detail in the third section of this chapter, the demand for bioequivalence emerged in part in response to dawning scientific and regulatory understandings that chemical equivalence might not always be a good enough proxy for the (e)quality of generics consumed by actual bodies. And, as we'll see, there are certainly pharmacological reasons why one might look beyond chemical equivalence as a proxy for pharmaceutical sameness.

But, as with so many pharmaceutical matters, the facts underpinning this demand were also impossible to separate from the interests of patent-holding pharmaceutical laboratories (see Dumit 2012).[29] It was these laboratories that initially produced the evidence and the arguments that chemical equivalence might not be "same enough" in a bid, it has been argued, to raise the regulatory bar for their generic competitors (Carpenter and Tobbell 2011, 93–98). In the late 1960s and early 1970s, the question facing successive US congressional committees was thus, in part, the following: Was bioequivalence a crucial guarantor of generic medicines' safety and efficacy or was it, effectively, a contrived way for the innovator industry to make it more difficult and more expensive for their generics competitors to secure regulatory approval? The argument was settled in 1977 in favor of a blanket requirement that *all* generic medicines would have to meet a threshold of bioequivalence, a provision that became one of the backbones of the United States' foundational legislation on generic medicines, the Hatch-Waxman Act of 1984 (formally the Drug Price Competition and Patent Term Restoration Act).

In 1993, on joining NAFTA, the Mexican government effectively agreed to implement bioequivalence requirement for generics as part of a suite of new laws and regulations on intellectual property and data exclusivity—that is, as part of the new rules on pharmaceutical patents and on what happens when those patents expire (Zahl 2016). When generic medicines then came into commercial circulation starting in 1998, the transnational industry certainly made clear that they did not welcome the challenge to their share of Mexico's private pharmaceutical market. The powerful transnational industry trade association PhRMA (the Pharmaceutical Manufacturers' Association), made known its grave concerns about the dangers such competition posed (to itself) in a *Journal of Commerce* article in 1998:

> Legislation pending in Mexico for generic drugs could disrupt the sale of trademarked and patented products worth millions of dollars in exports to U.S. pharmaceutical companies. The pharmaceutical companies worry that, absent strict controls and regulations, their investment in research and development will be chipped away by the creation of a generics market in Mexico. . . .
>
> When Mexico became a partner in the North American Free Trade Agreement, its patent law and rule-making process became subject to harsher scrutiny. Regulations covering generics have been slow in coming, although officials had promised that they would be published by the end of last year [i.e., 1997]. . . . The U.S. industry is nervously awaiting the whole package of reforms that will define the market for generics. "*We want to be sure that these (generic) drugs fulfill the same requirements as we do,*"

said an executive at an international pharmaceutical company. "It's not the generics so much as the conditions under which they are introduced into the market." (Sutter 1998; my emphasis)

If the creation of a new market for generics threatened transnational market share in Mexico, the threat might be reduced, at least in the innovator industry's view, by demanding that the threshold for generic equivalence be raised to the standards demanded in the United States. So, for instance, whenever patent-holding companies make, say, a tablet version of one of their drugs that was initially approved as a capsule, they must undergo bioequivalence studies as well. Demanding "the same requirements" in the form of bioequivalence testing would effectively rule out most of the copies then in circulation (i.e., those that had been manufactured for the Seguro Social under a regime of chemical equivalence).

In this way, bioequivalence is geopolitics. And it makes markets. In many regulatory contexts—in Mexico, India, Brazil, Argentina, and elsewhere—bioequivalent generics are specific kinds of copies that are also recent inventions or even, in the view of some domestic manufacturers, "impositions." Bioequivalent generics are defined not (simply) or even primarily "against" or as substitutes for patented leading-brand drugs. Rather, they are (also) defined against, and as substitutes for, the copies that are already circulating within public and private sectors. In the sphere of generic and copied medicines internationally, US-driven demands for harmonization have required the addition of this specific iteration of the proper pharmaceutical copy—the (bioequivalent) generic—to an often already-robust presence of pharmaceutical copies long known by other names and calibrated to other equivalencies: *the drugs the Seguro gives you* in Mexico, *copias* in Argentina, *national brands* in India, and the official category of *similars* in Brazil. I can't help recalling here the dynamics that produced ten different definitions of generic medicines in ten different Latin American countries in the 2005 study I mentioned in the introduction. Despite its name, then, one of the things that harmonization produces is multiplication, or proliferation, even as it is supposed to rule out the copies already in circulation.

Some of the Latin American generics manufacturers from whom I have learned so much have contested the introduction of bioequivalence standards in precisely these terms, characterizing the regulatory emergence of (bioequivalent) generics not as a boon for access but as its opposite: a barrier to entry into their own, newly (re)configured pharmaceutical markets, keeping local firms, with longer histories of producing drugs under regimes of chemical equivalence on the wrong side of the line dividing the good copy from the bad. Central to this argument is the nontrivial fact that generics manufacturers bear the costs of equivalence testing, and submitting their drugs to a third-party laboratory for bioequivalence testing is a far more expensive proposition than testing their medicines for chemical equivalence.

The argument that bioequivalence is a boondoggle has certainly held traction in Argentina, where a robust domestic drug industry has thrived from the latter half of the twentieth century by making unlicensed copies of drugs often still under patent elsewhere (see chapter 3). Argentine physicians, health economists, and government officials told me in a series of interviews in Buenos Aires in 2006 that bioequivalence—which at that point was required only for a few classes of medicines, including antiretrovirals—might best be considered a transnational industry maneuver to keep domestic (Argentine) laboratories out of their own markets for as long as possible. The quality of Argentine *copias*, one national lab director told me, has been "proven repeatedly" without this contrived—and expensive—new threshold. Taking a spirited stand for the art and science of copying, Alfonso Ferreira declared with pride, "Our drugs are excellent, without having to prove bioequivalence. We copy to the letter!"[30]

The chief chemist of Víctor González Torres's Laboratorios Best made a similar argument to me in an interview. In her office in Mexico City, she laid out her company's initial objections both to the introduction of bioequivalence in the 1998 regulations and to the 2005 directive meant to implement this regulatory demand:

> But listen: you know that this [chemically equivalent] medicine has been sold [to the public sector] for fifty years. It's not just in one clinic: it's millions of people to whom absolutely nothing bad has happened. And why are you [Mexican regulators with the transnational firms behind them] *now* asking me for this proof of "quality"? Because you know it's very expensive, and you suppose that the national laboratories don't have the economic power to carry them out. But surprise! The national labs are doing it and they are demonstrating to the transnationals that they meet the proof perfectly well. So there can't be any doubt, anymore.[31]

Dr. Aguirre's defiant stance on the matter of the new "interchangeable generics" contained a notable pivot, from Laboratorios Best's (and hence the Similares enterprise's) rejection of the need for bioequivalence testing to a full-throated defense of "national" laboratories' abilities to meet this new standard perfectly well. (Indeed, around 2005, Similares started to proclaim, without much evidence, that it sells more "interchangeable [bioequivalent] generics" than anyone else.)[32]

Within that particular arc lies a further point about the relationship between a harmonized politics of equivalence and the politics of generic substitution. By including, for the first time, a bioequivalence requirement for generics, Mexico's 1997–98 reform to the General Health Law functioned both as part of a solution for improving access to cheaper medicines and as a belated response to US demands to raise Mexican parameters for generic equivalence, which it had been under pressure to do since NAFTA took effect in 1994.

At stake here, then, are competing versions of a transnational politics of generic substitution, *the same but cheaper*. Does the rise of the generic signal a reassertion of national pharmaceutical sovereignty or an accession to transnational industry and foreign demands? Echoing the anthem of this chapter, the answer might best be seen as both/and: they are versions of each other. We can see this in the state's initial embrace of categories that allowed both chemically equivalent and bioequivalent copies to circulate simultaneously as generics. Beyond the categories themselves, the regulatory language adopted by the Comisión Federal para la Protección contra Riesgos Sanitarios (COFEPRIS; Federal Commission for the Protection against Health Risks) also created space for such multiplicity. The US FDA states that a generic medicine is "identical—or bioequivalent—to a brand name drug in dosage form, safety, strength, route of administration, quality, performance characteristics and intended use" (US Food and Drug Administration 2021). The Mexican government's language was notably more capacious. Here is how the new regulatory norms defined the equivalence required of a generic medicine: "A pharmaceutical product with the same active substance and pharmaceutical form, with an equal concentration and strength, that uses the same route of administration and that, through the required regulatory tests, has demonstrated that its pharmaceutical specifications, dissolution profiles, or its bioavailability or other parameters, depending on the case, are equivalent to those of the reference drug" (Dirección General de Normas 1998b). The ample scope of possibilities here ("or its bioavailability or other parameters, depending on the case") makes the federal government's short-lived lime popsicle campaign all the more intriguing. With that unharmonious commitment to chemical equivalence, the state effectively took sides against "itself" but also against the demands of the "transnationals." A subtle form of post-NAFTA resistance in popsicle form, perhaps, this middle ground recomposed the puzzle of equivalence in regulatory form.

As such, Mexican regulatory approaches remind us that there is, in fact, no generic definition of a generic medicine. What, then, of the substance that cures?

Section 3: Zones of Tolerance

Thus far I have tried to show how commerce and the consumer market for generics in Mexico proliferate samenesses and how regulatory capaciousness, including the state's subtle, de facto assent to chemical equivalence, has produced multiple versions of equivalence. These conditions generated the substrate(s) in which generic alternatives circulate in Mexico, creating a crowded field of different kinds of copies that vie not only or even primarily with originals but with each other. Chemical equivalence, bioequivalence, interchangeability, and similarity have worked in Mexico's generics market as specific and competing forms of sameness—they are sites and sources of distinction.

These spectacular proliferations, I will argue in this final section, cannot be written off as Mexican aberrations awaiting normalization, Latin American irregularities demanding regularization, peripheral variations on a generic universal, diminished departures from a platonic ideal, or "bad copies" of equivalence itself. Rather, all that we have just learned shines a bright light on the terms and contestations that have long defined and continue to animate international trajectories of pharmaceutical production and regulation. The much-decried, confusing, chaotic "battles" in name and deed among Simi, various branches of the Mexican state, the transnational industry, and Mexican subsidiaries thereof are being waged in terms that are the history and the future of generics as the pharmaceutical's commodity form.

Let me explain by turning in more detail now to bioequivalence as a relation. Bioequivalence is the promised horizon on which rest liberalizing demands for generic harmonization; it is a relation that might well stamp out the "wrong" kinds of sameness and similarity. It was indeed specifically the promise of bioequivalence that Peterson pointed to when she noted her Nigerian interlocutors' hopes for at least a little bit of (pharmaceutical) equity in this unequal world.[33] Attending more closely to what bioequivalence is (meant to be), and how pharmacologists and testing labs bring it into view, opens up a third locus for the recomposition of the puzzle of equivalence.

The harmonizing moves discussed previously were meant to settle the problem of generic unfungibility by finally anchoring the same—lo mismo—in a proper measure of equivalence. Bioequivalence places into question the degree to which chemical equivalence can reliably stand as a proxy for an equivalence of outcome in actual bodies for some, if not all, drugs. With the invention of this measure in the 1960s (in the United States), and its variously harmonized introductions in a range of regulatory contexts, the physics and biochemistry of drug manufacturing, the relationship between active and inactive ingredients, the variability of consuming bodies and metabolisms, and even formulation differences in the same drug made by the same laboratory (shifting from a tablet to a capsule, for example) all come into view as factors that might in fact generate effective differences between chemically equivalent versions of the same drug.

In/active Ingredients: More Than a Copy

We can start to dive into these forms of differentiation by considering the possibility that the lime (or, actually, *the salt*, because pharmaceutical chemists often refer to active compounds as salts, since many of them exist in salt form) isn't the only substance that cures. First of all, attention to bioequivalence and bioavailability was, and is, premised on the possibility that inactive ingredients—the excipients, binding agents, and fillers, the vehicles that coat, encapsulate, and bind with the tiny amount of active ingredient—can differentiate the same drugs from each other, because they affect how the drugs dissolve and thus become "available" to the bodies that consume them. Think of the chalky tablet or the one that sticks in your throat, the one that goes down smoothly, the one that burns through your stomach lining, or *the one that takes longer to work*. Belying the message of the lime popsicle poster, bioequivalence is primed to tell us that "what cures" is (also) inactive substance. There is a potent disjuncture here between what patent law values—the active molecule—and what pharmacology would tell us to (also) value. Pharmaceutical companies are not unaware of this disjuncture. Even when a patent expires on a therapeutic molecule (the active substance) and that molecule may legally be manufactured by other laboratories, patent-holding companies often keep their inactive ingredients and delivery mechanisms to themselves, protected as trade secrets or otherwise not disclosed. Patents are, after all, "strategic documents that are generally incomplete and elusive" (Correa and Cassier 2009, 84; my translation).

The fact that an original drug's inactive ingredients, among other important details, are not disclosed in a patent matters quite a lot to the puzzle of equivalence as conventionally posed: Are generics *really* the same? It also matters to this puzzle's recomposition. We can get to both parts of this puzzle by asking, What *does* it mean to copy a medicine in such circumstances? Claudio Morales, one of the lead chemists in a large and well-respected generics lab in Guadalajara, Mexico, reflected on the matter with me one day in 2010, in Label's laboratories: "Actually, yes, we make 'copies,' but they are copies *only up to a certain point*." He did not mean that his lab's generics are diminished copies. He meant, and I am not taking license here, that they are more than copies: "Acquiring the active ingredient is the easy part [of making a generic drug]: you just buy it!" He continued, "You want chemical equivalence—the same salt [active compound] with the same level of impurity as the original." He laughed, and I laughed: "Well, yes, depending on how you look at it, that's what it is. The originals come with their own impurities; you don't want more [impurities], but you might get fewer."[34]

Even with the information from an expired patent in hand, and even when you purchase the active ingredient from a chemical company (the majority of Label's active pharmaceutical ingredients come from laboratories in China), the process of copying a drug is often of necessity, inventive and research-intensive. It can produce meaningful differences, and sometimes these differences register as improvements, just as your active salt might come with fewer impurities than that of the original. Morales elaborated on the process: after buying the active ingredient (the one no longer under exclusive patent control), "then comes the more difficult part, as you often have to reverse engineer the inactive ingredients to get optimal performance for your generics." Thus he emphasized that "the only 'sameness' is in the salt." His colleague, Graciela Tellez, echoed the point. Since "most of the time, the innovator firms keep their *excipientes* and inactive ingredients secret," she said, making generics is "like reverse engineering: you know where you want to end up, and then you have to develop the steps to get there."[35]

Across Latin America, the process of *developing the steps to get there* has entailed a range of practices of varying intensity, from choosing the optimal inactive ingredients matched to the lab's particular manufacturing equipment and expertise, as Tellez showed me at Label, to developing new pathways for synthesizing chemical ingredients that are not fully described in a patent, as Brazilian public laboratories have done in their work on antiretroviral medicines. Famously, in Brazil's formidable research labs such as Farmanguinhos, the work entailed in reverse-engineering drugs has at times resulted in copies that are, much as Morales suggested, more than: several Brazilian reverse-engineered antiretrovirals have been deemed by state regulators to be "better" than the originals—that is, they have had fewer impurities, better dissolution, more efficient biological action (thus enabling the pill in question to be smaller and hence easier to swallow), or a combination of these factors. A few of these not-mere copies have been patentable under Brazilian law.[36] As one biochemist told Maurice Cassier and Marilena Correa (2013, 26): "This means that the formulation cannot be the same. This means it's not a copy." As I'll elaborate in chapter 5, this kind of inventive copying is the stuff of which much postcolonial science and technology studies is made.[37]

But even at the more mundane, less research-intensive level of "simply" manufacturing off-patent copies, the process of copying must contend with a host of contingencies that require close attention and that can produce consequential differences. According to Morales, "The innovator product might be a tablet and you might be making a capsule," which already entails differences in how, and with what inactive ingredients and binders, the drug is assembled. "But imagine you are making a capsule to match a capsule. Even there, there are all kinds of variables. A lot depends on the flow of the powder, the molecular weight of the material, the speed of the machine." Morales had walked me through his company's plant prior to this conversation, giving me a glimpse of some of the machinery through which the *substances that cure* flow through a giant funnel, are formed and compressed, and emerge on the other end in a tumble of round white tablets. "Imagine," he said to me, "you've seen all that powder flowing down into the part that compresses it into tablets. There has to be an adequate flow so that it flows evenly, that you get the same amount of material [active and otherwise] in each capsule or tablet."[38] These are the contingencies that manufacturers have long addressed under the rubric of good manufacturing practice and quality control, a set of metrics that is called on to account for the consistency and stability of product (i.e., ensuring that the active principle ingredients do not degrade over time). Such contingencies suggest that even in chemical and physical terms, drugs are dynamic, as tablets, capsules, and pills respond to environmental conditions (temperature, humidity, light). But medicines are also relations with the bodies who/that consume them, and Morales and Tellez's company, as is the case with most of the major generics laboratories in Mexico, committed (whether begrudgingly, as with Laboratorios Best, or proactively, as with

Label) in the early 2000s to "optimize" its generics and production processes to this new threshold.

Bioavailability and Bioequivalence

To talk about the "sameness of drugs"—to dwell in the puzzle of their equivalence as if it were a property (even a comparative one) of drugs themselves—is to presume a vast sameness of bodies and metabolic function (Landecker 2013). And that is too much to concede, not least but not only because at least half a century of statistical medicine has been premised on the idea that it is folly to treat any drug as an isolated, self-identical object (Dumit 2012). Pharmaceuticals are effects or relations rather than isolated substances (Gomart 2002). Although one could make such a case "even" in merely chemical terms, the argument is particularly vivid when considered in biological and pharmacological terms. Drugs' efficacy comes to matter most when absorbed into bodies (animals, humans), and at the very least these bodies may have different metabolisms, or may be on other drugs, or smoke, or have genetic differences that matter to a drug's action, or eat different food, or weigh more or less than other bodies. These variables can affect many things, including how, or how fast, drugs are absorbed into yours, and others', bloodstreams and hence, arguably, how well they work. As a scientific-regulatory threshold, bioequivalence is different from chemical equivalence in its insistence that these interactions and relations are important. But then it must somehow come to terms with those relations' confounding effects. As soon as equivalence shifts from being a matter of the substances within drugs themselves to average comparative effects in variable human bodies, we move from the tools and idioms of chemistry and physics to the medium of blood and the measurement effects of (bio)statistics.

As a biostatistical formulation, bioequivalence can be apprehended only when run through the blood of human subjects, the workings of more and less sensitive measuring devices, and a suite of state-authorized statistical parameters and software packages (Niazi 2014; Steinijans and Hauschke 1993). This is why I said earlier that bioequivalence testing requires entirely different testing apparatuses, labor practices, and forms of expertise than does chemical equivalence. In Mexico, generics manufacturers contract with a suite of government-authorized third-party laboratories, whether university labs or state-approved, private-sector facilities, to undertake these tests.

In the barest outline, here is how bioequivalence is currently made visible in Mexico, as well as in the United States and Europe: it is a comparison of the extent and rate of drug absorption into the bloodstreams of a smallish number of healthy volunteers (in Mexico, the *n* is 24). The drugs being compared are "introduced" (taken by the volunteers) one at a time over a relatively short period, leaving time for the first drug to fully exit the subjects' bloodstream before the second can be swallowed and its presence in the blood measured. Each person is in a sense their own control.

The technicians, scientists, and statisticians working in bioequivalence laboratories in Mexico, as in the United States, are essentially measuring two things: the maximum concentration of active substance in each person's bloodstream (C_{max}) and the overall extent of this compound's absorption over twenty-four hours (usually), quantified and visualized as "the area below (under) the curve" (ABC in Spanish, AUC in English). The two drugs being measured in figure 1.5 are deemed bioequivalent by the FDA.

When laboratory technicians aggregate and plot these absorption data next to each other, excising the outliers that any given experiment may have churned up—"deleting data due to vomiting," for example, is a reminder of the nontrivial bodily work of being a test subject—they generate two average curves: one for each drug across twenty-four humans. These two curves almost always produce a space of difference between them.[39] The lines, in other words, are extremely unlikely to map exactly onto each other. The difference between them—that zone of tolerance—is the space-time of bioequivalence.

Look at those two curves (figure 1.5) again. With this image of comparative bioavailability in view, we might come to terms with a statement that at first seems a bit arresting: bioequivalence in Mexico, as in the United States and Europe today, indicates that a drug displays similar bioavailability to that of the reference product, within a margin of plus or minus 20 to 25 percent (Niazi 2014). In other words, the "availability" of the tested drug should not be calculated at less than 80 percent nor more than 125 percent of the reference drug.[40] *Más o menos* interchangeable, the relationship between the two curves will never be exactly the same, but it should be close enough, good enough, same enough.

This is one of the many ways that uniform bioequivalent interchangeability can be a difference machine: it both holds within it and can generate samenesses that are also differences. This point in itself is not surprising from the point of view of science and technology studies or the anthropology of science. But we must continue to ask, What are its implications? Let me note just a few. First, if we stay conceptually and politically attached to a zero-sum (either/or) proj-

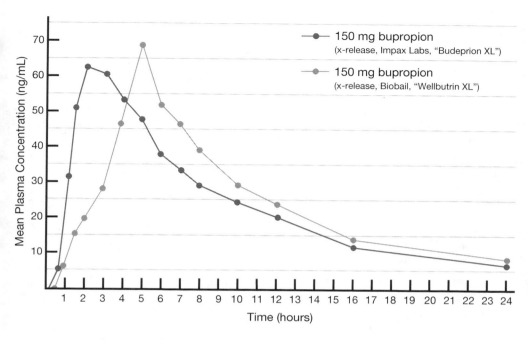

1.5 A buproprion bioequivalency comparison. Source: FDA data. Design modified.

ect of equivalence, this feature of bioequivalence could be at the very least disconcerting; at most, it could seem like a scandal (see also Peterson 2014; Hayat 2021). In the early 2000s, several IMSS physicians debated the merits and trouble spots of the new bioequivalence requirements in a heated written exchange in IMSS's public bulletin, the *Revista Médica IMSS*. Internist Guillermo Murillo-Godínez pointed to bioequivalence's zones of tolerance as a way to cast doubt on the prospect of generic (e)quality at all. Not only could the FDA's requirements (which Mexico's COFEPRIS was adopting, more or less) allow for the inequivalence of any given generic, he suggested, but this potential difference could hypothetically just keep amplifying across Mexico's crowded field of generic copies. "If a generic's demonstrated bioavailability cannot be more or less than 20–30% of the original's," he wrote, "two generic versions of the same molecule can be up to 60% different from each other!" (Murillo-Godínez 2006, 371–72). It's a difference that just keeps differencing, as Gabriel Tarde might say (Vargas 2010). Perhaps Murillo-Godínez was stretching things a bit in order to cast doubt on generic equivalence and hence quality, but he was also making a point worth considering in its broadest implications: What if bioequivalence as a measure doesn't just mask or contain differences? What if it intensifies or extends them?

There is a second question suggested by all this contingency, pointing in nearly the opposite direction: To what degree do bio(in)equivalencies actually matter? In much of the scientific literature about bioequivalence, the existence or even size of the "area under the curve"—that zone of tolerance—does not matter absolutely, that is, in or for itself. It matters because data about drug concentration (pharmaco*kinetics*) are used to point to or guess at the biological effects of the drug(s) in question (pharmaco*dynamics*), and these observations in turn serve as a proxy for expectations of how well the drugs work in bodies in the world. Since 1967 and still today in pharmacological research and regulatory debates, the relationship among these measures has been a pressure point in the United States and internationally, a site of contest that is periodically reactivated. How much do differences in drug concentration (shown by the points measured in that graph—maximum concentration, or C_{max}, and the *area bajo la curva*, ABC) actually matter to drug effects (Karalis and Macheras 2003)?

When bioequivalence testing was first contemplated by the FDA in the late 1960s, the stance among some regulators and legislators was that drug concentration and solubility could make a difference in the biological effects (pharmacodynamics) of some drugs. But it was not initially posed as a blanket requirement for all generic approvals. Chemical equivalence was initially seen as good enough for the majority of drugs. Thus, a 1967 US government task force concluded, "On the basis of available evidence, lack of clinical equivalency among chemical equivalents meeting all official standards has been grossly exaggerated as a major hazard to the public health" (Greene 2014, 119). The committee's position did not deny that there could sometimes be substantial differences in drug absorption; rather, it argued that this difference didn't necessarily or even usually make a difference in how (well) a particular drug works. This more measured stance did not hold in subsequent regulatory negotiations. As I noted previously, by 1977, the United States had made bioequivalence testing a blanket requirement for all generic approvals, and that blanket requirement travels with "bioequivalence" as a harmonized regulatory threshold.

But the question of what a lack of bioequivalence *actually* tells us still drives research agendas and global pharmaceutical politics. Perhaps, in fact, bioinequivalence does not (always or even usually) produce a difference in therapeutic effectiveness. When Mexico first issued its regulatory framework for bioequivalence, María Luisa Hess (1998), then a postgraduate student at Cinvestav, Mexico's premier science and technology research university (and home to one of the laboratories approved by the state to run third-party bioequivalence testing), ran a massive simulation in collaboration with a Universidad Nacional Autónoma de México (UNAM; National Autonomous University of Mexico) pharmacologist. Their project explored whether drug concentration actually has a linear relation to the duration and intensity of a drug's therapeutic effects. That is, if a generic's maximum concentration in the bloodstream shows up at 25 percent less than that of the reference drug, is the generic 25 percent less effective? Having run more than seventy thousand simulations based on pharmacodynamic and pharmacokinetic data, Hess and her collaborators concluded that basing bioequivalence on the concentration of the drug in the bloodstream (the C_{max} as required in the new regulations) could declare inequivalent many compounds that could, in effective (pharmacodynamic) terms, be considered bioequivalent.

The question of what bioequivalence actually means was also at the heart of the Indian Supreme Court's now-famous ruling on a case brought by the multinational drug company Novartis. Dwai Banerjee (2014), Stefan Ecks (2008), Amy Kapczynski (2013), and Kaushik Sunder Rajan (2011, 2017) have tracked in detail the complex politics and implications of this case, in which the court declined to grant Novartis a new patent for a minor modification on the cancer drug Gleevec (also called Gleevic). Novartis's claim was that its modified version showed more bioavailability than the original and hence it deserved a new patent on that drug. (Filing for a new patent on a minor change is a much-criticized corporate practice known as *evergreening*.) The Indian court was not convinced by Novartis's argument. Drawing on India's 2005 patent law, which demands that drug makers show meaningful differences in efficacy in order to secure a patent (a markedly higher requirement for patentability than that of the United States), the Supreme Court ruled that Novartis's increased bioavailability data did not necessarily mean the ("new") drug was more therapeutically effective than its prior version (Kapczynski 2013). Bioinequivalence in this case did not register as a difference that mattered enough to grant Novartis a new patent.

And finally, let's broach the question of access (boon to access or barrier to access?) once again. The demand for bioequivalence in generics has always carried with it the distinct possibility that bioavailability and economic availability could run in opposite directions. As I've suggested, extending the bioequivalence requirement to all generic approvals, first in the United

States and then in emerging markets via NAFTA and the WTO, has been seen simultaneously as an intervention in the name of drug safety and efficacy and, arguably, as a way for the innovator industry to try to protect its market share against generic competition. In the United States in the 1970s, some industry analysts argued that the bioequivalence requirement was a gift to Big Pharma: they predicted that the cost of bioequivalence testing, placed directly on generics manufacturers, would defeat the point of generic competition by limiting the number of companies in the field and raising prices (Greene 2014, 123–24). Argentine and Mexico City–based drug manufacturers and others involved in the generics industry made similar points to me. The director of a government-authorized, private bioequivalence testing laboratory in Guadalajara, Mexico, told me in 2010 about the concerns of his clients (Mexican generics laboratories) regarding the costs of this new regulatory demand: "You know, a lot of the labs here, being family labs and all, the owners initially said, 'Hey wait a minute, why are you asking me to go through all of this? I've been in this business over twenty years and *no se ma ha muerto nadie!* [not one person has died on me!].' But now, the costs of doing these tests are normal, included in their estimation of the costs of bringing a drug to market."[41] Bioequivalence does come at a (new normalized) price: bioequivalence testing costs Mexican generics manufacturers roughly US$100,000 (2,003,420 pesos) per drug. That is not a trivial sum, and many of the manufacturers with whom I spoke in the mid- to late 2000s observed that this cost was running some smaller labs out of business. But, following the federal decree in 2005, the bigger companies have committed. What does this commitment mean for retail drug prices? In 2008, as more and more certified bioequivalent generics were making their way to the market, a new commercial claim started to call forth from pharmacy storefronts and billboards: "Generic medicines, up to 38% cheaper!" A study commissioned almost a decade later by the Mexican federal government found that GI prices in Mexico in the mid-2000s were, on aggregate, not significantly cheaper than name-brand medicines, often hewing closer to around 30 percent less expensive (Comisión Federal 2017). The radical changes in affordability promised by generic medicines indeed started to diminish on aggregate as the decade wore on. We will return to this point at the end of the book.

Quality Control: Originals Are (Not) the Same

Beyond the specificities (and contingencies) of measuring equivalence in drug availability and efficacy, the fact that pharmaceuticals are mass-produced goods leads us directly to one last crucial dimension of the recomposition of equivalence: bioequivalence tests routinely show that original medicines can differ from themselves.

Pronouncing an enalapril (a hypertension medicine) as bioequivalent or, as it is said in Mexico, an interchangeable generic is meant to compare ("same") drugs made by two different labs: Label's generic enalapril versus Merck's enalapril (Renitec). It is this comparison that structures the burden of proof for conventionally understood generic equivalence. *Serán?* Are they *really?* But as a statistical concept, bioequivalence is derived from the history of quality control more broadly in which the equivalence and interchangeability at stake rest within the same factory or assembly line: it is meant to mark the "consistency of product" within the same laboratory. Quality control within the same facilities in industrial production is thus where we first see the equivalence or interchangeability of manufactured products redefined as equivalence within upper and lower limits, or within statistical zones of tolerance (see Slaton 2001).

True to this legacy, generics manufacturers in Mexico have to contend with the fact that original drugs, as with all objects of mass production, are not even or always the same as themselves. This bare fact of mass production was built into the reinvention of industrial quality control as a statistical project in the 1930s, and in the United States it was folded into drug regulation following a 1937 safety scandal involving the contamination of a sulfa drug. The shift to understanding quality in statistical terms drew directly on the work of statistician Walter Shewhart (1931), who was on loan in the 1930s from Bell Telephone to the US Department of Agriculture, which then housed the nascent FDA.[42]

Shewhart's prior experience with telephone systems had made clear that, when you make thousands upon thousands of the same thing, there is no way that each part will come off an assembly line as identical "with respect to any given quality" (2).[43] Explaining why he thought it was important to move from the quixotic search for exactitude toward a more probabilistic notion of quality as equivalence, he argued, "Manufacturers soon found that they could not make things exactly alike in respect to a given quality; moreover it was not necessary that they be exactly alike, and it was too costly to try to make them so" (2–3). Shewhart noted that not only was it difficult to impossible to make them so, the prospect of knowing that it was so would in fact be expensive and ridiculous. Often, a sample must be destroyed in order to test it, as when grinding up a pill to test its mix of active and inactive ingredients.

The closest alternative—random sampling—only guarantees that the particular pills tested hold the desired qualities.

Shewhart's reconceptualization of quality control made two significant imprints on the exigencies of mass-producing medicines today, generic and otherwise. First, this statistical notion of quality control made "process" prior to product: that is, since testing each and every item that rolls off an assembly line is not feasible, the environment of manufacturing was controlled instead—the process, the machinery, the inputs, the practices (i.e., the labor), and accounting structures themselves (Cochoy 2005; Daemmrich 2004). This principle and these practices are the basis of good manufacturing practice (GMP), a powerful idiom in the harmonization of regulatory regimes for mass production across the globe.[44] In Mexico, as in the United States, new equipment requires new certification processes—not just of the new equipment but of the "old" product produced with the previous equipment. José Martín Palomar, the director of Label, told me about the near-death and resurrection of his father's generics company, one of the biggest in Guadalajara. At the end of the twentieth century, he and his brothers had taken a deep breath, he said, and decided to update all their equipment in anticipation of the new generics law and (in turn) the invention of a new consumer market for generic medicines. But then they faced the prospect of getting all of their existing products (a fifty-year inventory) recertified. The absence of the prior machinery made the prior drugs unreadable to auditors.[45]

The constitutive priority of process to a drug's quality helps explain why, in the time I have spent in generics laboratories in Mexico City and Guadalajara, my hosts have insistently drawn my attention to things I otherwise would have overlooked. While I strained, with earnestly misplaced desire, for a glimpse of drugs themselves in production, my hosts kept showing me where to *really* look to see the quality of their products: in the seam where walls meet floors, which are not squared off but curved so that dust cannot accumulate; in the rigorous separation of dry and wet manufacturing areas; in the several layers of sanitary control between zones. Even equipment out of service was pointed out to me with pride, since GMP requires that certain pieces of machinery be cleaned and serviced every six months.

Second, and perhaps just as fundamentally, Shewhart had made an eloquent case that the redefinition of interchangeability, which is the same within upper and lower limits, was not a weakness—something to be explained away—but a strength and a new tool in the economic rationalities of mass production.[46] This underlying principle—that mass production *cannot* make things exactly alike with respect to a given quality—helps us understand some of the pragmatic concerns that Mexican generics laboratories must navigate as they seek bioequivalence certification for their products. As a matter of course, they know that the reference (original) drug to which their generic is being compared can differ from batch to batch. The directors of Label and other Mexican generics laboratories usually contract an authorized laboratory to conduct a pilot study to assess whether their product stands a good chance of passing a bioequivalence test, before investing the $100,000 in a full study. They consistently told me that it is very important to do a pilot test and subsequent tests with the same batch of the reference drug, so that "you're not up against an unpredictable reference point," as Palomar told me at Label's factory.[47] Like any medicine, Palomar said, different batches of a reference drug can give different bioavailability results, which could of course churn up some destabilizing surprises in efforts to show how equivalent a drug is to the original.

The annals of bioequivalence are indeed rife with examples of, and arguments about, variation within an original lab's drugs.[48] Thus, for example, in trying to staunch the sensationalism surrounding a few instances of generic bioinequivalence, the head of the National Formulary in the United States noted, in 1967, that "successive batches of the same brand-name drugs could differ among themselves by as much or more than the brand-name drug differed from the generic" (Greene 2011, 493). In other words, differences within "the same" can be greater than the differences across drugs produced by different labs. We know the form and content of such an argument from the histories of classification, of race and gender, of population genetics. This scenario is both counter and a counterpart to IMSS internist Murillo-Godínez's scenario noted earlier, in which he contemplated the nightmarish statistical prospect of ever-amplifying differences across successive versions of generics. Here, bioequivalence tells us that it is the original that might just *keep differencing*.

The multinational structure of major pharmaceutical laboratories adds another layer to the ways in which this variable sameness is experienced by Mexican generics manufacturers. Ingrid Medina, the director of a small but rapidly growing generics lab in Mexico City, recounted for me how a product of hers had recently "failed" its bioequivalence test in Mexico because her drug's bioavailability curve was too far above that of the reference drug she used in her test. The reference medicine was manufactured and sold in Mexico by the Mexican subsidiary of a major US-based transnational lab. She then repeated the test by having her drug evaluated against the version of the original that the company sells in the United States. And sure enough, she told me, the curves were "equal." The innovator labs' reference drug—the one they made and sold in Mexico—had a different dissolution profile than the one they sold in the United States, and hers looked more like the US version. She pointedly raised the next "obvious" question: "Are they making shittier versions of their drugs in Mexico?" I asked her, given that experience, if she "believed" in bioequivalence—an odd question, perhaps, but one that took shape in the context of our conversation about how the state's aspiration to turn all generics into bioequivalent interchangeables felt like it was off to a rocky start. Medina replied, "In Mexico? In the US? Anywhere?" She laughed and started to sing, jokingly, in English: "Somewhere, over the rainbow—No, not really. Because the process can tip the balance in ways that aren't necessarily fair to generics companies."[49]

Conclusion: Recompositions

A robust legacy of work on standardization within science and technology studies and anthropology would certainly prime us to expect that the closer we look at any particular regulatory-technical standard or threshold the more elusive, contingent, and heterogeneous its foundations will reveal themselves to be (Alder 1998; Bowker and Star 1999; Slaton 2001). *Of course equivalence is turtles all the way down*, to throw in a Geertzian cliché. But in this chapter I am not just arguing that underneath (pharmaceutical) equivalence lurks a host of contingencies, specificities, or differences. There is a close affinity between that kind of analysis and the ways we have often addressed the commodity form: one of our most readily available moves is to contest the sheer force of commodification and its relentless, often violent, abstractions (equivalence among them) by showing how concrete specificities irrupt or persist within (see Mazzarella 2003; Stengers and Pignarre 2011).

But the experience of dwelling in Mexico's generics landscape has made me less invested in demystifying equivalence than in taking seriously its explicit, even spectacular, proliferations. In all we've seen thus far—in Mexican pharmacy slogans and acts of similar kind-making; in consumers' arguments, speculations, and certainties; in the regulatory doublings and the unharmonious harmonizations that configure transnational and domestic markets—the multiplicities that make pharmaceutical equivalencies have been explicitly named, set loose, and further materialized. Interchangeables! Similars!

Generics! *Equivalentes! Lo mismo!* Not turtles all the way down, then, but specific equivalencies proliferating.

What are the implications of all this unfungibility for the question of access and for the composition of the pharmaceutical's commodity form? These spectacular excesses have certainly been among the most important and visible consequences of turning to generic substitution in Mexico as a market-pharmacological principle. Far from simply resolving the problem of access, the introduction of a consumer market for drugs that are *the same but cheaper* has generated a crowded, stratified, differentiated, and anything but generic field of generic alternatives. For regulators, physicians, generics manufacturers, and consumers, the matter of generic substitution has thus become a question of navigating and redefining the samenesses that matter.[50] In a slight modification of Jane Guyer's (2004) important argument that "inequivalence" is actually a key generative force within some of political economy's most cherished abstractions, here we start to see how an equivalence that is constitutively more than can become a vivid locus of valued distinction.

This scenario feels unexpected, confounding; it might even seem dangerous or unsettling. It seems unsettling because these multiplying iterations of that which is same and not the same rearrange the either/or burden of regulatory certainty on which assessments of generic quality are supposed to be based. But it is also unsettling because the generic is not "supposed" to be a site or source of such spectacular commercial exuberance, such that the interchangeable generic becomes a hybrid commercial/regulatory mark or that similarity itself becomes, in Dr. Simi's hands, an auratic stamp of distinction. Indeed, the importance of generics to a wide range of politics of access is that for the most part they are not attached to name brands, to marketing budgets, or to the distinctive aura of commercial actors. They are, as the World Health Organization (WHO) says, "meant to be interchangeable" regardless of their source (World Health Organization 2005). It is this lack of distinction, their severance from the operations of marketing and commercial fecundity, that is key to their affordability (at least in contexts where IP laws allow leading-brand drugs to be priced exuberantly) and hence to the promise of access. For these reasons, pharmaceutical industry insiders understand genericization as a fall from protected grace; it is what happens when your patent expires and your drug is at risk of becoming merely a commodity.

But Mexico's generics market—a composite, bumpy mix of post-NAFTA regulatory formations, chemical and biological equivalencies, a notably fecund commercial sphere, and not least the contagious and compelling operations of Dr. Simi—suggests another understanding of the generic as commodity. For just as generics are commodities, then, intriguingly, it is genericness itself that emerges here as a site of enchantment. The regulators, consumers, and entrepreneurs who are making this market are explicitly naming, activating, and transforming the many equivalencies that have long constituted the contested field of generics in Latin America, in the United States, and in international or transnational trade negotiations. The generic is, in other words, a site and source of more-than fungibility. As such, the peculiar abundance characterizing Mexico's generics market is not some kind of unharmonized outlier; rather, it reminds us that it is not fungibility but its spectacular excess that composes, or constitutes, this commodity form.

Simipolitics 2

STATE AND NOT THE STATE

The lack of a stable and well determined attribute is the problem posed by any *pharmakon* [a drug that may act as a poison or a remedy], by any drug whose effect can mutate into its opposite, depending on the dose, the circumstances, or the context, any drug whose action provides no guarantee, defines no fixed point of reference that would allow us to recognize and understand its effects with some assurance.
ISABELLE STENGERS, *COSMOPOLITICS I*

I'm Che Guevara in a Mercedes!
VÍCTOR GONZÁLEZ TORRES, A.K.A. DR. SIMI

For what, exactly, are generic medicines substitutes? When generics were introduced to the Mexican public in the late 1990s and early 2000s, their potency was embraced by one notable private-sector protagonist—the famous Dr. Simi, avatar of pharmacy proprietor Víctor González Torres—as a tool for fighting the economic inaccessibility and the ideological power of the foreign brand-name drug. In one of his more clever double entendres, Dr. Simi/González Torres encouraged potential customers: "Defend your domestic economy!" With such claims, Simi's version of generic substitution initially evoked explicit resonance with the state populism that took shape under Mexico's regime of import substitution industrialization (ISI), which reached its apogee in the 1960s: a national(ist) politics and defense of the nation built around the figure of the domestic substitute, or the domestic copy.

But, like drugs-as-pharmakon, the politics of pharmaceutical substitution can also readily mutate, and so can its protagonists. Their attributes are not fixed. For many of the people with whom I spent my time in the course of this research, the act of going to a generics pharmacy or to a Similares does not serve primarily as an alternative to buying expensive, leading-brand drugs. It is, rather, a choice set directly against the prospect of going to the facilities of the public-sector health clinics, especially the Instituto Mexicano del Seguro Social (IMSS; Mexican Institute of Social Security), where understocked pharmacies and long waits to see physicians had been sources of serious complaint. *Los genéricos*, like similares, are kinds of drugs, certainly, but they are also places, as in "Me voy a los genéricos" (I'm going to the generics [pharmacy]), just as one might say, "Me voy a Similares." And they have become places for reasons exceeding their inventories of cheaper generic, similar, and interchangeable medicines: a staggering number of these genéricos and Similares pharmacies also have primary-care clinics adjacent to them, offering low-cost consultations with physicians (at between twenty and thirty pesos per consult, or US$2 to US$3), up to twelve hours a day, six and even seven days a week.

This potent combination—cheap medicines and cheap medical attention—has made generics pharmacies into an infrastructure-like and infrastructure-light force that, in turn, has propelled a powerful recomposition of the landscape of health care in Mexico. In chapter 1, we saw how copied drugs can work as more than substitutes for expensive, leading-brand drugs; generics, similars, and interchangeables have been set in motion alongside and against each other in a crowded market of different equivalencies. In this chapter, I will argue that drugs are not the only locus of such dynamic substitutions and proliferations. In the context of mounting pressure on, expansions of, and dissatisfactions with Mexico's public-health institutions (especially the IMSS and the Seguro Popular), the commerce in generic drugs has, in many respects, come to serve as a substitute for the state. And, just like replacing one medicine with another, this substitution has generated plenty of excess.

A great deal is at stake in this opening observation. Not least is the very big question, What are the implications of turning to a cheap consumer market as the answer to the problem of access to medicines on a mass scale? Following the threads of a robust literature in Latin American cultural studies on neoliberalism and globalization (García Canclini 2001; Yúdice 2001; Sarlo

2001) or the work of anthropologists on global pharmaceutical politics and the right to health (see Biehl and Petryna's [2011] excellent work on judicialization in Brazil, among others), we can certainly imagine where such a substitution might lead: the market subsumes and encroaches on the state; erstwhile "citizens" become atomized "consumers"; forms of collective solidarity are displaced by marketized idioms and mechanisms of individual rights and individual choice (Biehl and Petryna 2011).

Mexico's commerce in generic medicines has certainly taken up residence at the very center of these familiar and important tensions between state and market, public and private sectors, and the broader imaginations of consumers and citizens. But I'll argue that far from delivering us to a generic critique of neoliberalism and its effects, these developments bring us to an analytic opening—a Simipolitical opening, I'll call it. For, while the processes I am tracking are diffuse and have unfolded on a broader scale, Dr. Simi the composite actor (person, mascot, corporate entity, pharmapolitical juggernaut) looms peculiarly large. Dr. Simi/Víctor Gonzalez Torres has vividly theatricalized, thematized, a broader dynamic in which the low-cost consumer market for pharmaceuticals and medical attention has come to both double and trouble the state—to compete with it by copying and even becoming something like it. Though this dynamic does not belong to him alone, González Torres has made it spectacular, visible, vexing, and oddly his: he made his mark by selling copied drugs while simultaneously copying a version of the Mexican state—the classically clientelist PRI state—precisely at a moment when the PRI's hold on power first seemed to be coming to an end. This pharmapolitical dynamic is what I propose to think through the idiom of *Simipolitics*.

Like Dr. Simi himself, the term feels perilously cartoonish. But also like Dr. Simi, it's no joke. Simipolitics immerses us in the mechanisms and discourses of an as-if populism in which the potency of copying, the multiplications of equivalence and that which is "same and not the same," are not just generic-pharmaceutical matters. In Simipolitics, these pharmaceutical relations reverberate in and as politics. Simipolitics thus brings into view two arguments or interventions. First, the term helps me name the way that the low-cost consumer market for generics doesn't just work as an atomizing force set against the state as a locus of solidarity or care. In Dr. Simi's hands, the market in generics is meant *to crowd*—it gathers its crowds in the name of and with the similar, in the name of and as-if the state. Far from simply individuating citizens as consumers, Simi hails his consumers as if they were his citizens, expanding his market through recognizably populist political tactics of gathering-to. Second, and by extension, Simipolitics (and all that has happened through the generics market in Mexico) issues yet another reminder: that state and market are not stable, preexisting entities locked in battle. That argument can take a generic form, so to speak. We know very well that state and market are never diametrically opposed to each other; rather, they have always been intertwined. But it also takes on a particularly vivid character where Mexico's health system is concerned. Tara Schwegler's (2008) insightful work on Mexican social security and pension reform characterizes larger transformations in IMSS not as a straightforward, top-down form of privatization but a hybrid, complex mixture of governing rationalities. The rise of the generics market in Mexico, in its Simipolitical forms, provides another window into how the landscape of health care is being rearranged in Mexico. With it, the elements of state and market themselves are also being rearranged, or recomposed.

Crucial to these arguments is the fact that if the state has arguably become a target of generic substitution, it is also a radically moving target; it has expanded and shape-shifted alongside and in ways that are fully entangled with the cheap(er) generics market. Let's recall that, since 1943, Mexico's major public health system has, on the guild-based model common to many twentieth-century welfare states, provided health coverage and pension support to salaried workers—people with formal employment—and their dependents. By far the largest pillar in this system is IMSS (see figure 2.1). It was joined in the 1950s and 1960s by similar institutions for state workers such as the Instituto de Seguridad y Servicios Sociales de los Trabajadores del Estado (ISSSTE; Institute for Social Security and Services for State Workers), members of the military, and employees of the state-owned petroleum company Pemex (see Schwegler 2008; Martínez et al. 2009). But IMSS and ISSSTE, especially, have had their shortcomings, from the underfunding and medication shortages plaguing their clinics and pharmacies in the late 1990s (and continuing to the present) to the more-than-biopolitical problem that by late 1990s, half of the population did not count with formal work and thus over fifty million people were excluded from state coverage in the first place. The creation of the generics market in 1998 was one dimension of the state's answer to the resulting problems of widespread access to medicines and health care.

But it wasn't just a market that was invented to address this problem. Under President Vicente Fox (2000–2006), his Partido Acción Nacional (PAN; National Action Party), and Secretary of Health Julio Frenk, the state also expanded, with the introduction of *another* Seguro. Frenk's signature

2.1 IMSS's logo, an eagle gathering an Indigenized woman and infant under its protective wing, rendered in statue form on the central IMSS campus, Mexico City, 2008. PHOTO BY AUTHOR.

intervention, the Seguro Popular, was introduced in 2003, part of a constellation of international experiments—including in India, France, and arguably in the United States with the Affordable Care Act under President Barack Obama—to promote "universal coverage" in a diverse array of hybrid public-private "experiments" (Reich et al. 2016; Knaul et al. 2012; Tichenor and Sridhar 2017; Frenk, Gómez-Dantés, and Knaul 2009). But this Seguro has had its difficulties too. For many critics on the left, it worked and sounded a little too much like a market, and for others, including many among its target constituencies, it felt a little too much like the state. Just as Dr. Simi inserted himself firmly in the middle of the new generics market, he has also been right in the thick of the expansion of the state-as-Seguro Popular, both foil to this morphing public sector and, as I'll argue at the end of this chapter, an essential condition of possibility for its emergence.

In the pages to come, I will explore how Simipolitics emerges in two intimately entangled registers. First, I tell the story of how Simi made a mark on

Mexico's pharmapolitical landscape not only by copying drugs but by becoming a domestic copy of the political itself in Mexico. We will see how Simi has activated a potent, sometimes troubling but certainly recognizable litany of political tactics and aesthetics, often in the register of a populist appeal to the care for the health of the Mexican people. In the process, Simipolitics draws our attention to the centrality of copying to theories of populism itself. In the second part of the chapter, I explore how those Simipolitical relations have unfolded in the terrain of health care in particular. Here, I will show how the Simi enterprise doubles the state while the state's expansion takes on characteristics of a market. "State and not the state" might well describe both the Simi enterprise and the Seguro Popular—another locus of excessive doubling.

Simipolitics, Part 1

To understand the moves I am making in this chapter, it may be helpful to recall that the 1990s and early 2000s were a time of multiple "transitions" and transformations in Mexico. I noted in the introduction that Víctor González Torres emerged in 1998, re/born as Dr. Simi, in the midst of several consequential diversifications or "openings." NAFTA had radically extended the "opening" of national industries and economic sectors to transnational capital (land, telecommunications, agriculture among them)—a globalization with many primary and side effects, from the ascendance of Mexican drug cartels to the well-documented decimation of the Mexican countryside, sending people both to major urban centers (Mexico City, Guadalajara, Ciudad Juárez) and to the United States in search of work.

There was, at the same time, an opening of the political field. The PRI lost the presidential election in 2000 to PANista candidate Fox, marking the first time in seventy-one years—since the advent of the revolutionary state—that a party other than the PRI would run the country. The right-leaning PAN victory generated a cautious optimism for many, even on the left; it seemed to signal the possibility of multiparty democracy, and it was a sign, too, of new openings for a nascent civil society (see Poniatowska 1988; Lomnitz-Adler 2000; Sahuí 2009).[1] Importantly for the story I am telling here, Tara Schwegler has argued that the (temporary) end of the PRI's reign—and the election of the former CEO of Coca-Cola México, no less—also marked an end to the PRI's long-standing marginalization or exclusion of the private sector and the business community from politics (and political office) in Mexico (Schwegler 2004; Camp 1989).[2] Meanwhile, another opening—that of the licit pharmaceutical market with the introduction of generic medicines for commercial sale—meant that the transnational drug companies were facing the loss of their monopoly in Mexico. And, as noted previously, with the invention of the Seguro Popular in 2003, there was the further diversification of a health-care system that was already multiplied. The openings were many, and González Torres took them all.

Víctor González Torres is a strange and important figure, both singular in himself, it would seem, and a composite who combines and plays back a pitch-perfect inventory of Mexican political history, aesthetics, and modes of political pageantry, including at times a familiar kind of mercenary clientelism. The González Torres family can be considered one of Mexico's many minor dynasties, with a notable presence in the pharmaceutical business, in elite institutional circles, and in party politics (Anderson and López 2008). Víctor, who started identifying as Dr. Simi soon after the opening of his first pharmacies in 1998, is the great-grandson of the founder of Laboratorios Best, one of the many labs established in the 1950s to manufacture nonbranded drugs for the major public-sector health institutions of Mexico. Víctor's grandfather was the head of purchasing for ISSSTE. Víctor's brother Javier was the founder of one of Similares' biggest competitors, the pharmacy chain Farmacias del Ahorro (Pharmacies of Savings). Another brother was rector of the prestigious private Universidad Iberoamericana, on the outskirts of Mexico City (Anderson and López 2008). Still another brother was the founder of the Green Party of Mexico, a party that is infamous for being very dubiously green (see Johnson 2012). Mexico's version is the only Green Party in the world to support the death penalty, for example. It also happens to have developed a sizable interest in promoting state policies favorable to the generics market.

Farmacias Similares emerged directly from this stew of pharma-family networks and political entanglement. Víctor, trained as an accountant, was given leadership of the family's Laboratorios Best in the mid-1990s. Given all that I just mentioned, it is perhaps not surprising that he proved uncannily well-placed to take advantage of the major regulatory shifts initiated by the federal government in 1998. Just as Ernesto Zedillo's secretary of health announced new policies to allow generics into private circulation, González Torres announced the opening of the first eight branches of Farmacias Similares—a chain that would sell only copied drugs, either made by its own Laboratorios Best or purchased from other generics companies that were largely but not exclusively Mexican. In only a few years and on the back of an exceptionally robust franchising practice, the initial eight storefronts had multiplied to two thousand, and then three thousand; outlets now number over thirty-five hundred in Mexico, and Farmacias Similares dominates the private Mexican generics market (Célis 2016). The total number of Similares pharmacies surges to over four thousand if one counts storefronts in Chile, Guatemala, and elsewhere in Latin America (see Garzón Ortiz 2006).

But in all this market expansiveness, we should not lose sight of the fact that the Simi enterprise began in the form of a Mexican generics lab that, like roughly two hundred smaller and larger generics manufacturers in Mexico, had counted the Seguro Social and allied public-sector institutions as its primary client and buyer from the 1950s until 1998. In 2002, an industry analyst described the effect of the new generics market thus: "Some of the suppliers to the public sector have partially shifted their production to the private market" (J. González 2002). That is a dry, seemingly unremarkable observation, but, as we saw in chapter 1, this simple shift—same drugs, new market—is precisely where generics started to become spectacular. In their multiplication and excess, as I've argued, they became more than (mere) commodities. But I am not only invoking the spectacular to point to those multiplications of equivalents, sames, and similars; *the spectacular*, in this book, is a pharmapolitical term. The excess to which it points, and which it gathers, lies in the ways that a private market for generics helps bring into view a series of doublings, of the more than, at multiple registers simultaneously—including in the (Simi)political. There is no better way to explain or exemplify these multiple registers of spectacular excess than attending to the ways that Víctor González Torres took Mexico's "generic" openings and claimed them as his own, over and over again. As we saw in chapter 1, he did so in part by making the very principle of generic substitution—the same, but cheaper!—into his own unmistakable, ubiquitous slogan. His auratic presence made the similar, and his similares, into proper nouns, sites and sources of distinction. This chapter explores how he did so.

González Torres did not lay claim to this market or even to similarity itself by advertising or marketing specific drugs. In fact, generics manufacturers typically do not advertise particular medicines since their drugs, as commodity drugs, are not supposed to be particular at all. Instead, González Torres announced himself, from the start, as a pharmapolitical actor. When Dr. Simi opened his first pharmacies, González Torres carefully picked his first political fight(s)—not only raising a quasipopulist pharmaceutical challenge to "the transnationals" but staging an attention-getting tussle with the Catholic Church. One of Simi's first major publicity campaigns was for the Simicondón (the Simi condom), which provoked the Church hierarchy into wan attempts to stifle the campaign and the condoms, which in turn gave Simi an opportunity to ridicule the Church. If the condom campaign seemed to provoke an antiquated oligarchic power center, it was arguably also a pilot proxy war with the new party in power: the party that had dislodged the PRI from the presidency in 2000, the PAN, was closely tied to the Catholic Church in Mexico.

While going on the attack against new and established seats of power, Dr. Simi used the commerce in domestic copies to reanimate a kitschy and consequential version of the nationalist and populist idioms of the 1960s and 1970s in Mexico, asserting himself as a new vehicle for delivering the older promises of the receding corporatist state. Indeed, González Torres/ Dr. Simi's iteration of pharmapolitics included a series of moves, in the early 2000s (just as his pharmacies were taking off), to (re)create the ingredients of what we might call a Similar social state. The tentacles of Simi's wide-ranging enterprise, gathered under a nonprofit foundation called the Best Foundation, came to extend far beyond Farmacias Similares, its adjacent clinics, and its thousands of outlets across the country. Deploying the familiar tactics of clientelism under the PRI, and echoing the many-faceted offerings of IMSS itself (Schwegler 2011), the Simi enterprise busily and loudly established "social assistance programs" for the poor, the Indigenous, the elderly, and the disabled.[3] The Similares enterprise hosted *fiestas populares* in city and town *zócalos* (squares), with costumed, dancing Dr. Simis handing out the classically popular/populist commodities of rice and beans. When the price of corn, and hence tortillas, spiked in the mid-2000s (one of the many perverse effects of NAFTA'S opening of Mexico's market to US-grown corn), Farmacias Similares started selling tortillas too—at a steep discount.

Further confirming its intention to occupy the now-underdetermined role of benefactor of the Mexican people, the Similares enterprise (again, gathered under the auspices of Foundation Best), would receive petitioners for aid or assistance at their corporate headquarters in Mexico City. On one of my visits to Foundation Best's offices in 2005, the then director of public relations, María José Gutiérrez, was about to usher me to my next appointment when a woman in her early thirties was brought to her door. Gutiérrez suggested I stay, as I might find the conversation interesting. This other visitor, Carmen Pérez, looking a bit nervous, had come to follow up on a written request she had made to Foundation Best on behalf of her organization. Together with a few other women in her corner of Iztapalapa, a sprawling poor to working-class zone of the city, Pérez had started a small child-care center to help the women in the neighborhood who worked during the day (many as domestic workers) but whose children were still too young to be in school. The center, she summed up in her bid to Gutiérrez, was hoping Dr. Simi's foundation might help with a donation of funds or supplies.

Gutiérrez pulled out the file and made a noncommittal gesture toward in-kind assistance, noting that they would not be able to just give money. But, she noted, "We could give you a franchise, which you could operate. And then you'd have a source of revenue." "A franchise? Of the pharmacy?" Pérez asked. Yes, a franchise of the pharmacy. My jaw dropped ever so slightly, as did Carmen's (she demurred, saying she would bring the proposal to the other women). I followed up with Pérez a few weeks later, visiting her at her child-care center, a repurposed two-story house located on a quiet, narrow street precisely in the midst of the kind of *barrio popular* that Simi officials encouraged franchisees to seek out as ideal locations for their pharmacies. "No, no, we didn't take the pharmacy, of course," Pérez said quietly. "We considered it, but that's not what we were looking for; we're not really set up for that." But, she added, "They did help us a little with some basic supplies—cooking oil, soap, rice." "Why did you approach Simi?" I asked. She explained that when the child-care center was set up, the city government (under the left-leaning Partido Revolucionario Democrático [PRD]) had made grants and support available for operating expenses for social assistance organizations such as hers. But, she noted, "Those funds aren't there anymore." The city government no longer provided avenues for support, nor did the federal government under the PAN'S decentralizing mandates. They were thus scrambling to keep things going. She had heard that Simi's Foundation Best provided social assistance to organizations, so they decided to give it a try. "It helps a little," she shrugged.[4]

Gutiérrez, at Foundation Best, told me at the time that Pérez was certainly not the only person to lodge such a request. People were arriving frequently at her door with personal entreaties because "they heard," in Gutiérrez's words, "that Fundación Best, represented by Dr. Simi, *"tiene un compromiso con los que menos tienen"* (has a commitment to helping Mexico's neediest).[5] Such requests and such bequests—whether in response to in-person, direct petitions for support or on a mini mass scale in well-publicized acts of distribution (as in the fiestas in public squares or rice-and-bean giveaways at Farmacias Similares)—are famously the stuff of which the PRI's everyday corporatist clientelism was made (see de la Peña 2000, 123), not to mention the foundations of a more spectacularly charismatic populism (I think of Eva Perón in Argentina, receiving thousands of supplicants and promising them *electrodo-*

mésticos [household appliances], a mattress, shelter) (Auyero 2001).[6] These transactional relations were certainly already politics by a *Similar* name.

But González Torres's pharmaceutical incursions quickly became even more explicitly political. One dimension of this emergent Simipolitics was a notable shift in the target of González Torres's declarations of war. By the early 2000s, Dr. Simi was no longer primarily seeking to defend the Mexican people from the transnationals (the multinational pharmaceutical companies) but rather against the Mexican state itself in the form of IMSS and successive secretaries of health, which and whom he accused of not meeting their commitments to care for "the people." González Torres launched an all-out publicity war on IMSS via unceasing, multiplatform criticism of what he (though not he alone) condemned as critical shortfalls in the state's public health institutions—not least, medication shortages. On TV, in full-page ads in Mexico City dailies, and on the radio, González Torres/Dr. Simi amplified allegations of corruption in public-sector medication procurement. He also proposed a pointed remedy, with a dramatic offer to fill prescriptions for free for any IMSS beneficiary who could not fill their prescription at IMSS pharmacies. For its part, IMSS did not take this lying down, and the institution refused to continue to buy medicines from Laboratorios Best (González Torres's generics lab), citing problems with their quality.

Dr. Simi's "war" on and with IMSS soon further crystallized in the form of an anticorruption movement as he attached himself to an obligatory and persistent cause for Mexican civil society actors and political reformers. Thus, under the banner of his generically named National Movement against Corruption, González Torres began to stage marches in Mexico City throughout 2004 and 2005 "in defense of the Mexican people" against the corruption of IMSS and against Secretary of Health Julio Frenk, formerly of the WHO, whom González Torres accused of being "more comfortable in the offices of the international bureaucracy" than he was caring for the health of the Mexican people (Grupo Por Un Pais Mejor 2005). These marches managed to gather thousands of people on the Paseo de la Reforma, a common staging ground for political demonstrations at the heart of Mexico City. One (very) sympathetic account of an early rally at the major transit hub, Cuatro Caminos, gave a crowd estimate of fifteen thousand (*Macroeconomia* [Mexico] 2005). The marches portended a move that seemed to many pundits, customers, and politicians simultaneously inevitable, worrying, and risible ("Lo mismo, pero más idiota!"): they were prelude to the announcement that González Torres/Dr. Simi (singular) would run for president in 2006. If he was now defending the Mexican people against both the transnational drug companies and against the Mexican state itself, he would do so in the name of the state and by trying to become (like) the state. "Let's save IMSS!" was the rallying cry for his attacks on IMSS and on Julio Frenk (Grupo Por Un Pais Mejor 2005).

Simi-candidato

Caramba! Politics just took a not-exactly-unexpected turn towards the pharmaceutical: Dr. Simi has become, or wants to become, the interchangeable generic candidate for the Social Democrat party, substituting for the similar Patricia Mercado.
—ENRÍQUE GALVÁN OCHOA, "CANDIDATO GENÉRICO INTERCAMBIABLE"

With his attempted entry into electoral politics at the national level, González Torres/Dr. Simi began to illuminate some of the key dimensions of what I am thinking of in this book as a spectacular pharmapolitics. Hailing "his" popular masses simultaneously as customers and an as-if electorate, Dr. Simi showed us more broadly how difficult it is to distinguish between the two. This is Simipolitics, as a both/and proposition: "Simi-candidato" showed how the rise of consumer markets doesn't just atomize, turning erstwhile citizens into individualized consumers; it also gathers its crowds by pointing to the ever-elusive promises of a *state that cares*.

For all this, his electoral efforts were not without their complications, which troubled any idea that there might be a distinction between a "real" campaign and a "simulation" of one. Dr. Simi's bid to stand as a proper political candidate ran into some trouble at the outset, not least because he could not find an established party to accept him as their own. The Social Democrats declined his offer to substitute himself for their existing candidate, but González Torres was not deterred. Claudio Lomnitz-Adler (2001) has written about the constitutive place of ritual, and ritualized performance, to the Mexican presidency, and certainly the familiar trappings of Mexican political candidacy and (anticipated) executive office seemed to come easy to González Torres/Dr. Simi, even without a party to call his own. We could count among these trappings Simi's corporate flag, the bouncy corporate hymn, and Simi's tricolor sash (green, white, red, the Mexican national palette), not to mention the weekly press conferences, ubiquitous television

2.2 Press conference at Grupo Por Un País Mejor, Mexico City, with Victor González Torres (Dr. Simi) in the center, June 2005. PHOTO BY AUTHOR.

presence, and ever-increasing attacks on prominent political figures in 2005 and 2006 (see figure 2.2).

The political campaign was based at the headquarters of the umbrella organization Grupo Por Un País Mejor (Group for a Better Country) that housed a multitude of González Torres's projects, from the pharmacy enterprise, to the social assistance programs, to Laboratorios Best, and still more. I spent some quality time in Grupo's headquarters in 2005 and 2006, where the wall along the central stairway was decorated with a cartoonish (there is that word again) rendition of Diego Rivera's famous stairway murals in the National Palace in Mexico City. Rivera's murals depict the revolutionary state's version of the long sweep of Mexican national history and its socialist future. Simi's version explicitly gestured to Rivera's masterpiece while including a picture of Dr. Simi the mascot handing out pills alongside other iconographic highlights. Among its many offices—the office of Laboratorio Best's chief chemist, the corporate publicity office, the export/import licensing office, the philanthropic operations office—Grupo's headquarters also housed a buzzing media monitoring operation. The frenetic energy of this space felt very much to me like what one would expect to find in a political campaign's war room, as Grupo employees busily tracked and compiled every single mention of Farmacias Similares and González Torres—positive, negative, indifferent, and academic—in the national, regional, and local press.

Dr. Simi's presidential bid took other recognizable forms as well. Former and then-current employees of Simi pharmacies and Foundation Best (the "philanthropic" arm of Simi's enterprise) with whom I worked and whom I interviewed both during the period of Simi's run for presidency and many years later, painted a vivid picture for me of the ways that the Simi enterprise used their pharmacies to suture together some of the many established tactics of patronage, employment, and gatherings-to that so powerfully defined the PRI's twentieth-century run. Guillermo Delgado, who was pursuing a PhD at one of Mexico City's premier research institutions when I met him, talked to me at length in 2010 about what he found to be a harrowing experience working for the Simi enterprise in 2005, squarely in the buildup to the 2006 presidential campaign. He had, in 2005, just finished his undergraduate degree in psychology and was looking for work. He found himself unexpectedly landing a job as a psychologist in Simi's counseling services ("I just got my degree; I had never counseled a patient in my life!").[7] The counseling services, themselves a short-lived experiment, were offered only in major Simi "service centers" (this one was in Colonia Doctores in Mexico City); they were not offered in franchised outlets. In fact, this service center offered a wide range of services: there was a Farmacias Similares, of course, and physician consultation offices as well as the new clinic for psychological counseling at twenty-five pesos an hour (US$1.25), staffed by people like Delgado. But there was also a "consumer protection office," set up to receive complaints about pharmaceutical products. Indeed, Víctor González Torres had started to position the Similares enterprise in polemic public pronouncements not just as *subject to* state regulation but as a Simi-regulatory force itself, claiming to be the only chain that independently surveils the labs from which they buy medicines. This office and the state-like potency it sought to project—Simi the regulator, Simi the protector of the consumer—didn't quite attract the kinds of complaints the enterprise seemed to want or expect: "Mostly people came in to complain about the Simi condom—it breaks, apparently! So they closed that down."[8]

Simi's service center, Delgado recounted to me, had also started to function very much as a political campaign headquarters and a party office (even though Simi had yet to find a political party to accept him) open to the public.

Beyond being offered a chance to counsel people when he had no experience doing so, what really concerned Delgado was the way this service center began to function as a place for recruiting people for González Torres's presidential campaign: "They would get the information (names, addresses) of people who came in to use their *consultorios*, or who came into the pharmacy, and then browbeat them into participating in *mitines*," he told me. "Browbeat how?" I asked. He answered, "By reminding them how much the company does for them, how much Dr. Simi helps them, insisting that they should give back something in return to this company that 'gives so much to them.'"[9] Mitines are gatherings that are something between a mass march and a mass meeting; they are a key display of public power enacted by political parties in Mexico. Party leaders or delegates usually assemble the enrolled/faithful in smaller meeting places and then scoop them up and bus them to the zone of assembly, such as the Zócalo, the massive central square in Mexico City, or Paseo de la Reforma, where Simi staged several of his marches in 2005. Seeing this familiar manifestation of politics reproduced via Simi's service center was upsetting to Delgado, in part because of the way that people who had come in seeking health services had been corralled into participating in political activity, and in part because of who these people were: they were "mostly old people, left standing or sitting around the Simi service center for hours and hours waiting to be picked up, just left there, no chairs, nothing, and it was cold."[10]

Was this a "real" political campaign or a simulation of one? Was Simi using politics—including the distribution of social assistance and staples to those who have the least—as a clever marketing ploy for his pharmaceutical enterprise? Or was the pharmaceutical enterprise an elaborate front for gathering, even browbeating, loyalties for a political project? There is, at this point, every reason to refuse the imperative or temptation to try to disentangle the pharma from the politics, to try to discern the real nature of the enterprise. Simipolitics is a constitutively both/and proposition, a vivid reminder that the spectacle of politics *is* the spectacle of mass-mediated markets (Baudrillard 1994). In Simi's pharmapolitical enterprise, one thing is certainly clear. In the astute words of anthropologist Casey Walsh, who has long worked and lived in Mexico and with whom I have discussed all of this at length over the years, Simi was ratifying the common political sense that to get anything done in Mexico, you need to gather your masses.[11]

Simi was in fact cultivating the popular masses as both customers and an as-if electorate, another register of same and not the same. In so doing, he also made clear that it has become harder and harder to disentangle the two. In Simipolitics, then, it is not just that erstwhile citizens, subjects of the state, and beneficiaries of the Seguro Social were now being hailed as consumers (though certainly this was happening). Dr. Simi doubled this move back on itself, mobilizing consumers as-if they were (his) citizens, as Simi-populist political actors. This is just one of the ways that Dr. Simi suggests how a rapidly expanding, private, low-cost consumer market in medicines and health care doesn't just atomize. It crowds. It *gathers to*.

This pharmapolitical mobilization manifests in the examples I have just discussed: the festive, ritual distributions in city squares; the surveys in Farmacias Similares asking people to signal their willingness to vote for Dr. Simi should he run; the nominal, in-kind bequests to petitioners; the anticorruption marches and mitines. My interviews with former and current Simi employees, which spanned the period from 2005 to 2016, also paint a picture of González Torres's agility in other familiar tactics for gathering masses to a cause. If they seem at least a little bit mercenary, this also makes them perfectly recognizable as properly political (de la Peña 2000, 120–24).

Sociologist Guillermo de la Peña (2000) has shown how, in the context of very little labor protection, one of Mexican clientelism's chief modalities has been its gatekeeping functions in relation to work and employment. In other words, "employment" becomes a way for parties to lay claim to workers as an electorate. Simi has not neglected this tactic either. Former Simi employees, whose names and identities I am deliberately keeping very vague here at their request, recounted to me how the company was essentially blackmailing them in 2006: if they did not hand over their voter registration cards so that González Torres's enterprise could vote on their behalf they wouldn't receive their fifteen-day salary (this vote-by-substitute was in fact legal). Similar tales were never far from the surface whenever I spoke with people who had worked in various parts of the sprawling Simi enterprise; these stories repeatedly came up unsolicited. A woman who had once worked for Foundation Best as a regional representative told me she had started to become wary of González Torres's *prepotencia* (arrogance), finally quitting once the foundation put "all this pressure on us to participate in mitines."[12] Another current employee told me of a tactic, to which she had been subject, that helps bind together the little coercions of employment and politics: "If you go to work for them directly in their own branches [i.e., not in franchises] or in headquarters in Mexico City, they make you sign your letter of resignation when you come in." My response was a shocked, "What?" Her response: "Yes, so you can't accuse them of firing you illegally."[13]

All this unseemliness is of course not a deformed "bad copy" of real politics in Mexico. A vast social science library on corruption and Mexican politics (some of it quite thoughtful in its refusal to use the term *corruption* as an accusation or to signal a lack) has been dedicated to trying to understand the ways in which clientelism, the distribution of personal favors or assistance, the organization and control of work itself, and the "informalization" of formal institutional practices (de la Peña 2000) long served as the glue holding together something like a social contract between the PRI and its "people" (Erfani 1995; Lomnitz-Adler 2001; Morris 1991). Over the last several *sexenios* (six-year presidential terms), after the PAN took the presidency from the PRI, and even more so in the hotly contested 2006 election between Felipe Calderón (of the PAN) and Andrés Manuel López Obrador (of the Left party, the Partido Revolucionario Democrático [PRD]), it became clear that the PRI did not hold a monopoly on such tactics. The cautionary tales of many analysts watching the temporary demise of the PRI in the early 2000s reminded us that these practices have long constituted politics more broadly in Mexico, not just one party's version thereof (see Morris 2009).

Simipolitics, Populist Politics

From the mitines to the anticorruption marches, from the fiestas populares to the distribution of small favors to petitioners, Dr. Simi was busily mobilizing widely recognized tropes and practices of both the Right and the Left in Mexico; he was deploying the operations of ruling and opposition party politics; he was both civil society and a pretender to rule. In the occupation of so many positions at once, Simipolitics paints in the palette of populism. That is, González Torres/Dr. Simi animates—sets in motion, deploys, evokes, and invokes—many of the things that occupy political theory and political science's accounts of, and concerns with, populism. And, I'll argue, he does so not only politically but pharmapolitically. The generic multiplicities that occupied us in chapter 1—the ways that generic equivalence became swamped by, and proliferated into, a crowded field of multiple similarities or samenesses that are also not the same—are not merely pharmaceutical relations. They are the currency of many theories of populism (Sánchez 2016; Laclau 2005). As Rafael Sánchez (2016) has shown in his work on populism in Venezuela, theories and practices of populism themselves paint in the palette of the copy, of imitation, of a fragile equivalence that is, as Dr. Simi has already shown us, so much *more than*.

I want to build up to this argument first by acknowledging how not useful, or at least how frustrating, the term *populism* can be. A rapidly proliferating literature on populism in sociology, political theory, and anthropology since the early 2000s (given new urgency and vigor in anglophone worlds since Donald Trump, Brexit, and the rise of right-wing ethnonationalism more broadly) has grappled, serially, with the underdetermined nature of populism in the world. As a term, it seems to point to such a wide range of political formations and ideologies, from Left to Right, from democratic to authoritarian, that it might in fact mean nothing at all (at least, that is the preoccupation). In much of this literature, populist movements or regimes have no fixed attributes in terms of content, except the one that Dr. Simi invoked in his efforts on behalf of the *pueblo mexicano*: an appeal to "the people."

Is Dr. Simi *really* a populist? If so, is he a *good* populist or a *bad* populist? *If* we wanted to get some traction on such questions, anthropologist Jean Comaroff (2011) has argued, careful contextualization might be the only way forward.[14] But political theorist Ernesto Laclau takes the opposite approach. Laclau sets content and deep context aside, turning instead to form, and in so doing opens the door to a Simipolitical understanding of populism as theory and practice. In *On Popular Reason* (2005), Laclau suggests we read the constitutive move of populist logics formally or structurally. That is, he argues that the notion of "the people" serves as the basis for a logic of equivalence and identification such that radically different demands can become equivalent—*equivalente!*—at least temporarily. Such equivalencies can be defined in relation to a common antagonist, internal or foreign (i.e., the transnationals or IMSS); an appeal to the people; or an attachment to the figure of what Simi employees indeed called, in my visits to corporate headquarters in Mexico City in the buildup to the 2006 election, "our leader."

I do not normally opt for formal structural analysis. I like my deep contextualizations but something hails me here. Part of what compels me in Laclau's analysis is the itinerary he took to arrive at this argument. He builds his understanding of these "operations of equivalence" on the back of an engagement with the excesses of copying, imitation, and suggestion that animate late nineteenth-century crowd theory. The crowd theorists whom he engages—including Gustave LeBon, Gabriel Tarde, and Sigmund Freud—were profoundly attuned to the potency of imitation and contagion, of similitude and copying, as the signature modes of crowd emergence. Even so, Laclau reads those crowd theorists as if copying essentially leads to or produces a (temporary) field of equivalence, homogeneity, and sameness. Rafael Sánchez builds on this crowd literature to push Laclau's analysis much further, proposing a theory of radical populism: in Venezuela, he argues, there has long been a serial alternation between liberal aspirations to citizenship based on equivalence and interchangeability, on the one hand, and crowd emergence, on the other, in which such equivalencies dissolve into, and are swamped by, an excess of imitation and copying (Sánchez 2016, 6, 11).

With Sánchez, I suggest that in the crowd theory that Laclau engages, and in the world of Simipolitics, imitation, similarity, and copying lead us to a more spectacularly exuberant formation. If we try hard enough—if we read Laclau Simipolitically—we might indeed hold onto some of that vexing liveliness. For, at the center of Laclau's argument is the way that equivalencies—the same! *lo mismo!*—are made and then fall apart again. They cannot stand still; they do not hold for long; and when they do not, something else, something more, emerges. The story of Peronism in Argentina provides what I find to be one of his more compelling examples. In Argentina, the figure, the idea, or at the very least the name of Juan Perón has been able to gather or attract a remarkably wide range of political visions from 1944 until the present. This was the case in Perón's presence in Argentina, in his absence (exile), and then again perhaps even more strikingly after his death. In these various moments, Peronism (and Perón the leader) was claimed by right-wing antilabor militants, by left-wing prolabor parties, and many factions within and beyond. If they claimed Perón, he claimed them as well, as "the people" whose demands, sovereignty, and representation would be fulfilled in his rule. But such articulations—the making equivalent of radically divergent claims, demands, and positions—are contingent. The moment they are called in or made real—the moment when the empty signifier must be attached strongly to a particular signified—is often the occasion for their collapse. When Perón returned from exile in 1973, for example, the identifications of different groups with him, and in Laclau's terms the "chain of equivalencies" that they had established with each other through a claim on him, could no longer hold. The people fragmented (again) into contentious factions (Laclau 2005, 214–21).

If the ultimate realization of a people fully unified with its leader is impossible, this tells us something too about the "logics of identification and equivalence" on which this unity is based, at least in Laclau's terms. They cannot be full, total, or lasting. Francisco Panizza (2005), commenting on Laclau's analytics, notes indeed that such "identification always fails to produce full identities" (28). In its failure, equivalence dissolves into something that is potentially less than. But we might also argue, Simipolitically, that these failures are also productive: they generate more—more disappointment, demands, reclamation, mobilization, and hence more politics (28). The equivalence at the heart of this formal understanding of populism is a relation that, in its full impossibility, is constitutively more than. It is spectacular.

We already have grounds for thinking this relation "generically" and thus Simipolitically. For, as we saw in detail in chapter 1, Laclau's description of the logics of populism is also a description of how the "operations of equivalence" work in the terrain of generic pharmapolitics in Mexico. The relations of equivalence that anchor the regulation and sale of generics keep fragmenting within and across the registers of science, regulatory thresholds, and commerce—chemical equivalence, bioequivalence, interchangeability, similarity. This fragmentation is confusing, certainly, but it isn't necessarily a failure; rather, the very proliferation of equivalencies that animated the prior chapter, as with Dr. Simi's operations in this chapter, provide an idiom and a substrate for understanding how (generic) equivalence is not an either/or proposition; it is a both/and multiplication. Víctor González Torres's Dr. Simi has been, from the start, squarely in the middle of this activation of equivalence as meaningful, proliferative difference: "Same, but cheaper"; same and similar; same and not the same.

In this light, it feels impossible not to see in Simipolitics shades of a lively analytics of populism. After all, Simipolitics is precisely an operation and exercise in form. Dr. Simi has hailed the people in ways that seem to exhaust the incoherent checklists that so frustrate political theorists trying to get a handle, empirically, on what populism *really* is, from mobilizing the people against enemies within (the corrupt state) and without (foreign companies) to distributing goods (from employment to tortillas) and demanding loyalty in return. In González Torres's articulation of a pharmaceutical populism, he/it/they (the person, the mascot, the enterprise) loudly and cheerfully proclaim to be all things to all people simultaneously—state and market, civil society and private enterprise, nationalist defender of the country and leader of a Bolivarian Latin American revolution, champion of those who have the least and champion of those who earn a lot. "I am," González Torres has often declared with a wink, "Che Guevara in a Mercedes."

In a distinctly pharmapolitical turn, he has done all this while explicitly laying claim to the multivalent principle of equivalence itself (lo mismo!). Dr. Simi's operations are dizzying not just because of their scope, their diversity, or their uncanny echoes of established political tactics. They are also dizzying because he/it/they perform(s) a rousing rendition of populist politics explicitly in the name of an equivalence that dissolves into something else, into something more. González Torres's Simipolitics can take the shape it does, even or especially as a target for ridicule ("Lo mismo pero más idiota!"), only because of its resonance within particular zones of tolerance—what an anthropologist might call *context*, or what a pharmacologist might call *the area below the curve*—in which "same and not the same" is not a failure but rather the very route to potency.

I began this chapter by invoking Isabelle Stengers's restaging of the idea of the pharmakon—a remedy that can, depending on the dosage, become its opposite (i.e., failure and potency, poison and remedy). I did so precisely because, in Stengers's thinking, the pharmakon is a both/and formulation of pharma(political) potency. It disallows the question of whether any given drug is really this or really that and instead insists on the proliferative possibility of that which is both/and. But when, and how, and in what form does one kind of potency become another?

Dr. Simi did not, of course, win the Mexican presidency in 2006. The more serious contender in that election was Andres Manuel López Obrador. Amlo, as he is called, had been a very popular, left-leaning mayor of Mexico City and at the time was a leading figure in the Left party, the PRD. When PAN-ista candidate Felipe Calderón was (barely) declared the winner of the 2006 election, López Obrador vigorously contested the close results: he declared himself the legitimate president and asserted that he would run a parallel government from the street. Over the next year and a half, Amlo periodically mobilized up to one hundred thousand people in marches and occupations that brought Mexico City to a standstill—much bigger, we might note, than Dr. Simi's marches in the buildup to that election. Two elections later, in 2018, López Obrador won the Mexican presidency, with his own new party, called Morena. His candidacy and then victory triggered warnings from centrist and right-leaning pundits and business leaders in Mexico, the Americas, and Europe that Mexico was running the risk of electing a dangerous left-wing populist as president.[15] From the 2006 election to the present, it could be tempting to see Dr. Simi as a curious and possibly cynical political sideshow, a pharmapolitical simulation of a presidential candidate eclipsed by the fact of several actual campaigns and dueling "legitimate" presidents. But Dr. Simi was not incidental to that 2006 electoral contest, nor to subsequent claims to parallel legitimacies, same and not the same. His endeavors have in fact been central to, and a spectacularly visible version of, an ongoing reconfiguration of the coordinates of the Mexican social state where health is concerned. This point delivers us to Simipolitics, part 2.

Simpolitics, Part 2: The Seguros

As has become evident by now, in Víctor González Torres/Dr. Simi's hands, selling generic medicines was never merely a business proposition; the Similares project was always something more than that. Of the many things it has been, Similares has been part of a serious reorganization of health care for sectors of the population that the state has called, respectively, the "social" and the "popular."[16] The Seguro Social in Mexico, as with social security and pension systems across Latin America (not to mention the United States), has weathered decades of shrinking state support and growing political attacks on its legitimacy, with privatization consistently looming large as threat and alternative (see Schwegler 2008, 2011). Raquel Pêgo, a researcher of Latin American social security systems based in Mexico City, generously shared with me her views on the matter in the early days of Dr. Simi's emergence. She argued that the combination of disaffection with IMSS on the one hand and the vast swathes of people left uncovered by its embrace (however imperfect) on the other created a vast "unorganized market" of the uninsured.[17] In the early 2000s, the federal government and Dr. Simi both set out to organize this unorganized market, to enroll the unenrolled, and to hail Mexico's more than fifty million uninsured people as a population, a market, and a constituency.

This development brings us to our second Simipolitical opening, in which the commerce in generic medicines has come to compete with the state by doubling it, specifically in the provision of primary care and pharmaceuticals. Let me, then, return to the question with which I opened this chapter: For what are generics substitutes? For the vast number of people who earn low wages (not to mention the very poor), private doctors and *medicinas de patente* are manifestly out of reach and hence are not necessarily the targets of generic substitution or alternation—this, or that? Instead, the contrast and hence the "choice" that has emerged repeatedly in my work over the past decade is that between Simi or the genéricos, on the one hand, and the consultorios and pharmacies of the major public-health institutions, on the other. And the substance of comparison is, in many ways, "care," lived intimately as attention and accessibility.

Attention is the concern that animated many of my interlocutors' descriptions to me of their itineraries, decisions, and experiences when they seek out medical attention—for gastritis and indigestion, for a pain in the right wrist, for a cough, for diarrhea, for fever, for vitamin B12 injections, for their hypertension, or to keep tabs on their diabetes. Dolores Salcedo, a domestic worker in her late thirties, explained to me a few years ago why she had become a loyal customer of Dr. Simi. We were in the midst of a lengthy conversation that also included her aunt; they work together for the same upper-middle-class family in an affluent Mexico City suburb near the exit to Toluca. Her aunt has worked for this family for close to thirty years. Dolores had recently joined her, to help out in the household. Though their own work does not give them access to the Seguro Social, they both have (or have periodically had) access to its clinics, doctors, and medicines through their husbands and fathers.

Dolores, the younger of the two, declared in no uncertain terms that Simi beckons to her in large part because she has no patience left for the Seguro Social and its mode of (in)attention. The doctors in the Seguro, she said, "don't even want to get anywhere near you. One told me: 'stay there' [on the other side of the room] with a hand up. 'I don't need to check you over, I know what you have from what you just told me.'" Dolores felt insulted and angry. But the Simi doctors are different. "Me atienden bien," she explained to me: "They take good care of me; they pay attention.... The doctors in the Simi [pharmacy] are very, very good. They weigh us, they look at us, they check us. If you compare doctor to doctor, I definitely opt for Simi or the genéricos." Her aunt, Eugenia, joined in: "The [Simi] doctors also prescribe you vitamins, liquids, help you think about what to eat, like recommending a lot of fruit, depending on how you're doing and how you're feeling or what's going on."[18]

This difference in attention also accrues in the twinned questions of time and space—of how quickly you can be seen, of how easily you can get to the doctor's clinic or the pharmacy. Mexico's deregulated commercial space has directly produced something that is lived by so many as a substantial improvement in access and hence care. In the country as a whole, there are no regulatory restrictions on how many pharmacies can operate in any given area, and the requirements for who may open and operate a pharmacy are effectively quite loose. The result is the pronounced sense that low-cost pharmacies are "everywhere"—a provisional everywhere of course—but whether in dense concentration or simply in their one-off presence in what might otherwise get called "underserved" areas, the visibility and presence of these low-cost pharmacy-clinics stand in stark contrast to the centralized and much more concentrated geography of the Seguro's facilities. It is a difference that matters. It's not just that the Simi doctors "take good care of me," Dolores noted: "Wherever I am, they are there—right on my normal route. I just have to hop off the bus, no need to go looking for one." Eugenia assented, noting that in fact she often goes to a genéricos rather than the Simi because the former is right on her route home; the Simi is another few blocks away. In any case, Dolores continued, "The Seguro doesn't even have a clinic near my house, and there, the doctor might not even arrive, and you have to make another appointment, after waiting all day, for another day." This inaccessibility is a key part of the constellation of disregard that Dolores associates with the Seguro: "They also always tell you need to lose weight." "And they're all fat themselves!" chimed in her aunt with a laugh. Dolores continued, "The service in the Seguro is really bad. I don't even want it anymore."

The contrast that Dolores highlighted, between Simi's attention to her specificity and the Seguro's insulting depersonalization, is recognizably part of wide-ranging and long-running discourses of market-oriented critiques of state institutions, especially where health is concerned (see Day 2015).[19] The market, we are so often told, is what provides the privilege of having your specificity attended to, as when the Simi doctors *prescribe you vitamins, liquids, help you think about what to eat, depending on how you're doing and how you're feeling or what's going on*. Anthropologist Emilia Sanabria (2010) explores this nexus beautifully in her work on the relation among class, contraceptives, and the heterogeneity of citizenship in Brazil. Her analysis elicits the stark differences many people articulate in Brazil between the indignities of mere formal equivalence before the law—that to which the interchangeable masses are relegated—and the personalized or special treatment that is "due" those who see themselves as part of Brazil's middle or upper classes.[20] Sanabria notes that this broader dynamic has become materialized vividly in the domain of health care, particularly contraception. The rhetorics and practices of formal civic (in)equivalence become pharmaceutical: the urban poor are given standardized treatment (the same dosage, the same method of delivery) in contrast to the personalized care and tailored choices that middle-class women demand, expect, and often receive in private clinics. In this dynamic, I might say that equivalence before the law (that provided by universal state care) is *mere*-d. Mere equivalence is for the masses; privilege, on the other hand, is the privilege of having your uniqueness attended to.

The matters of class and (in)equivalence in Mexico certainly resonate with this story, though it would be a mistake to simply transpose the framework. Part of Dr. Simi's efficacy resides in how he both taps into and tries to amplify an analogous sense of depersonalization and bureaucracy that some people—not all by any means—associate with the state in the form of the Seguro Social or ISSSTE. This is especially the case for those who have reached their limit with its long waits, "insults" and (in)attention, and locations far from their daily routes of circulation. Simi's intervention (and those of others copying his model) is to offer the possibility of being "attended to" personally, when and where you need such attention; as such, this market offers a similar antidote to the classic critique of state or bureaucratic depersonalization. Crucially, though, this antidote is aimed not at the economically advantaged; rather, it is aimed directly at the popular classes. Offering the privilege of a certain kind of recognition, as attention or care—"They'll suggest things that take into account details about you like, 'This one wouldn't be bad for you, at your age!'"[21] another Simi-loyal customer explained to me—this low-cost, infrastructure-light form of health care is aimed precisely at those who have resolutely not had access to expensive private health care.

But lest we cede assessments of the public sector and its shortcomings to the younger generation, Dolores's aunt, Eugenia, was much more sanguine, as were a number of the people with whom I spoke who have had longer relationships with the Seguro Social. Part of an older generation (she was in her sixties when we spoke), she has had a long-term, on-and-off relationship to the Seguro, and she has a real loyalty and appreciation for what it has meant to have access to its services, doctors, and not inconsequentially, its surgical expertise—a kind of attention, with its attendant infrastructures, that Simi and the genéricos can certainly not provide. Eugenia talked me through her relationship to these forms and sites of health care: she had access for a long time to the Seguro Social through her husband, and so she'd go to the Seguro, especially if she had something serious, such as the wrist problems that required surgery a number of years ago: "And they have been very good, the Seguro. The problem," she continued, "is if you lose your job, like my husband did. Then you're not covered anymore."[22]

That is indeed a problem, often in a particularly gendered way. And it is precisely the problem into which Simi and the state, in the form of the federal government, both tumbled, headlong.

"Universal Coverage": The Seguro Popular
In 2003, González Torres announced that Dr. Simi would debut a new facet of his pharmacy and health-care enterprise, with his very own Sistema Similar de Seguros (SSS) or el *Simi Seguro* for short. Patients would pay fifty to sixty pesos a month (US$2.50–3) and receive free medical treatment and half-price

medicines at Simi clinics and pharmacies. The program did not last long, but the timing of its debut was, as ever, pointed. With the Simi Seguro, Simi was doubling the state at a moment when it, too, was multiplying, by gathering the uninsured into its embrace.

In the same year (2003), under the administration of PANista Vicente Fox, Julio Frenk, the secretary of health, had introduced a now-famous experiment in state insurance expansion, called the Seguro Popular. Frenk's name will be familiar to chroniclers of global health actors and institutions; he is particularly well known for his expertise in evidence-based health policy (see Frenk 2006). Prior to serving in Fox's government, he was the executive director of Evidence and Information for Policy at the WHO. Following his post in Mexico's federal government (which he held from 2000–2006), he took a leadership position at the Bill and Melinda Gates Foundation, served as executive president of the newly established Carso Health Institute in Mexico City—a Latin American "answer" and alternative to Gates, funded by the Mexican billionaire Carlos Slim—ran Harvard's School of Public Health, and then went on to a post as the president of the University of Miami. The Seguro Popular, which I'll discuss more, became a major touchstone and reference point in the recent annals of global health—a key experiment in turning mass lack of health insurance into universal coverage, often through expansions (and redefinitions) of the state (Wirtz et al. 2012; Pueblita 2013; Bonilla-Chacín and Aguilera 2013; Martínez, Aguilera, and Chernichovsky 2009).

Frenk set out in 2003 to achieve the rather staggering enrollment goal of fifty-two million people. The program was meant to provide those who do not otherwise have access to existing social security plans "subsidized insurance" that would be comparable to what was available through the Seguro Social and ISSSTE. Unlike the Seguro Social, however, it did not provide pension benefits (World Bank 2008, 1). Also unlike the Seguro Social, the Seguro Popular asked beneficiaries to directly pay premiums, though the poorest 20 percent were not asked to pay anything at all.[23] In exchange, Seguro Popular enrollees were promised access to a set of benefits that would be free "at the point of service" (a key principle for many experiments in universal coverage [Yates 2009]) and administered by *existing* state public health clinics, hospitals, and other facilities.

This latter point is crucial. The Seguro Popular was itself a kind of shadow or double of the Seguro Social. Unlike the latter (and unlike Simi and the genéricos), the Seguro Popular was not thought of as a place; it did not have its own facilities. It was conceived as a portal of sorts: an insurance plan that granted subscribers access to the (same) facilities, clinics, doctors, diagnostic capacities, surgeries, preventive care, and medicines that were managed through existing Seguro Social facilities managed by state (as in not-federal) governments.[24] In other words, as a federal regulator explained the scenario to me, "The Seguro Popular promises coverage but has no infrastructure of its own."[25]

This structure has posed its share of challenges. Some are definitional. The overlay of same and not the same versions of the Seguro (a collective noun, like the generic, that keeps multiplying) compounds the confusions that many analysts and users have identified in an already fragmented (public) health system, "which includes several health insurance schemes offering different benefits packages and having their own sources of funds, their own provider networks, and little communication among them" (Bonilla-Chacín and Aguilera 2013, v).

Granted, not everyone finds this situation as vexing as it sounds. "Yes, lots of people I know have the Seguro," a young domestic worker named Beatríz Gómez told me in 2007 in an interview in Mexico City. "Seguro Popular?" I tried to clarify, "or the Seguro Social?" "Yes, the Seguro!" While I was confused, Gómez was not: if you have the Seguro Popular, then you have the Seguro (Social), sort of. At the same time, not all potential subscribers found this near-equivalence between the two Seguros compelling or reassuring (see also Pueblita 2013). Elly Yglesias, a former airport employee and an aspiring psychology student hoping to study at UNAM, was, when I talked with her in 2013, working as a child-care provider in a private home. Yglesias dismissed the Seguro Popular, almost out of hand: "It doesn't really appeal to me; I haven't paid it much attention." We returned to the matter later, and she spelled out her objections in stronger terms:

> It's not worth what I have to pay, to invest for them to see me, if they don't treat me well. Because it's the same. An uncle had it, paid I don't know how much to have the coverage. And you end up the same as if you had the normal Seguro—they leave you waiting there, until they see you dying [she laughed sharply], and that's how it goes. It's the same. *Es lo mismo.* The quality is the same. It's bad. So, the truth is, I wouldn't pay for that.[26]

It was lo mismo but bad—and for a premium. Why pay for the Seguro Popular when (all) it buys you is access to the Seguro Social? Yglesias's view on the matter was not unique; a growing cottage industry of assessments of the program identified among the Seguro Popular's "challenges" the significant question of quality and consistency of care, which have tended to vary quite radically from state to state (Wirtz et al. 2012; Nigenda et al. 2003; Frenk, Gómez-Dantés, and Knaul 2009). One particularly telling analysis documented the relation, state by state, between election seasons and upticks in funding allocated to Seguro Popular–related services and employment, placing the program fully within a recognizable catalog of state patronage practices (Pueblita 2013).

At the same time, though, people *did* enroll, and its massive enrollment numbers initially qualified the Seguro Popular as a global public health success story. Pilot programs in 2003 and 2004 first generated two million members, quickly growing to five million. By 2012, Frenk could declare victory—universal coverage—as the target number of fifty-two million enrollees had been met (Knaul et al. 2012). The possible relation between massive enrollment and an uneven quality of care—perhaps fruit of a program offering access without its own infrastructure—was not lost on those analyzing the program. José Carlos Pueblita (2013, 3) pointedly suggested that the goal might shift from measuring progress in terms of "universal enrollment"—access as a good in itself—to measuring the provision of "universal effective coverage," in which enrollees have equal access to high-quality care.

In other words, remarkable as it was, the nominal enrollment achievement of universal coverage did not, of course, preclude gaps in health care. Nor, by extension, did it revoke Dr. Simi's or other generics pharmacies' invitation to this market. After musing on the Seguro Popular's shortcomings, Elly Yglesias brought the point back around: "I think the Seguro Popular hasn't worked out the way they imagined it. And that's where Dr. Simi's clinics come in. Because the other alternatives are the expensive private clinics, but—the lower class doesn't go there. It's not an option, obviously. You can't afford that."[27] Indeed, as Yglesias observed, the real-world, uneven effects of universal coverage, in the form of the Seguro Popular, were in fact a condition of possibility for Simi and other generics proprietors' continued success.

We could certainly say, in one sense, that Dr. Simi and the Seguro Popular were in direct competition for the same constituency, and there were, in some respects, zero-sum (either/or) relations between the two. Unhappiness with the Seguro Popular, as with unhappiness with the Seguro Social, brought people to the door of Dr. Simi and a wide range of genéricos pharmacies—*this*, instead of *that*. But, I will argue, a now-familiar multiplication effect was also at work here, a both/and proposition. In many ways the expansion of the private consumer market in generics and their similars was an essential condition of possibility for the Seguro Popular's expansion. Medicines and their provision are crucial to this story and to the Simipolitical rearrangements at stake here.

State and Not the State

The emergence of a vigorous commercial market for cheaper generics and the public health system's simultaneous expansion through the Seguro Popular held complex relationships to each other. Medicines—in their scarcity and their peculiar abundance—are key to these relationships. Given the conditions that gave rise to the private market for generics, it is perhaps not surprising that the provision of medicines was, early in the Seguro Popular's existence, the single most important benefit that low-income families hoped to draw from the new program (Nigenda et al. 2003). That hope, documented in an early study, prompted the study authors to issue a caution for policy-makers: do *not* encourage people to think of the program as primarily an avenue for access to medicines (Nigenda et al. 2003, 272–73)! Why? In part to avoid the "overdemand" for medicines, they argued, and in part to prevent "false expectations" (272–73). On the latter point, the not fully equivalent relationship between the Seguro Social and the Seguro Popular was a potential source of disappointment: the Seguro Social provides a significantly higher percentage of its medicines for free (78–89 percent) than the Seguro Popular (60 percent) (Nigenda et al. 2003).

But there was also the question of available supply, which is what threatened to make overdemand a problem. Given the structure of the Seguro Popular, as an overlay of access on top of the already-taxed Seguro Social, we might not be surprised to hear that the specter of "medication shortages" haunted the Seguro Popular, too. Dr. Simi had spent the first several years of the twenty-first century amplifying the charge that, due to "corruption," public-sector pharmacies were too often out of medicines. Many people who had rerouted their pharmaceutical consumption through low-cost generics pharmacies continued to decry public-sector medication shortages to me— "they don't even have medicines!"—as part of their experience of going to the Seguro, well into the second decade of this century. Exploiting this sense of shortage quite early on, Dr. Simi had baldly offered additional discounts to those Seguro Social or ISSSTE patients who could not get their prescriptions filled in the public sector's pharmacies.

Around 2012, such bare-knuckled tactics pitting private, low-cost pharmacies against public-sector pharmacies became, like the 1910 revolution, institutionalized. Channeling consumers/citizens from the public sector to private pharmacies—Dr. Simi's and others—became a project of the state. In the context of allegations that the Seguro Popular was (also) having trouble providing prescribed medicines to enrollees, the Green Party of Mexico (PVEM), a distinctively González Torres family concern, began floating a controversial "vales for medicines" program during the long buildup to the presidential elections of 2012 (i.e., between 2006 and 2012) (Rangel 2015). *Vales* are essentially coupons—substitutes for money that have long formed part of the monthly salary of many kinds of regularly employed workers, from white-collar office staff and university faculty, to airport workers, to supermarket and pharmacy employees, and beyond. Thus, as part of your monthly paycheck, you might receive three hundred pesos (thirty dollars) worth of vales that can only be used for groceries, for example (*tortibonos* [sandwich bonuses], they are often called).

The PVEM's proposals were to create vales that beneficiaries of the Seguro Popular, Seguro Social, ISSSTE, and other public-sector health services could exchange for medicines (for free) in private-sector pharmacies, if the public pharmacies could not fill a prescription. The political rationale granted to this move was the same one that accompanied the Seguro Popular: universal coverage. In the name of guaranteeing pharmaceutical access to all, the proposal was adopted by PRI presidential candidate (and soon to be president) Enrique Peña Nieto, as part of his campaign platform. A pilot "vales for medicines" program was initiated in 2012. An announcement in the national press read as follows: "'Seguro Popular beneficiaries who do not receive all of the medicines they have been prescribed can complete their prescriptions in private pharmacies,' announced the president of the Mexico's National Association of Pharmacies, Antonio Pascaual Feria. 'This program . . . has as its objective to meet the commitment to Universal Coverage, not only regarding services, but also regarding the supply of medicines'" (Organización Editorial Mexicana 2012). In other words, the vales program was represented as helping meet the Seguro Popular's commitment to universal coverage precisely by channeling public funds and public-sector beneficiaries to private-sector providers. Commentators and critics, including Andrés Manuel Lopez Obrador's new political party, Morena, called foul again and again, connecting dots and proxies that by now may not read as a surprise (Morales 2012).[28] To begin, the primary instigator of the vales for medicines program, the PVEM, was itself a González Torres family enterprise. Its head was Jorge Emilio González, the so-called Niño Verde, nephew not just of Víctor Gonzáles Torres, but also the nephew of the owners of two other major pharmacy chains: Javier González Torres, proprietor of the competing generics chain Farmacias del Ahorro, and Jorge González Torres, proprietor of Farmacias el Fénix. The argument was that no one stood to benefit more from the vales scheme than this family, whose pharmacies now counted among the most successful in Mexico. Indeed, the PVEM had boldly declared itself "the party of access to medicines" (see Morales 2012).

Moreover, by substituting wholesale for retail prices, the vales scheme ensured that "the public" would pay twice. That is, the government had to promise that it would reimburse private pharmacies for the vales that these pharmacies redeem for drugs. But at what price? This is a small-scale and a large-scale question. The vales scheme seemed poised to further bleed IMSS, ISSSTE, and the Seguro Popular dry, for the government would be reimbursing private pharmacies for medicines at prices much higher than those commanded through the wholesale bidding system for the public sector (Moise and Docteur 2007). Economist Raúl Enrique Molina-Salazar and colleagues (2008) documented the frequently striking differences between public-sector wholesale prices and retail prices in private pharmacies (Molina-Salazar, González-Marín, and Carbajol-de Nova 2008).

There is certainly every reason to agree with outraged pundits that the vales for medicines program represented nothing less than "a logic of privatization" (*Emeequis* 2012; Morales 2012)—a cannibalization of the public sector by state actors themselves, whose ranks included members of the González Torres family. As such, the vales schema laid bare some of the larger Simipolitical shifts underway, in which state and market were expanding together, the one similar to the other. But so, too, did the Seguro Popular, critiques of which were also proliferating. As with Yglesias's assessments noted previously, some potential beneficiaries certainly felt that its problem was that in the end, the Seguro Popular was too much like the state—and at a cost, no less: "You pay a premium and all you get is access to the Seguro?" For others, the problem with the program was that it acted and sounded too much like a neoliberal, marketized intervention. Critics from the Left, especially, were wary of the program's ideological orientation, signaled in the Seguro Popular's keywords *decentralization* and *responsibility*. Decentralization (a shift away from the power and funding of the federal government) has been a consistent tendency in Mexico's neoliberal shifts over the last two decades (indeed, since the debt crisis of 1982), and the Seguro Popular was as much an experiment in financing models—shifting funds and accountability away from the federal government and toward state governments—as it was an experiment in the delivery of health care (Frenk, Gómez-Dantés, Knaul 2009). Within this decentralizing mandate, the Seguro Popular also trumpeted, from the start, an insistence on government-individual (or family) "co-responsibility" (Knaul et al. 2012, 1265). The appeal to responsibility was a red flag for many critics, manifest explicitly in the fact of the Seguro Popular's requirement that (many) beneficiaries pay for state coverage to which, critics noted, people should by right have access for free (Lara and Campos 2003).

Such critiques did not just come from an identifiable political Left. One of the loudest voices on this point was Víctor González Torres/Dr. Simi, who claimed, from the start, that the Seguro Popular would fail. In the early 2000s duel over the market population of the *popular*, the tenor of González Torres's attacks on the Seguro Social and the Seguro Popular was *not* to argue explicitly that the private sector, or the market, could perform better than the state or that the state had no business providing health services. Rather, in denunciations of this program in Mexico City daily newspapers in 2004 and 2005, González Torres argued that the Seguro Popular was an abdication of governmental responsibility to the poor, "who have a fundamental right to receive care from the state free of charge."[29] Since the state was failing to meet this responsibility by asking those with fewer resources to pay for their own care, González Torres was happy to make his own bid for how to guarantee the well-being of the Mexican population, which of course entailed offering to the poor and increasingly the middle class the opportunity to pay for their own care. Denying accusations that he sought to compete with the public sector, Víctor González Torres promised to provide a viable "complement."

Cynical as it sounds, in many ways González Torres's Simipolitical promise—a viable complement, an as-if state, "caring for the people" through cheap consumption—was perfectly descriptive of the mutually entangled relationship between the Seguro Popular and the private market in generics. The Seguro Popular, without a doubt, provided a mechanism for drawing millions of uninsured Mexicans into the state's transformed embrace. But how could the state provide access to public insurance at the massive scale at which it did—fifty-two million enrollees—when it did not also provide a correspondingly massive expansion in state infrastructure, much less a correspondingly massive investment in the purchase of medicines? The Seguro Popular couldn't expand at the rate that it did without the low-cost private market in generics—and their clinics, and their doctors—to take the overflow (see Chu and García-Cuellar 2007). As Yglesias had noted so astutely, "The Seguro Popular hasn't quite worked as planned, and that's where Simi comes in."[30] The rapid, extraordinary expansion of this state program could not "work," even in the provisional way that it did, without Simi and other generics pharmacies in place to absorb the effects of bottlenecks, shortages, and a lack of dedicated public resources. This relationship is Simipolitics in motion.

Neither Seguro nor Popular

Thus, we might ask, What is the state, what is the market, and where does "responsibility" lie where the provision of health and medicines are concerned? What and who serves the public, the people, and the popular sectors? What version of public provision is legible and workable today? Such questions remain vividly alive in Mexico as I write this, in 2020. Much like Dr. Simi and myriad other critics, the current president of Mexico, Andrés Manuel López Obrador, has forcefully attacked the Seguro Popular for its abdication of the state's responsibility to care for the Mexican people. Indeed, when López Obrador began his presidential term in 2018, he debuted a potent refrain: "*Ni seguro, ni popular!*" The Seguro Popular is neither! ... "It's not security" (it does not provide real coverage), "nor is it popular" (that is, it does not truly care for the popular classes) (Político MX 2018; Macías 2020).[31] Dr. Simi promised/threatened a viable complement to the Seguro Popular through a Simipolitical market intervention. López Obrador now has his own power to offer an alternative through what he described as his own act of "substitution" (CNN 2018). In January 2020, he announced that he had discontinued the Seguro Popular. In its place would be built (is still being built) *his* version of a recentralized, differently universal health system: INSABI, the Institute for Health and Well-being. This system will offer, López Obrador has promised, free medicines and health care to all, from cradle to grave.

The Seguro Popular is thus officially no longer. The other long-standing pillars of the public health system (IMSS and ISSSTE) are in an increasingly precarious state following severe budget cuts that López Obrador initiated in 2019 (see Martínez Cázares 2019). López Obrador's new universal system is getting off to a halting start, not least given the timing of its debut just months before the 2020 novel coronavirus pandemic hit Mexico and the rest of the world with such force. Meanwhile, Dr. Simi and thousands of other generics pharmacies remain vigorous as ever, selling medicines, prescriptions, B12 injections, generic Viagra, vitamins, supplements, natural products, and, not least, health consultations at a "cheap" price and mighty clip.

Simipolitics is central to the trajectory through which generic medicines become spectacular. With its many doublings and recompositions, Simipolitics shows us how the excessive potency of copying redounds simultaneously in the multiplications of same and similar drugs, in and as politics, in and through multiple excesses of substitution. The idea of Simipolitics is peculiar, of course. It draws its potency from the specific, mass-mediated, political-market interventions of the rather singular, though not self-identical, Víctor González Torres/Dr. Simi: the cartoonish, nostalgic appeal to the iconography and promises of the clientelist, one-party state; his vivid animation of an as-if populism built out of the excessive potency of equivalence itself (lo mismo!); his canny moves to hail "the Mexican people" simultaneously as consumers and citizens. Dr. Simi in all of his particularity has shown how "the people" and the hypothetically unmarked "generic" might be aspirationally gathered into particular political and commercial trajectories, narratives, niches, spaces of reclamation, and excessive, doubled identifications.

But for all of the vivid specificity of Dr. Simi's often controversial interventions, Simipolitics is not merely about González Torres's tactics and projects. What Dr. Simi's interventions have done, in part, is loudly announce and even spectacularly perform a much broader suite of transformations in the provision of health care and medicines. In Mexico, Dr. Simi's pharmacies and clinics constitute only a part of the rapidly expanding, relatively new commercial sphere of generics pharmacies offering low-cost medicines and consultations with physicians. That is, to Simi's thirty-five hundred outlets, we must add the tens of thousands of other such pharmacies across the country, each, in turn, part of the complex and changing constellation of "access" that competes with, doubles, and even enables the state's own precarious and contested expansion. In this light, Simipolitics draws our attention to broader questions about how a politics of access to medicines, grounded in generic substitution, reverberates in unexpected ways. Not least, here, it has become part of a post-NAFTA politics of the domestic copy, or the domestic substitute; far from reproducing a populist, protectionist state-led politics ("Defend your domestic economy!"), Simipolitics announces a reimagined twenty-first-century politics of the copy.

In its vivid instantiation of a pharmapolitical, as-if populism, of a complicated both/and relation between state and not state, Simipolitics certainly reverberates with broader dynamics in Latin America. I am thinking in particular of the ways that the early twenty-first-century "return of the state" (a pharmapolitical turn often entangled with the rise of the generic) might in fact be better described as something else: a recomposition of state forms in and through neoliberal or marketized idioms (Biehl 2004; see also Gago 2014, 5).[32] The provision of medicines directs a bright spotlight to such dynamics, providing a way to understand how particular kinds of scarcity can morph into what I have been calling the peculiar abundances and contradictory effects of turning to mass consumer markets. Neither neoliberal logics nor state populism quite capture the relationship at work here (see Gago 2014). Simipolitics names this *something more*, this complicated both/and exuberance and its pharmakon-like implications for the politics of access.

To say that Simipolitics might well resonate beyond Mexico is not, however, to claim that it is effortlessly fungible, whether as an analytic or as pharmapolitics. Simipolitics (like the generic itself) might well travel across contexts, political and otherwise, but as we will see in chapter 3, it certainly does not seamlessly replicate itself.

No Patent, No Generic   3

Mexican soap operas are known all over the world. The struggle between the good brother and the bad, the selfless one and the selfish one. Now, this classic Mexican melodrama is making a splash in Argentina. But this time it's not on television; it is happening in real life. The fight [is] between the brothers Víctor and Javier González Torres, two millionaire Mexican businessmen, owners of Farmacias Dr. Simi and Dr. Ahorro, who are extending their businesses and their disputes to Argentina, [and] it's coming to you, live!
"DR AHORRO VS. DR SIMI," UNIVISION, FEBRUARY 5, 2005

In 2004, Víctor González Torres/Dr. Simi arrived in Buenos Aires seeking "to repeat the formula," as one news account aptly phrased it, which had proven so successful in Mexico and beyond (*Clarín* 2004). González Torres had, in fact, expanded his pharmacy franchise to El Salvador, Guatemala, Chile, Argentina, and Peru as part of what he was calling his "Bolivarian revolution"—a continental project of "liberation" from foreign drug makers, bringing cheaper medicines made by a variety of Latin American manufacturers to "those who have the least." The Farmacias del Dr. Simi have indeed become a well-known Mexican export throughout the region, like soap operas or cement. But in Argentina, the irrepressible Dr. Simi encountered a peculiarly fitting problem: Dr. Simi arrived in Buenos Aires already doubled. Víctor's younger brother Javier, proprietor of the pharmacy chain Farmacias del Dr. Ahorro (literally, Dr. Saving's Pharmacies), had already established a presence in Buenos Aires, immediately following Argentina's tremendous economic crisis of 2001 to 2002. When Víctor/Dr. Simi attempted to open his own pharmacies in Buenos Aires, Javier/Dr. Ahorro immediately requested and received a legal injunction against his brother (Víctor insisted they are "ex-brothers") (*El Ojo Digital* 2010). The Argentine Department of Justice forced Víctor to cover up the marquees on the Farmacias del Dr. Simi temporarily, ruling that Simi's slogan, "The same, but cheaper!," was too similar to Ahorro's slogan, "It's equal but more economical!" (*Cronista* 2004). In Argentina, Víctor was seen to be copying his brother who, in Mexico, seemed to be copying him.

The Argentine press had a field day with the melodrama, and it became a kind of public joke. "Vienen los hermanos mexicanos peleados!" (Here come the fighting Mexican brothers!) crowed a young clerk to me in a high-brow Palermo shop one day in May 2006, making fun, in one easy pass, of Mexican soap operas, *lucha libre*, and what many Argentines consider Mexico's hilariously high-pitched, nasal Spanish. Of course, as in lucha libre, the spectacle (here of the tussling brothers whose fight spills over borders and across a continent) had its real effects. Víctor/Dr. Simi certainly has a public profile as a commercial-political brawler in Mexico, as we saw in chapter 2. And while he and his brother Javier/Dr. Ahorro are considered substantial competition for each other there, Dr. Simi's most concerted "fight" in Mexico was with the public health institutions and the secretary of health. But here, in Argentina, the fight between brothers arrived as a formula, repeated: "The same fight that two businessmen brothers have in Mexico over the pharmaceutical market has just come to Argentina" (*Clarín* 2004).

Not surprisingly, and surely not unwelcome to Dr. Simi-the-second-comer, one effect of the media spectacle was that the two chains became, for many members of the Argentine public, largely indistinguishable from each other. The kind-making work of nation, kinship, family business ("It's all going into the same pocket, no?" more than one person said to me), and the stickiness of scandal quickly made it difficult to mention Dr. Ahorro without tangling it/him up with Dr. Simi, and vice versa. Thus, when I asked people in Buenos Aires about Farmacias Similares, they often responded as if I'd asked about Farmacias del Dr. Ahorro. The two chains became interchangeable in everyday talk. And so we arrive, again, at the ever-expanding question that animates this book. In an interview in her office in Buenos Aires in 2006, Sylvia Brunoldi, a health advocate for people with diabetes, recounted some of the saga for me: "Dr. Simi arrived here three years ago, more or less. Parallel to Dr. Ahorro." Then she paused and asked me: "Son lo mismo? [Are they the same?]"[1]

What does it take to *trasladar*—to bring across borders and repeat—generics, the similar, a market, a business model, a formula, a family feud? This is a kind of question that animates global business strategy, not to mention the syntax of a comparative social science. Pharmaceutical sector analysts note that generics now represent the biggest growth area in what they call "pharmerging markets," by which they mean "emerging markets for pharmaceuticals" (Ribbink 2011). Both Víctor and Javier González Torres have found their ways into this emergence across Latin America, staking their claims together in battle over diverse market niches organized around low-cost generic medicines. What *does* it take to expand a market for generics?

Thus far in this book, generic substitution has essentially come into view as a pharmacological instantiation of the market philosophy of competition by price: *the same, but cheaper*. That, certainly, is how generics emerged in Mexico as new kinds of pharmaceutical commodities in the first years of the twenty-first century. In Argentina, however, the emergence of a politics of generic substitution was grounded in a very different composition of the generic as a pharmaceutical kind, not least because pharmaceutical patents were not at the time (nor are they now) widely granted or enforced. The effective "absence" of patents raises the distinctively ontopolitical question, Do generics even exist without patents? The promotion of generics in Argentina thus raised some particularly intriguing questions about how we might define generics at all. At the same time, the notion of the generic was just one of the elements of Dr. Simi's formula that came into question in Argentina. So, too, did the pivot to "the market" and cheap consumption as an answer to the problem of pharmaceutical access. Indeed, in both respects, generics were seen, at least to some voices on the Argentine Left, as accessions to the neoliberal marketization of fundamental rights. Thus, as we'll see, neither the generic nor market competition served as particularly self-evident principles on which Drs. Simi and Ahorro might stake a claim in Argentina. This chapter examines how the very premise and promise of generic substitution has been composed in Argentina, with Simi and Ahorro in view. In so doing, it provides another set of coordinates for rethinking the fungibility of the generic as both a pharmaceutical commodity and a pharmapolitical relation.

At first glance, though, the conditions for the emergence of generics in Argentina seemed remarkably similar to the conditions that presaged the emergence of generics in Mexico. The formula-in-common included crisis (economic) and shortage (pharmaceutical) and a subsequent regulatory turn to generic substitution as a response to both. Thus, Javier-the-brother, proprietor of Farmacias del Dr. Ahorro ("The same substance but more economical!") established a strong presence in Buenos Aires and in a few other Argentine cities immediately following the 2001–2 economic crisis, during which currency devaluations, the rapid flight of foreign capital, and bank closures paralyzed the country. Though crisis has long been repetitive or serial in Argentina (Gago 2014; see also D'Avella 2014), the events of 2001–2 retain a certain claim to distinction—this crisis marked, at that point, the largest sovereign government debt default in the world—and its magnitude was felt especially where health and pharmaceuticals are concerned. Exorbitant drug prices, medication shortages (prominently including insulin), and hospital and clinic closures were instrumental in bringing events to a head in December 2001 and January 2002, with health advocates forcing the government to declare a health emergency (Rossi and Varsky 2002).[2] The paralysis of pharmaceutical commerce was one indication of the problem: in a 2004 speech delivered in Peru, then minister of health Ginés Gonzáles García noted that "in 2001, there was a 42% fall in the sale of medicines across Argentina—an indication of a terrible lack of access" (González García 2004).

Among the priority recovery measures established by González García were two initiatives meant to ensure or at least improve people's ability to acquire medicine, from antibiotics and hypertension medications to insulin and beyond. Programa Remediar was established in 2002 to distribute free medicines, often sold at low cost to the program by multinational corporations, to the poorest Argentines (Tobar 2004).[3] This program, aimed at those who could not afford medications no matter how low the price, was accompanied by a 2002 law promoting generic prescriptions. The Law for the Promotion of Use of Medicines by Generic Name was meant to drive medication prices down by requiring that prescriptions contain the generic name of a drug—the name of a molecule, such as enalapril—rather than a specific brand name (Bergallo and Michel 2014, 73; El Senado y Cámara de Diputados de la Nación Argentina 2002). This move should sound familiar.

The Argentine generics decree was indeed similar to Mexico's prescription decree, as was its goal: to pry open the monopoly-like hold that leading brands have on physicians' prescribing practices and on patients' consumption. One physician in Argentina described the law to me as an intervention into "neoliberal prescription practices."[4] Again, the idea was to create the conditions for the substitution of low-cost alternatives to expensive brands. "Lo que cura no es la marca!" (What cures is not the brand!) the director of Programa Remediar (the program distributing medicines for free) told me emphatically.[5] If the Mexican government conveyed the substance of this message via its lime popsicles and Dr. Simi via his contagious slogan, "The same, but cheaper," the Argentine government popularized its decree with a no-holds-barred declaration of radical equivalence as equality: Todos son iguales! (All are equal! Or, They are all the same!).

In Mexico, Dr. Simi's version of this message, like his brother's, vividly instantiated generic substitution as a market principle. That is, generic substitution *is* competition by price ("The same, but cheaper!"). And yet, in Argentina, both the generic and the market principle of substitution were de-composed and put back together again in a different way. The relations between originals and copies, brands and generics, price and access, and bioequivalence and "the same" are all at work in this story but on different terms than we have seen thus far. This difference left the notion of the generic, as well as the Mexican brothers' direct appeal to the principle of market competition, looking somewhat impoverished or perhaps a bit ill-fitting. Departing slightly from the recurrent question, Are they the same?, we might do better to ask, What does it mean to sell only generic drugs in a context in which *generics do not exist*? To compete on a message of price in a context in which *no one competes by price*? To incur into a market *wrongly imagined*? The formula must change if it is to be repeated; indeed, the formula had already changed in its repetition.

Re(re)composing the Generic Question

Before we can ask about the fates of Drs. Simi and Ahorro in Argentina, there is some serious conceptual and definitional work to do. That work constitutes the bulk of this chapter's intervention with the previous discussion of Simipolitics in Mexico firmly in view. If Simipolitics tells us anything, it is that we gain little from treating the fecundity of pharmaceutical copies as if they reproduce of their own accord (much less of capitalism's own accord).

To the contrary, the notion of Simipolitics has helped me propose a way to gather Mexico's generic multiplicities, in form and content, into and through very particular political histories, tactics, "openings," and even aesthetics. The market for generic medicines in Mexico has been arranged through a particular constellation of familiar populist and nationalist tactics, commercial practices and aesthetics, and transnational dynamics. Asking about Dr. Simi's fate in Argentina requires turning down the volume on Dr. Simi and his kin for a moment in order to attend to a distinctive constellation of pharmaceutical populism differently organized around the domestic copy. There are other triangulations and globalizations at work in Argentina and distinctive mobilizations of the defense of the pharmaceutical national interest. Contemplating these differences will require still another set of analytic recalibrations and hence a recomposed vocabulary for the relation between originals and copies, the proper copy and its improper counterparts, and market and state.

Let me begin to lay out these interventions simply by repeating what I was told repeatedly in Buenos Aires as I followed Dr. Simi's bumpy adventures there: in Argentina, *there are no generics*. They simply do not exist: "En la Argentina, no hay genéricos!" Generics do not exist there because drug patents also do not exist (or, more precisely, at the time they were rarely enforced). The Argentine policymakers and economists with whom I spoke emphasized that the concept of a distinct market for generic drugs can make sense only if there is a market for patented drugs. Just think about the intellectual property-saturated, common-sense understanding that trips off the tongue in the United States: a generic drug is that which comes into circulation once the patent on the original has expired. That sequence of events structures the generic question in the United States and in Mexico to a strong degree. But in a context in which pharmaceutical patents have been roundly resisted and refused, the after-the-patent generic is an impossibility, a non sequitur. It is out of sequence. When the epistemological architecture, semiotics, and temporalities of patent law are configured otherwise (i.e., when pharmaceutical patents do not have traction), the generic as a distinctive kind slips out of frame as does the power of the original, which has little standing as such. As I've argued elsewhere, the epistemological and political elements must be rearranged, because to speak even casually of a market for generics would be to ratify the normative view of the world as it exists under, or within, patent regimes (Hayden 2010). And that normative view is not the starting point in Argentina.

This scenario, on which I will elaborate, is the product of the assertion, throughout the mid- to late twentieth century and into the twenty-first century, by Argentine drug laboratories and successive legislatures that pharmaceuticals are a "public good" and should therefore not be subject to the monopolies granted by patents (Katz and Burachik 1997). This nationalist, protectionist relationship to drug patents, long embraced by various Peronist administrations, laid the foundation in the mid to late twentieth century for a powerful domestic drug industry based largely on copying pharmaceuticals that were, and are often still, under patent elsewhere. Argentine laboratories often copy these drugs, or reverse-engineer them, without a license.

Patent-holding multinational corporations and the entities backing them up (including the Office of the US Trade Representative and the WTO) have long denounced these acts of copying as piracy, and in the 1990s and early 2000s, Argentina was subject to sanction by the United States for breaching the patent rights of major drug companies (see Bergallo and Michel 2014). But these pirate domestic laboratories, and their pirated domestic copies, have been perfectly licit in national terms. In fact, they dominate the Argentine pharmaceutical market. And they are very firmly *not* generics. To the contrary, they are among the "leading brands" against which generic substitution is now set up as competition. Thus, generic substitution is a puzzle of a radically different sort than the puzzle as we have imagined it thus far. Do generics exist, or don't they? Against what might they compete? With what politics are they aligned? What is a copy, and what is the copy of?

Given the point of departure that generates these questions—a nationalist, protectionist assertion that generics don't exist in Argentina and a powerful domestic industry making leading-brand copies—we can begin to imagine that some difficulties might await a Mexican generics entrepreneur or two attempting to make a play for Argentina's generics market. But it was not only the definition (or existence) of generics that caused them some trouble, nor did the challenge simply rest at the restaging of national(ist) difference through protectionism. The invocation of the consumer market as the solution to problems of access, so powerful in Mexico, was also a source and site of critique in Argentina when the Law for the Promotion of Use of Medicines by Generic Name was introduced. During the Menem years (the late 1980s and into the mid-1990s), the government had lifted pharmaceutical price controls, precisely in the name of market deregulation (Lakoff 2005, 137–41). This was one of the many demands of the United States under the Agreement on Trade-Related Aspects of Intellectual Property Rights (TRIPS) provisions of the WTO. The effect was a dramatic surge in drug prices across the board, including for domestically made copies, as leading Argentine laboratories took advantage of the opportunity to raise their prices (Lakoff 2005, 2006; Bergallo and Michel 2014). Post-2002 Argentine government efforts to encourage generic substitution were meant to address these problems in price. But the move sparked strong criticism from some physicians and activists about the consequences of turning to the (recently deregulated) market as a solution to the problems that "liberating the market" had itself created: "Clearly, the 'politics of generics' as we have heard it explained by the Ministry of Health is nothing more than one of trusting the Free Market or Free Competition to lower prices. Trust the Free Market? In this country? Have the prices of medicines increased 300–900% in this country because of the lack of the Free Market? . . . Aren't we taking the patient out of the frying pan and dropping her in the fire?" (Varsky 2002). The argument, as articulated here by physician Carlos Varsky, is that a politics of generic substitution and competition ("The same, but cheaper!") looks more like a capitulation to market logics than a solution to their inequities. (Similarly, speaking of "a market for generics" epistemologically accedes to the normalization of patent regimes rather than contesting them.) The argument is one that many of the physicians and policymakers with whom I spoke were actively batting around—some referred to it as the argument that generic substitution was a neoliberal project. My interlocutors did not always agree with the critique, but it was in the air, and they were grappling with it in one way or another, as we will see at the end of this chapter.

At the heart of these two unresolved matters—the (non)existence of generics as a distinctive kind and the politics of generic substitution as a market principle—lies the domestic copy in Argentina's vacillating Peronist governments. Dr. Simi's Simipolitics did not "trasladar" easily into this formation of state, copy, and market.

The Domestic *Copia*
What market *were* the Drs. Simi and Ahorro vying for? The fighting Mexican brothers arrived in an Argentine pharmaceutical-political space already dominated by copies. *Copias*, to be precise. Argentina is home to one of Latin America's most powerful domestic pharmaceutical industries, second only to Brazil's. While the Brazilian industry has largely been funded by the state (Biehl 2004; Cassier and Correa 2007), domestic companies in Argentina have primarily been funded by private Argentine capital (Katz and Burachik

1997), though the public sector does have some labs as well.[6] Throughout Argentina's period of import substitution industrialization in the mid- to late twentieth century, this domestic industry flourished under a set of conditions characterized by a high degree of state protectionism: regulation favoring national companies in the processes of authorizing and launching new products, high import tariffs, and the "weak" protection of international intellectual property rights (Katz and Burachik 1997, 87) or, better said, the strong protection of the right to copy (da Costa Marques 2005; Cassier and Correa 2007).

Indeed, the Argentine pharmaceutical industry has been proudly built on the manufacture of copies, precisely in a context in which pharmaceutical patents have been roundly resisted (Lakoff 2005, 2006). Argentine firms have thus risen to domestic dominance by copying drugs developed elsewhere and marketing them under their own brand names. These Argentine copias have been known to beat their patented counterparts into the domestic market and hence to become the leading, dominant brands. For example, the US-based pharmaceutical company Merck Sharp & Dohme developed and held a patent on the hypertension compound enalapril, which it markets as Renitec. In the two years before the expiry of its US patent (in February 2000), Renitec was Merck's second best-selling drug worldwide. But in Argentina, the leading brand, for several decades—that is, from the time enalapril was developed in the United States—has been Lotrial, made by the Argentine laboratory Roemmers (González García 2004). This is what Argentine economist Daniel Maceira meant when he told me, "In Argentina, leaders can quickly become followers."[7] Domestic labs have consistently commanded over 50 percent of the pharmaceutical market in the country, with Argentine laboratories including Roemmers often figuring as overall market leaders (ahead of US, European, Brazilian, and other Argentine companies). Major multinational patent-holding firms, accustomed to being the "leaders," have often either ceded this market altogether or else tried to play catch-up to the domestic brands that were given first entry into the market. This pharmaceutical context is thus, as Andrew Lakoff has remarked, "a peculiar one" in the so-called Global South (Lakoff 2004, 196). It is certainly markedly different from Mexico's: Argentina joins the United States, Germany, Switzerland, and Japan in a list of "the only countries whose domestic [pharmaceutical] producers have a greater market share than foreign ones" (196).

In a 2004 speech in Peru on Argentina's National Policy for Medicines, Ginés González García (the architect of the prescription decree) argued that such an orientation places Argentina in good company in the annals of global industrial development:

> Copying has long been central to the production of medicines, worldwide. Our industries [in Latin America] have been defined as copycat industries. There is nothing bad in this, from a historical point of view; the way I see it, "copying" has been at the foundation of history. Any empire that wants to get ahead copies that which, in a given moment, is most developed. In no way would England have become England [in the domain of pharmaceuticals] if it hadn't completely copied the chemistry from Germany. In no way would the United States have become the United States if it hadn't copied everything from the English—it's just that later the US made cheaper products. In no way would Japan have become Japan if it hadn't copied everything from the United States. In no way would China be en route to what it is becoming if it weren't copying everything from everyone. (González García 2004)

The closing nod to China's ascendance is not incidental. The rise of the Chinese economy, and the dominance of copying thereto, is becoming central to many Western reimaginations of scale in commodity production and not a few anxieties about the demise or reconfiguration of authenticity itself (Wong 2014). But González García is not exoticizing China's adroitness at copying; rather, he is placing what Ackbar Abbas (2008) has called China's "fake economy" (which is very much the real economy) firmly into a global lineage of industrial innovation that has come into being by copying that which preceded it. There is also a defiant, nationalist narrative in many Argentine articulations of the (il)licit copy, particularly where pharmaceuticals are concerned. "The history of Argentina is the history of contraband!" (Lakoff 2006, 112). The ability to copy *well* is a source of pride in the pharmaceutical sector.

The value of copying, and copying well, has not figured so positively in the United States' late twentieth-century and early twenty-first-century big-stick discourses or practices on trade and intellectual property enforcement. To the contrary, Argentina's official politics of copying have generated indignant accusations of piracy—and sanctions—from the US government and transnational pharmaceutical firms for decades.[8] The accusations against Argentina's copycat industry were particularly pointed in the 1990s during the Clinton administration, when expanding multilateral trade accords (particularly the Uruguay Round of the General Agreement on Tariffs and Trade [GATT] in 1988) placed a premium on the protection of intellectual property rights as a trade priority. At stake in the GATT and TRIPS (and even more so in negotiations for successor agreements) was explicitly the curtailment of what former Argentine trade negotiator Carlos Correa called developing countries' "relative or total freedom to imitate" (Correa 2000).

Indeed, alongside the pressures on Argentina from the GATT and TRIPS negotiations, the radical experiments in market liberalization and deregulation initiated by President Carlos Menem in the late 1980s and 1990s—following the military dictatorships that had already made Argentine markets available to foreign capital—seemed poised to put an end to Argentina's practices of pharmaceutical copying on several fronts. With Menem's election in 1989, the United States thought it had finally found a willing partner in its project to "open" the Argentine economy to foreign investment, competition, and intellectual property protection in a number of arenas, with the large prescription pharmaceutical market—ranked twelfth in the world at that time, with a value of $3 billion—as a key object of transnational industry desire (Lakoff 2005). Reflecting Menem's stated willingness to implement pharmaceutical patents, Argentina signed on to the TRIPS accord of the GATT in 1994, and the legislature subsequently passed a national patent law in 1996, which included pharmaceutical product and process patents. Yet, strong pressure from the domestic industry kept its implementation very much at bay (Bergallo and Michel 2014).

Argentina thus technically has had a patent law but effectively has not granted (many) pharmaceutical patents; that is, the law has not been widely enforced for pharmaceuticals (Bergallo and Michel 2014, 79). Physician Patricia Silva described the dynamic of this "special" patent arrangement in our 2006 conversation in her office in Buenos Aires: "Now, what happened? Well, a patent law depends on the office that patents. The patent office here, how much has it patented? *Poquísimo! Patentó repoco*. Very, very little. This is very Latin American—you lose the battle on one side, so you go and fight back on another."[9] Via one avenue or another, Argentine researchers and public officials have thus continued to make the case that copying has been essential to constituting a pharmaceutical public good (Bergallo and Michel 2014, 79).

These copies, in turn, are generally regarded as high-quality drugs. They are copied well. Néstor Carbajal, a psychiatrist in private practice, explained to me: "The Argentine drug laboratories are very good laboratories. They have very good technology, and they do good work overall. Thus [speaking of the period leading up to the crisis] they copied down to the very letter; they worked perfectly, and they produced a drug that was useful."[10] But confounding any easy equations we might start to draw here between domestic copies and affordable medicines, the prevalence of domestically made copias has not necessarily guaranteed an abundance of affordable drugs. "Those labs might have produced excellent copies," Carbajal continued, but "what they didn't do was lower their prices."

In fact, in the midst of these geopolitical fights over the right to copy, leading-brand Argentine copias became relatively expensive, a development enabled by the removal of price controls for drugs. Copista firms have also happily embraced the power of the brand name to build attachments to their products; thus, theirs is not an anti-intellectual property stance in general but an anti-pharmaceutical patent stance in particular (Hayden 2011). Domestic copias have thus come to occupy the slot, in many drug classes, of the expensive leading brand(s). It is this situation that helped define the postcrisis problem of "lack of access." The goal of requiring physicians to prescribe drugs by their generic name has been, effectively, to create a demand for less expensive copies of leading-brand copias.

No Patent, No Generic

Intellectual property regimes are fundamentally tools for regulating the act of copying.[11] In the Global North, broadly defined, we do not often enough lead with this foot when explaining what patents (or copyright) do; more often, we begin by talking about how patent law defines protectable innovation. And certainly, this is part of what patent regimes do. By granting temporary monopolies on molecules or formulations that are deemed to meet specific thresholds of novelty and nonobviousness, drug patents produce relations of sameness and difference, dividing the world of chemical entities into those that are deemed "merely" copies (of nature, and of previous innovations) and those that are deemed innovative (different). These relations of sameness and difference have a powerful temporal inflection, one that readily becomes naturalized (and yet that must be constantly defended and performed) in IP-saturated contexts, not to mention in a broader platonic metaphysics: originals come first, and copies follow. In the case of pharmaceutical patent regimes established and required of others by the United States, generic manufacturers must wait twenty years from the issuance of an initial patent before they are able legally to secure the information necessary to make their own versions of the drug (effectively, twenty years often become ten years of monopoly on the market, as a number of the initial years of a patent are absorbed into the research, development, and clinical trial phases of a drug).

The harmonization of pharmaceutical patent regimes through multilateral trade conventions has meant that nations such as Mexico, Brazil, Thailand, India, and others are now required to concede twenty years of monopoly protection on pharmaceuticals before the patented molecule becomes part of the public domain and thus becomes (legally) available for manufacture and commercialization by other laboratories.

Yet patents do not only produce a (contested) line between original and copy. We could just as readily understand patent regimes as primarily defining the line between proper copies and their improper counterparts: the *good copy* versus the *bad copy*. One of the intended effects of the introduction and enforcement of intellectual property regimes in new regulatory contexts, as with the entry into force of pharmaceutical patents in Mexico in the 1980s, in Brazil in 1996, or in India in 2005, is the creation of precisely this line between the good copy—the generic that by definition does not enter the market until after a patent expires—and its improper counterparts: the pirated drug, the illicit copia, and, increasingly, the specter of the "counterfeit" (Hornberger 2018). These are often the same drugs, renamed or reclassified. For if, as Tobar suggested to me, what goes up must eventually come down, and drug patents will eventually become more broadly enforced in Argentina, then the leading-brand, domestic drugs will by law be reclassified domestically too as improper copies set in contrast to legal, regulated generics.

Still, as we have already seen so vividly in Mexico, such regulatory and classificatory acts of rezoning do not always or simply imprint themselves on the world, organizing things, temporalities, and relations according to their own schedules and classifications. Argentina's copista orientation, despite the patent law "on the books," scrambles intellectual property's epistemological and temporal order of things in a number of ways. When pharmaceutical patents are not granted the capacity to organize and naturalize relations of firstness and secondness, the ideological furniture is arranged differently, and so is the market.

One implication of Argentina's politics of patenting *repoco* (very little), as we've seen, is that there is no such thing as a generic. Argentine pharmacoeconomists, physicians, consumers, pharmacists, and policy-makers insisted to me repeatedly that in the absence of an enforced pharmaceutical patent regime, "the generic drug," as a distinctive kind of thing, cannot and does not exist: "Sin patente, no hay genérico" (Without a patent, there is no generic). This double refusal casts further critical light on the politics of generics as a politics of harmonization: in the normative world inscribed in intellectual property regimes, generic competition (properly) begins only when a patent ends. The only proper counterparts to patented drugs are thus off-patent generics. And thus the scenario that so readily trips off tongues in the United States, or in Canada, or in Europe—if a drug is not a patented original, then it must be a generic—is the effect of some fairly dense normative commitments, not merely a description of the self-evident order of things. Recognizing this point, and dwelling in it for a moment, requires some recalibrations in our analytic languages.

Without patents, copies can readily emerge first, and leaders can become followers. Moreover, while pharmaceutical brands certainly hold power in Argentina, they do so without being attached to the aura of originality and innovation bequeathed by patent offices; brands are instead "divorced from the patent."[12] And when brands are divorced from patents, "originality" has little bearing in everyday acts of distinguishing between versions of the same drug. In the United States, it is the patented drug—alone on the market for ten to twenty years, backed by a massive marketing apparatus—that has a well-known brand name; thus, we colloquially distinguish generics from the brand-name drug. But this distinction does not hold in Argentina, not only because there is no distinctive juridical category of generics. It does not hold because decoupling patents from brand names has already scrambled the temporal coordinates necessary to create the singular aura of the brand; instead, brands multiply simultaneously, copiously, laying bare the peculiar fecundity of consumer markets in chemical compounds, same and not the same. There is certainly a consequential leveling effect to this market-mediated copiousness. As my interlocutors (customers, pharmacists, physicians, and public officials) explained to me often, and forcefully, all drugs are brands, and at the same time, all are copies, in the serial sense of being one of many: *Todos son de marca; todos son copias*. This is a radical declaration of equivalence—*todos son iguales*—functioning not in reference to the substance that cures but rather in reference to the more-than fungibility of the name.

A Singular Name
The juridical terms of intellectual property regimes are the first key, then, to the de- and recomposition of generics in Argentina. It is the absence of (enforced) drug patents that prompted my interlocutors to assert that "there is no such thing as a generic" in Argentina. And yet, in an uncanny analogue to the similares that "don't exist" while selling very well in Mexico, there *are* many Argentine pharmacies that advertise generic medicines (genéricos),

pharmacists who sell them, patients who seek them out, and consumers who consume them. In the years following the 2001–2 economic crisis, Drs. Ahorro and Simi were among the commercial outlets appealing to people seeking less expensive medicines under the generic name, as was the large and rapidly growing Argentine chain Farmacity. But what, exactly, circulated as a generic, and where did such a thing fit in this copy-saturated space in which generics cannot exist? The relation between a thing and a name—yet another enormously storied analytic stomping ground, alongside equivalence itself—is the second question we must contemplate in the composition of Argentina's generic problem space.

As I was told emphatically by Federico Tobar, the energetic and thoughtful pharmaco-economist who at the time directed the secretary of health's Programa Remediar, the unique approach of Argentina is that it did *not* create a new market for a new thing called generics. Rather, it simply renamed all existing drugs. No drug is a generic in juridical terms, but every drug, he reminded me, has a generic name. Here, the contrast with Mexico surfaces again, and this time the question of copying versus innovation surfaces, playfully, at the level of national policy. Tobar told me:

> Mexico was a copy. That is, the Mexican policy is a copy of the American policy, right? The only pharmaceutical politics [policy] that was truly innovative was ours. In what sense? Well, the United States created an additional market, we could say. It created two markets: one market for original drugs under patent protection, and one market for generic medicines. Argentina's innovation was that the law we passed, 25-649, does not produce a market in generics, like what the United States, Mexico, and Brazil did. It only decrees that you must use [prescribe] drugs by their generic name. . . . So, we didn't create a market in generics. What we did, by decree and by force, was *turn all medicines into generics*.[13]

All drugs are copies, all are brands—and, in Tobar's assessment, in one fell swoop, all became generics as well. That is, all drugs on the market already have a generic name (the name of the molecule on which the drug is based) and it is this name that now must be prescribed. The 2002 law was thus meant to enable and encourage physicians, pharmacists, and consumers to rename existing products and thus to rethink their relation to each other.

Prescription by generic name (e.g., enalapril rather than Renitec) is thus an intervention in a material and representational politics, navigating the tensions between abundance and singularity. Seeking to put a limit on the fecundity of copies as brands, Ginés González García described the law of prescription by generic name and the associated pedagogical project of reorienting physicians' knowledge and training back toward generic names and away from brand names, as a kind of purifying act of de-duplication, in the way that my colleague Lawrence Cohen (2019) uses the term—to signal a state's aspirational intervention into "improper" multiplications, to weed out excess in the name of good governance (here in the form of prescription practice).[14] That is, good prescription practice entails an aspirational return to singularity, an anchoring of these endlessly multiple iterations of branded copies back in the singular, unique name of the drug. Unlike the strategies of major corporations, which seek to affect precisely this singularization by creating and defending a unique brand name (under which, of course, millions of copies will be consumed), González García placed this de-duplicating burden and promise squarely on a compound's generic name. He has described the proposition this way: "Forty-five percent of doctors (in Argentina) don't know the generic name of what they're prescribing. This creates the need for a broad campaign that we're conducting together with universities and physicians' associations to improve prescription quality, starting where you must start: *putting the true name on the drug . . . , returning to the drug its singular name.*"[15]

There is indeed a term for this singular name in global pharmaceutical governance: the international nonproprietary name (INN), which the WHO denotes as "a unique name that is globally recognized and is public property. A nonproprietary name is also known as a generic name" (World Health Organization n.d.). Enalapril, carbamazepine, lorazepam—these compounds, known by their international nonproprietary/generic names, may circulate under as many as twenty-seven different brand names on the Argentine market. It is worth noting that in Argentina, the term for brand name is *nombre de fantasía*. The move impelled by González García—a move of getting back to the truth of the singular name—is meant to reattach "fantasy names" to a material truth, where a radical politics of equality as equivalence declares that they belong. *Todos son iguales* (all are equal) can be true only if there is, underneath it all, one true name: the generic, international nonproprietary name.

And yet, despite this commitment, when Drs. Simi and Ahorro started to ply their trade, medicines in Argentina continued to be sold by brand name, even if they were (also) prescribed with a generic name. In 2006 when I began tracking this dynamic, the promise of singularity was not yet remotely on the horizon, as generics were described by most people with whom I spoke—pharmacists and clerks in pharmacies, physicians, people looking to buy medicines, policy makers—simply as "lesser" brands, or what the marketing director of a leading domestic industry denigrated as "second or third brands" (i.e., those behind the leading brands, or "first-tier" or "first-level" medicines as they're often called). Hierarchies and differences are indeed very much in operation within Argentina's abundant field of copyness as much for people who buy drugs as for those who make them and those who sell them. The truth of the singular name is confounded by differentiation among these drugs, all of which are brands, all of which are copies, and all of which have generic names.

How, then, are differences among these same things organized? Unlike in Mexico, the differences that matter here do not cluster around the axis of the original versus copy, or the foreign versus the national, much less around the matter of equivalence as a material-technical-regulatory question. They cluster around *nombres de fantasia* and the potency of the laboratories associated with them. In pharmacies across Buenos Aires—from the Simis and the Ahorros in outlying *villas* and the city center, to smaller private neighborhood pharmacies, to bigger Argentine chains such as Farmacity in more-transited thoroughfares—I talked at length with pharmacists about how they make recommendations to their customers, especially in well-populated classes for which they might stock six, or nine, or thirteen different brands of the same drug. Pulling out a used envelope and a pencil, Norma Verastegui, the head pharmacist at Farmacia Constitución in Congreso, near the seat of the federal government, answered my question by drawing up a list of all the hypertension medications (all versions of enalapril) that she stocked. There were nine in her inventory that month. Then she started grouping them. The drugs made by reputable "big labs" (Roemmers, Bagó, Merck, Duncan, Bayer) came out at the top of her list. In this category, importantly, the domestic (Roemmers, Bagó, Duncan) and the foreign (Merck, Bayer) mix easily, without distinction. They were interchangeable. "These, yes, I trust and recommend. They're good," said Verastegui. "The others?" I asked. "Those?" She frowned in disapproval: "Those are from little labs that no one has heard of."[16] In this particular case, these were brands of enalapril made by smaller Argentine laboratories and a few Brazilian labs as well.

The distinction between big labs and little labs emerged often in my discussions—a reflection of the power of the leading laboratories (domestic and foreign) with their marketing budgets and *detallistas* (the sales representatives who visit physicians) and their sophisticated means of courting and tracking physicians whose loyalty in prescribing is highly prized and closely surveilled, as Andrew Lakoff has shown so vividly (2004, 2005).

In Villa Burano, a working-class neighborhood on the outskirts of Buenos Aires, a pharmacist in a Farmacias del Dr. Simi, which exclusively sells generic medicines under its too-similar slogan, "The same, but cheaper," explained the difference to me in a way that echoed Tobar's own sweeping assessment: "Well, the thing is, they are all the same. Everything on these shelves is a brand. What happens is that if people don't recognize a drug from TV [he gestured toward the television mounted high in the corner of the small storefront], then it must be a generic."[17]

This is it, precisely: the pharmacies that advertise generics are selling drugs made by the small labs that no one has heard of, with little to no marketing presence. These drugs sell more cheaply than many of the well-known copias made by the bigger Argentine labs, most of which have a vivid presence on billboards, on advertisements in the subway, on television and radio, and in physicians' carefully cultivated loyalties. While this Simi pharmacist insisted that they're all the same because everything is a brand, the thoughtful young pharmacist at Dr. Ahorro several blocks down told me the same thing, only differently: "Any copia is a generic." He was uneasy, though, about the implications of such a sweeping act of leveling, which seemed to run into a problematic limit. Any copy is a generic, he continued, "But I don't like the sound of it. It sounds like you are devaluing it. I don't think that generics exist. It's the same. So why call it a generic? It makes it seem *less*."[18]

This pharmacist selling generics was certainly not the only person who articulated a concern that calling something generic, in the midst of a plethora of well-known branded copias made by well-known laboratories, named it as both different and less than. If they really are all the same, why single out any particular drug as merely generic? His sensibility seemed closely attuned to that of his customers, many of whom come to him (behind the counter at Farmacias del Dr. Ahorro) with the box they bought last time and ask for that exact medicine again. Estéban Navarro, the pharmacist, summed up the situation for me: "If they are all the same, why not stick with the brand you like?" Reminding us of the capacious equivalencies operating even in the midst of these particular attachments, he was agnostic about who might have manufactured the brand one likes: "Who knows? It might even turn out be a generic!"[19]

In these discussions, equivalence was less an organizing regulatory-technical idiom than a statement about the transferability and interchangeability of names, a markedly fluid economy of signs. In this context, González García's aspirational de-duplicating project—the hope of reuniting a drug with the singular truth of its singular name—was elusive. It was all the more so given how tricky names themselves had come to feel in a globalized Argentina and posteconomic crisis—even or especially the names and identities of domestic and foreign companies.

Names are a site of fungibility, by which I mean, in the spirit of the analysis underpinning this book, not exact interchangeability but multiplying slippage. My conversations with physicians, pharmacists, health care workers, and pharmacy customers, as well as incidental conversations with neighbors in the building where I was living or with friends of friends, would often steer me directly to the larger matter of names as a notable site of swappable instability. That is, as soon as I mentioned that I was in Argentina to understand the question of generic medicines and Dr. Simi's presence there, it did not take long for the question of the name to come to the fore as a site of slippage, deceit, or hidden truth. Mauro, a pharmacist in Villa Burano, mused on the differences (and similarities) between Drs. Simi and Ahorro and then scaled up the question of who is who and what is what: "The truth is, people here don't know . . . let's be realistic: there are foreign [drug] companies that have subsidiaries here and they say that they're from Argentina, but in reality it can be a foreign laboratory."[20] Another such conversation unfolded in an Argentine (i.e., non–González Torres) pharmacy as I waited for the pharmacist who had agreed beforehand to meet me to talk about medicines. Edgar Lozoya, also waiting for the pharmacist's attention, noticed my not-very-Argentine Spanish and asked me what I was interviewing the pharmacist about. He also turned my interest in the trajectories of a Mexican pharmacy chain (or two) into a reflection on the hard-to-pin-down nature of names and entities, especially after 2002. Lozoya told me he had worked for a foreign private ambulance company before the 2001 to 2002 crisis. He lamented the loss of that particular job en route to reflecting on how names seemed to come and go, just like companies. "It was high tech, that ambulance: you could operate on people inside. The company had good relations with the *obras sociales* [insurance programs that contracted with ambulance services]. But when the crisis hit, the obras sociales stopped paying, and the company closed up shop and left the country." He continued, after some more small talk: "You know, Dr. Simi came here about a year ago but had problems with another pharmacy, and with Dr. K[irchener]."[21] Adding to the doctors in the mix, people often referred to then president Néstor Kirchner as Dr. K. The news had been full of Simi's allegations that Dr. Ahorro and the administration of Dr. K. were "in collusion." That is, Víctor González Torres accused Javier/Dr. Ahorro of making special deals with Kirchner's secretary of health Ginés González García, a point that will return at the end of the chapter.[22] After mentioning Dr. Simi's alleged problems with Dr. K., Lozoya continued:

> [Dr. Simi] had problems with their business, with society, with industry trade groups. They [Similares] put up a pharmacy but with no name [a reference to the injunction issued at Javier/Dr. Ahorro's demand when he argued that Simi's slogan was too similar to his own]. They started selling medicines but were closed down. *You can't sell drugs in a pharmacy with no name!* In fact, a lot of companies were here from abroad, like gas stations and supermarkets, but then when things got difficult with the country, they picked up and left. A lot have returned, but this time with different names.[23]

The ease with which such conversations about Dr. Simi's pharmacies (with and without a name) gave way to observations about companies that come and go, under new names or with names that belie another truth ("The people think subsidiaries are Argentine, but they're really foreign") is important here. If the appeal to substantive, regulatory "equivalence" was not going to easily stabilize Mexico's generic proliferations, an appeal to the singular name seemed unlikely to stabilize Argentina's proliferation of pharmaceutical brands. "The name," people told me in countless conversations about many different things, is precisely that which does not stand still. The equivalencies of names—"The thing is, they're all the same!"—was sometimes an affirmation, but it was also a lament ("But I don't like how that sounds!"). Echoing the prior chapters' argument that equivalencies can always dissolve into something else, and often into something that is more-than, "It's the same" or "They are all the same!" were assertions of how these things and relations proliferate unstably rather than stabilize. Here, equivalence and sameness index the effects of a pharmaceutical market and a political-regulatory arrangement in which nothing is original, everything is a brand, and everything is a copy. It is in this sense that so many people said to me, about medicines and their classification (as copies, and brands, and generics), and even about Drs. Simi and Ahorro: "Son lo mismo," or "Son iguales." They're all the same, precisely because they can so easily slip into or become something else.

(E)quality

For all this focus on names—the generic name, the pharmacy with no name, the companies that disappear and return only with new names—the questions of quality and even regulatory bioequivalence were not off the table in Argentina's generic problem space. They simply did not define the commercial semiotics and regulatory battles over genericness as they did so powerfully and explicitly in Mexico. How, then, did "quality" become part of the composition of genericness in Argentina?

While pharmaceutical patents did not hold enough traction to organize the question of quality, brand names on the other hand certainly did. Leading brands (with no necessary relation to originality) were often precisely what were tied to trust in the quality of drugs. This is not surprising. Patents or no, the relation between brand and quality is precisely what brand names were invented to secure (Coombe 1998; Lury 2004). These attachments could hypothetically (according to the Ahorro pharmacist I mentioned previously) generate loyalty to a cheaper brand (generic), but more often they seemed to militate against the kind of equalization that the generic prescription law was supposed to articulate and hence cultivate. "La gente de la capital son muy marquera" (People here in the capital are very attached to brands), Eduardo Alarcón, a building manager in the tony neighborhood of Recoleta, told me with exasperation.[24] In this context, he meant *attached to specific leading brands*. The point came up because he was recounting to me the lengths to which he must go in order to stretch his elderly father's supply of heart medicines. Alarcón makes very little money, he told me, and his father has even less at his disposal. But his father, with the very little money he has, is nonetheless suspicious of cheaper brands of his medicines and refuses to take anything but the leading national brand that he has come to know and trust from advertisements on TV and a recommendation of his doctor a while ago. Thus, Alarcón routinely sneaks a generic into his father's regimen by alternating the drugs: one day he gets the leading brand, the next day he gets a cheaper brand, and repeat. So far, he said, his father hadn't caught the subterfuge. Such interchangeability—a cheap brand for the expensive brand—is a tentative start to materializing González García's project of substitution by generic name.

The heads of the leading Argentine laboratories whose drugs are the targets of such substitutions were, in turn, not very different from the transnational, patent-holding laboratories in their efforts to resist such intrusions into customer and physician loyalties. In fact, the national industry was fiercely resistant to the emergent politics of generic prescription. This resistance sparked a telling alliance between leading Argentine companies and the transnational laboratories—two constituencies that had long been at odds with each other, as the latter had long accused the former of piracy. The potential rise of generic substitution was, however, enough of a threat to the manufacturers of leading brands, both Argentine *and* transnational, that these two sectors joined forces in the early 2000s to stave off the advent of generic competition (Bergallo and Michel 2014, 42; Vasallo and Falbo 2007). Their joint efforts ranged from coordinated lobbying efforts against the generic prescription law, to working together in supply and price-setting contracts with one of the largest institutional customers in the country (Bergallo and Michel 2014, 42), to the time-honored tactic of sounding warnings about the quality of medicines produced by their little-known competitors.

In May 2006, the marketing director for one of the leading Argentine labs sat down with me in a café in Buenos Aires, over a series of afternoons, to explain the generic situation as he saw it. On the matter of *which* brands (and hence, which labs) can claim quality, he was firm: "The generics market isn't the same in the United States as it is in Argentina. Here, a whole bunch of second and third brands emerged because of the crisis in 2001 to 2002. Yes, they represented a huge drop in price, but a lot of those second and third brands are of potentially suspicious quality."[25]

Of what, in this scenario, does quality consist? Or, more to the point, where might we find it? When Drs. Simi and Ahorro landed in Argentina, bioequivalence was only required for a few specified classes of drugs—notably antiretrovirals. In chapter 1, we saw how firmly regulatory equivalence and quality can become sutured together under particular political conditions of possibility: when both patents and regulatory equivalence are the reigning idioms structuring a market for generics, the question of whether they are the same (as originals) becomes the dominant, legible mode of asking about and affirming, or denying, the quality of generics.

In Argentina, quality was seen largely to reside in the name of the laboratory, whether innovator or Argentine copista: *these are the big labs that everyone has heard of*. Even in such assertions of better and worse quality, neither chapter 1's puzzle of whether the generic is really the same as the original nor its recomposed grammars of *same and not the same* were orienting devices. All that we have seen here puts into relief how strongly *that* version of the generics question is shaped by the conjunction of intellectual property rights and the demand to harmonize regulatory standards of equivalence for generic medicines. Argentina's protectionist defense of the right to copy, which gives no special status to originality, pulls one of the pillars out from under that formulation. But what of the latter, the question of equivalence, bio or otherwise?

Virtually alone among my many interlocutors in Argentina, the physician Patricia Silva, whom I mentioned earlier, homed in on pharmacological determination—that is, the question of bioequivalence as the other key piece of the puzzle, and hence the other reason why, in Argentina in 2006, "there was no such thing as a generic." When she started explaining the scenario to me, I thought I knew exactly what she was going to say, as just about everyone with whom I had spoken (from consumers to pharmacists to economists) had routed their explanations to me along a similar itinerary: "Everybody gets confused. They say it's a law of generics, but it's not; it's a law of prescription by generic name." But when I asked her what it would mean, in her estimation, to have a proper generics law (and hence proper generics), she moved beyond the question of the patent to invoke the relationship between IP and regulatory definitions of genericness—particularly the concept of bioequivalence. She essentially reverse-engineered a definition of *the generic that wasn't* (yet):

> I would say, you would have to delineate the characteristics of a generic, to lay out bioequivalence standards, to say what incentives there will be for companies to comply. What you find in Argentina is a strong national industry, which in many cases dominates the market. With any given drug, it might be that the top 10 selling brands are produced by Argentine labs. . . . They have to meet strict quality control standards, good manufacturing practice. Their quality is recognized as high. They are leaders in quality. But [*she paused for emphasis*] . . . their drugs are not generics. If there had been a patent, *and* the patent expired, *and* there is bioavailability . . . it has to have the definition of the generic of the World Health Organization. It's true, here, we don't have bioavailability for a lot of drugs [antiretrovirals were among the few classes of drugs for which bioequivalence was required in Argentina]. Argentine products are not generics. You have the medicines developed by multinational companies, and then you have those with an Argentine label on them: copies.[26]

Silva sketched the contours of a generic drug in a generic sense, as a class that must meet general criteria: in this case, those established by the WHO. If she can say that Argentine copies are not generics, it is because she is refusing to orient primarily to the nationalist stance grounded in both the de facto refusal of patent regimes and a limited regulatory insistence on bioequivalence as a threshold for locally made versions of drugs developed by patent-holding companies. Completely flipping the popular, operative hierarchies in which copias (leading brands) are better than generics (lesser brands), in Silva's hypothetically harmonized scenario, generics wouldn't be less than leading brand copias; they would be more, insofar as they would meet additional thresholds in the registers of intellectual property and regulatory bioequivalence. They would be proper generic copies.

If the national industry is not making generics, what are they making? Silva rounded out her argument with an assessment of another "underlying truth" of the domestic pharmaceutical industry: "What the national industry has been producing are similars. This is what those with an Argentine label, the copias, really are. Similars. And similars," she argued firmly, "are not generics."

And so the similar returns. In the multilateral harmonization and enforcement language circulating around bioequivalence, the term *similars* often refers to copied drugs that have not been subject to bioequivalence testing and that carry their own brand names. This description could fit equally well with Argentina's copias, leading brand or otherwise, the copied drugs approved explicitly as similars in Brazil until 2015, and (regular) generics as they have circulated in Mexico, including many of the medicines sold by Drs. Simi and Ahorro. These are the "improper" copies that are supposed to disappear, or be phased out, with the global harmonization of the (bioequivalent) generic.

But, crucially, let me emphasize one of the things that does not seem to be in jeopardy here: the quality of domestic copias. The divergence of Argentine *productos copias* from bioequivalent generics does not, in Silva's version of the order of things, cast doubt on their quality. After all, she noted, national labs "are leaders in quality." The absence of bioequivalence requirements is not, in her assessment, a question of quality but of classification, of harmonization with the idioms and regulatory structures of multilateral pharmaceutical governance. Just as "brands are divorced from patents" in Argentina, there is not a *necessary* relationship between (debates about) quality and (debates about) bioequivalence there either.

So, where *does* quality reside? It resides in the name—in the brand and hence in the source laboratory, and hence in a network of authorizing and legitimizing institutions, as science studies work on the politics of knowledge has long taught us to expect. The quality argument in Argentina is attached firmly to the reputation and familiarity of the leading labs, which are attached to the laboratories that make the drugs, which are attached, in turn, to marketing budgets, pharmaceutical sales representatives, and infrastructures of distribution. And these infrastructures have long been embedded in the institutions of Peronist governance. The bigger Argentine drug laboratories—and their products—have had a hold on brand recognition among physicians, pharmacists, and consumers not only through their marketing and sales efforts but also through robust and dense institutional networks. Crucial to this matrix is the leading laboratories' tight relationship with the obras sociales—the mutual associations that are a major form of social insurance in Argentina. Obras sociales provide medication coverage and health plans for most people who have or once had formal employment; these associations contract with particular pharmacy networks and offer 40 percent discounts on drugs to their members. The covered drug in any given category is often a *marca líder* (leading brand), which is often a national product. The power of such distribution networks should not be underestimated: the obra social for retirees, which is known by its acronym PAMI, alone accounts for almost 50 percent of the prescription pharmaceutical market in the country.[27] It is with this obra social, PAMI, that the leading-brand labs, foreign and domestic, made the "master agreement" to which I alluded previously, in their behind-the-scenes joint efforts to fight the new imposition of a generic prescription law (Bergallo and Michel 2014).

"Quality" (in these estimations) attaches to brands, and brands circulate through not-always transparent institutional arrangements; many of my interlocutors openly decried the leading labs' propensity to fix prices and enter into collusion with each other. This arrangement in turn opens up another front in the composition of the question of drug quality, generic and otherwise. If one doesn't trust those institutions, can one trust the drugs? Certainly, many of those institutions—and the broader question of the state that takes charge of health—had changed radically in the years prior to Drs. Simi and Ahorro's arrival. These changes technically preceded the 2001 to 2002 crash. Physician Susana Gaudi put it to me most starkly: "Ever since Menem privatized the country, the state has stopped taking charge of people's health."[28] She was referring to the ways that, under Menem and especially Minister of Finance Domingo Cavallo, Argentina had effectively become a poster child for the implementation of the Washington Consensus, with reductions in public spending, the privatization of state companies, and widespread deregulation, including the removal of state-sanctioned price controls over medicines.

In this context, the quality question might not be about cheaper brands (generics) per se, but about *all* drugs and the institutions and relations in which people in Argentina are meant to place their trust, such that they feel they can say something about the quality of any of the drugs they take—or prescribe. Néstor Carbajal, the psychiatrist whom I quoted earlier, gave me quite an extraordinary and extended condemnation of these institutions as he dismantled, piece by piece, every authorizing force meant to pronounce on the quality of a drug, any drug. He did so with an acute attunement to the ways in which quality serves, from the start, simultaneously as a pharmacological matter and a political economic argument. The question came up because he was rehearsing for me the "typical" response of transnational laboratories to the specter of generic competition and criticism of leading labs' high prices: "What argument is left for the international companies [to maintain high prices]? You've got the first argument, that they need to recoup their R & D costs, that this is how it works. But that's holding less and less weight these days. So what is their other recourse? That's when we get the quality argument."[29] Carbajal ceded, at first, that it is possible to "pay for quality," a sentiment about the relationship between price and the good-ness of a drug that did not remain intact by the end of his next ten-minute speech to me in the café where we met. The unraveling began gently enough: "But even if one can pay for quality hypothetically, *can* I really pay for quality? Can my patient? Not everyone can afford it." If price and quality seemed to travel together at first, things quickly became more complicated. He started with his own guild: "Compared to the United States, physicians' salaries here are very low. So, they are highly susceptible to being influenced by labs, internationals and domestics." It is therefore hard to trust a prescription if your doctor has been "bought" by a lab. But it is also hard to trust the regulators, not to mention the regulated:

> The regulatory agency, too, is susceptible [to being bought]. You can't trust them entirely; in other words, you can't trust the government entirely. And you definitely can't trust the companies. International companies: why are they losing ground? Well, they might have, let's say, 100 percent of the quality, but they are not showing me 100 percent of the information or the data. They maintain trade secrets; they are very cagey around publishing and withholding data. And then there's this thing where their patent is expiring, and then they come out with Prozac one-a-week or Paxil CR [controlled release]. These kind of antics [product-line extensions, meant

to extend the life of a patent through a new modification] contribute to the deterioration of their public image, reputation. And now I have to tell you my theory—and it's that, just my theory—but I think that with the invasion of Iraq, with Enron, with the Bush administration in general, people who before really bought into the Hollywood thing, the image of the US as good, as desirable, as defenders of freedom, et cetera . . . well, now they think, it's a lie, these folks are lying. With Iraq, the torture, Enron, Microsoft, like a domino effect, it's negatively affecting people's perception of the US. So, when I see a trademark from the US, well, people no longer trust it. They tell me the product is good, but if they are lying about all these other things? But I don't necessarily trust the *nacionales* either.[30]

Having dispensed with the transnational and national laboratories, the doctors, and the national regulatory agency, the National Administration of Drugs, Foods and Medical Devices (Administración Nacional de Medicamentos, Alimentos y Tecnologia Médica; ANMAT), Carbajal inevitably came to the question, How can you possibly evaluate quality? "Well, as a doctor, I have certain avenues at my disposal. If the patient has a particular, relatively simple ailment with immediately resolvable symptoms and the drug makes the symptom go away, I can say, 'Yes, it works.'" I wondered, briefly, if the cascade of calamities was going to cease at the feet of this particular doctor as the only authority one might trust, but here, too, I was several steps behind:

> But with drugs that need time to take effect [such as antibiotics], it's hard to evaluate. And if the patient doesn't get better, where does the problem lie? It's hard if you start to distrust every part of the equation. There are many aspects in which one might not have confidence. In the medicine: maybe the problem was simply not amenable to this solution. As a doctor, you might doubt yourself: maybe I'm just not a good doctor. In the patient: did they take the drug at the right time, for the entire time? ["This is what's called compliance," he spelled out for me. "It's hard sometimes with schizophrenic patients, for example."] You might not trust the information that the company gave you. Or maybe the problem lies in the "real world"—that is, the conditions in which the drug was tested were rather artificial, highly controlled. That is not the world of the patient, in which the patient is taking the drug.

So, he said, summing it all up with an understated punch line, "Quality is difficult to evaluate." With this careful anatomization of the contingency underlying pronouncements on the efficacy of *any* drug, this physician turned the spotlight away from second or third brands and provided, instead, a profoundly disenchanted diagnosis of quality as a broadly distributed and perilously elusive institutional effect.

What, then, are generics in Argentina? Here, as anywhere, the generic question is a pharmapolitical one. It requires a series of recalibrations as relations that ostensibly define generics as a distinctive kind of pharmaceutical commodity that come into view in relief; that is, they come into view through critical articulations of what they are not. *En la Argentina* (in Argentina), many of my interlocutors would say with a certain defiance, there are no patents, and therefore there are no generics. En la Argentina, leaders (transnational labs) become followers, quality and bioequivalence are different matters, and brand-name drugs are unmoored from the originality conferred by the patent. In such conditions, generics cannot be a distinctive kind of thing.

My interlocutors' insistence on that point was meant to *remind me* that to speak of generics as a kind is itself an argument and an assumption, even a neoliberal assumption. That is, to speak of the generic as a kind is an accession to the idioms and logics of patent enforcement. For those who insist that generics don't exist in Argentina, the premise of substitution points, instead, to an aspirational intervention in the politics of naming. This is a politics grounded in the elusive promise of a singular name, which might well equalize brands to each other. Todos son iguales!

Let us return, then, to the urgency behind the government's attempt to "return to the drug its singular name" in the early 2000s. For all the ways that Argentina's leading-brand, copycat pharmaceutical industry turns some of the basic epistemologies of intellectual property on their heads, what they still had not done, as one of my interlocutors had noted so pointedly, was lower their prices. The early to mid-2000s in Argentina, as in Mexico, saw notable challenges in the accessibility of medicines given a context of severe, widespread economic hardship. The government's attempt to promote the prescription and consumption (i.e., purchase in pharmacies) of cheaper alternatives to leading-brand medicines (often domestic copies) was a direct response to this situation. But, just as referring to generics itself is an argument and an assumption, so too is invoking "market substitution" as a solution to problems of access. The final section of this chapter elaborates on this point by bringing Drs. Simi and Ahorro back into view.

Bare Price

What room was there, given all of the preceding, for the Mexican Drs. Simi and Ahorro to make their entries into the scene? We could be forgiven for imagining that there would have been an opening and even a need for pharmacies selling less expensive medicines in the aftermath of the 2001–2 crisis. But we could just as easily be forgiven for imagining that foreign chains selling primarily cheaper generic brands might be up for a very difficult ride in a context in which the powerful domestic pharmaceutical industry dominated the market and had been vocally opposed to the politics of substitution by generic name.

In this rather complex context, Víctor González Torres/Dr. Simi was certainly attuned to the wisdom (necessity?) of taking domesticating measures. Reminding us that the nation-state is also a generic form, Dr. Simi's version of a Simipolitical nationalism proved interchangeable but not the same. First and most important, Dr. Simi's project of selling "national brands" had to mean, in this context, selling Argentine-made drugs. There is simply no way, my interlocutors were all utterly convinced, that he could bring Mexican-made pharmaceutical products into this protected market himself. But he did not cede his claim on "Mexicanness" either. Víctor/Dr. Simi's pharmacy openings featured Argentine tango *and* Mexican rancheras, empanadas *and* tacos, all in a kitschy essentialist fusion of national-popular cultures. The balloons were Argentine blue and white, and each pharmacy was adorned with a portrait of Víctor/Dr. Simi's grandfather (who was also, of course, Javier/Dr. Ahorro's grandfather). Right next to the similar *pater familia* in each new pharmacy, Dr. Simi had hung a portrait of Eva Perón.

Simi's domesticating attempts notwithstanding, there remained something different about his pharmacies and hence about Dr. Ahorro's pharmacies too. It was not (just) their Mexicanness but their message. And their message was price. How could it not be? The price of pharmaceuticals is of course one of the primary issues in global and localized politics of access. In 2009, the anthropologist Jane Guyer (2009) elaborated on both Karl Marx's and E. P. Thompson's famous insights on the "fiction" (or fetishism) of the price of commodities. Arguing that price cannot simply be understood as transparent or complete, she argues that it is "composite." Guyer notes, in other words, that price is always made or constructed; it is an effect of "narratives of creation, addition, and subtraction" (204), and hence it is a combination of many elements that are subject to negotiation, questioning, manipulation, resistance, and pressure. Indeed, she notes, "The questioning of simple equations between things and their prices is a sure sign of fundamental unrest" (204).[31]

The price of pharmaceuticals is of course one of the primary issues in access politics, whether we are thinking at the institutional level (say, large-scale purchased by public-sector health systems or private insurance companies) or individual, private consumption. Questioning simple equations between drugs and their prices has, over the last twenty years, been a sign of "fundamental unrest" among health advocates, activists, and (under pressure) policymakers and legislators in a wide range of contexts, whether in Mexico, or the United States, or Argentina, or Canada, or India, or South Africa, such that the act of decomposing or isolating and characterizing the components of drug prices has overtly served as a political act. Consider the public contests over the cost of innovation—or, rather, the costs of research and development (R & D) involved in bringing "new" drugs to market. R & D costs are routinely used as the justification for high drug prices in the United States. As the drug company Johnson and Johnson notes dryly in a 2017 report on transparency, "We have an obligation to ensure that the sale of our medicines provides us with the resources necessary to invest in future research and development" (quoted in Emanuel 2019). This is already one of the ways that Guyer might suggest prices are composite: in this story, high prices, guaranteed through temporary monopoly, are the cost society should bear in exchange for more "health" in the form of more new drugs or vaccines (see also Dumit 2012).[32] This argument is what Néstor Carbajal was referring to in the lengthy discussion of quality and distrust quoted earlier in this chapter: "What argument is left for the international companies [to maintain high prices]? You've got the first argument, that they need to recoup their [R & D] costs, that this is how it works. But that's holding less and less weight these days."[33]

Indeed, critics and analysts attempting to piece together the real costs of drug development—and hence to question the necessity of high drug prices—have argued that industry figures are inflated and misleading, and that, for example, much drug research in the United States is actually subsidized by federal and public funds, not by the companies bringing drugs to market (Hubbard and Love 2004; Yu, Helms, and Bach 2017). Moreover, actual R & D costs are opaque, as data on the costs of developing particular drugs for particular laboratories are "protected" (cordoned off) behind firewalls of corporate secrecy and proprietary databases. Trying to make visible these hidden data, counter analyses suggest that it is, rather, *marketing* that represents one of the highest costs incurred by pharmaceutical companies in bringing a drug to the public (i.e., bringing it to the market [including by cultivating the allegiance of prescribing physicians]) (Hubbard and Love 2004; Yu, Helms, and Bach 2017). To wit, Argentine drug company CEO Alfonso Ferreira told me, in our conversation in Buenos Aires, "The argument about high R & D costs? I dissent. A huge part of pharmaceutical lab spending is for tempting [buying the allegiance of] doctors. Otherwise, Dr. Simi would eat them alive."[34]

Generic drugs, as introduced (differently) in Mexico, Argentina, and in the United States, are of course meant to be interventions in the story of price, precisely because they materialize the market mechanism of competition: *the same, but cheaper!* They are not only cheaper in themselves, but the presumption (sometimes but certainly not always borne out) is that their very availability on the market (or as part of federal bidding processes for public institutions) creates competition, which could/should then bring drug prices down overall.[35] The market alternative is stark. From antiretrovirals to insulin, the persistence of monopoly pricing, with no cheaper or free alternatives available, is the stuff of which public health crises are made.

The emergence of generic drugs in Mexico, including Dr. Simi's widely copied price claims—"Up to 75% cheaper!"—helped create the conditions for public conversations about the composition of drugs and their prices: as in, What *are* we paying for when we pay so much more? Drs. Simi and Ahorro came to Argentina with the same message that had worked so well for both of them in Mexico. They claimed "up to 75% cheaper!" here too. And thus, "Their message," as Néstor Carbajal declared to me, "is price." The statement seemed so obvious to me at the time that I almost didn't write it down in my notes. But I quickly realized that he was not just describing the obvious; he was issuing a critique. He was commenting on the conditions under which the consumer market for pharmaceuticals actually operates in Argentina, which seemed unlikely to solve problems of access all by itself.

Let me explain. With their message of price, Drs. Simi and Ahorro were marked as out of place, for price in itself seemed bare and isolated from the distributional networks, accords, and behind-the-scenes channels through which many pharmaceuticals (and their consumers) circulate in Argentina. In fact, Carbajal had just told me, somewhat indignantly, that "nobody competes by price here." He was referring to two components of the storiedness of pharmaceutical pricing in Argentina. First, he was talking about what he and many others allege was overt collusion among the leading domestic laboratories; for example, he told me that there are "agreements" within Argentine labs and distributors to "keep prices 20 percent lower than imports."[36]

But he was also referring to the routes of circulation through which particular people end up in specific pharmacies consuming particular medicines. For people for whom purchasing a pharmaceutical is an option at all, there are a number of ways to arrive at a given pharmacy and at a given brand of drug. Price is not always the first or last word, nor is *brand*, per se. The obras sociales, the social insurance plans mentioned earlier, are a key part of this picture. Obras sociales have agreements with pharmacies that honor their prescriptions at a standard discount of 30 to 40 percent—a vividly composite price in Guyer's terms. The obras sociales cover (and hence provide at this discount) only particular brands of a given drug, which means that the pharmacies with which they contract might stock only those brands. Obras sociales thus channel their beneficiaries into particular pharmacies, but they are also central players in the close relationship between laboratories, national and otherwise, and the official intermediaries and wholesalers (*droguerías*, *mandatarias*) that help establish prices in the first place. The formal elimination of price controls mentioned earlier—the very reform that allowed leading domestic companies to raise their prices—combined with the power of the droguerías to work together in setting prices created a situation in which Carbajal could say with such confidence that "nobody competes (directly) by price here."

But *somebody* was certainly trying: competition by price was the only recourse for chains such as Simi and Ahorro, who were frozen out of these distribution networks. "It's a mafia!" a government official told me: "They would kill [Simi and Ahorro] before letting them in [to those distribution networks]."[37] But more importantly, Drs. Simi and Ahorro were not the only actors "excluded" from the networks mediated by the obras sociales and the droguerías. By no means do all Argentines belong to an obra social. Largely employment- or guild-based, the obras had, by the early 2000s when Drs. Simi and Ahorro landed in Argentina, left millions of people without coverage for health care or medicines. This scenario is not entirely dissimilar to the massive gaps in coverage in Mexico, which were precisely what provided an opening for Simi, Ahorro, and thousands of other generics pharmacies, as well as the Seguro Popular, there.

In Argentina, a number of schemes emerged in the early 2000s, just as Ahorro and Simi arrived, to help those without access to the obras sociales purchase medicines at similar prices—or, rather, at similar discounts. These schemes all spoke the same language as the obras sociales, offering discounts of 30 to 40 percent on a defined list of medicines. Among the many options that proliferated at the time, there were relatively low-cost *prepagas* (prepaid insurance plans that bring with them discounts, between 30 to 40 percent) on particular drugs at the specific pharmacies that honor them. At the same time, leading-brand drug laboratories had created their own plan, the Recetario Solidario (solidarity plan), which is something that preoccupied almost everyone with whom I spoke in 2006. This program emerged in 2003 just as the law of prescription by generic name was coming into effect. It constituted an explicit move by leading laboratories, mostly but not exclusively domestic pharmaceutical companies, to find a way to ensure that consumers, even those not covered by obras sociales, would continue to buy their own "first-line" drugs rather than cheaper versions made by smaller laboratories. An industry article from 2003, essentially an advertisement for the program, laid out the scenario:

> Facing the documented lack of health coverage for a large percentage of Argentines, a group of 37 leading laboratories generated a proposal to alleviate, somewhat, the precarious health situation of a large part of the population. The Recetario Solidario (RS) is distributed through physicians, together with a *pharmacopea* of more than 4,000 covered drugs. With a signed prescription in hand, all the patient has to do is go to a pharmacy with their RS sticker, in order to get a 30% discount on a large number of first line medicines. (IntraMed 2003)

Pointedly, the medicines covered under this plan were specific brands, not (any) drug under any generic name. Meanwhile, a public-sector agreement was announced in 2003 within the city of Buenos Aires, *also* offering a 40 percent discount on a list of fifteen hundred medicines in participating pharmacies within the city.

These private and public medication plans sought to extend access to medicines at the obras sociales' composite pharmaceutical prices, beyond the limits of the social security plans themselves; they were, in this respect, similar to the ways that, in Mexico, the Seguro Popular extended a recognizably similar form of health coverage to those who did not have access to the employment-based Seguro Social.

What did it mean, in such a context, for Drs. Simi and Ahorro to set up shop selling "second and third brands" at prices up to 75 percent cheaper than leading brands? To compete on price when "no one here competes on price"?

Certainly, for many of the physicians, pharmacists, lab directors, policymakers, and federal officials with whom I spoke, the Mexican brothers' intervention in price hit an off note. Dr. Simi's discounting language of 75 percent seemed garish, excessive. It was out of range. Physician Susana Gaudi put it starkly when I asked if she would send her own patients to Drs. Simi or Ahorro: "Absolutely not. I don't trust anything that's that cheap!"[38] The Argentine Pharmaceutical Confederation (representing the domestic industry) certainly gravitated to that message, warning that, with the Mexican brothers' price war, pharmaceutical "accessibility" was being "confused with a spectacular extravagance or *libertinaje* [excess]" (*El Universal* 2004). From some perspectives, then, these prices told the "wrong" story.

The *message of price* was only one of the ways that the Simi model looked, to many of my interlocutors, like a poor fit for Argentina. There *was* a niche for Dr. Simi to occupy, to be sure, but it seemed narrow, and by 2006, it was only getting narrower. Economist Daniel Maceira reflected on Simi's increasingly inauspicious prospects in my conversations with him in 2006: "Simi, what's he doing? Trying to occupy a niche, but my impression is that the niche is small. For people with very low incomes, there's Programa Remediar [the program distributing medicines for free]. For everyone who has obras sociales, the seguro social, they go with the brands. People prefer to stay with what they know. The space for Simi is relatively small. It's imagined for another market: generics are a market born of patents."[39]

The extreme appeal to bare price communicated a larger story: that Simi was imagined for a different pharmapolitical context, one that looked, not incidentally, more like Mexico's in the early 2000s. That is, Simi's model emerged from a context in which low-cost, private consumption was (prior to the advent of the Seguro Popular) the *only* recourse for the uninsured, as well as for the insured but underserved. Simi's no-holds-barred market intervention—*Lo mismo, pero más barato!*—was a model born of a context in which there was no safety net for the very poor or for those without the obras sociales, where there was no state-run Programa Remediar to distribute medicines for free, and where, not incidentally, generics actually existed because patents also existed.

Dr. Simi did indeed have a hard time replicating the success that he found so readily in Mexico. Víctor González Torres started closing up shop on some of his roughly forty outlets across the city of Buenos Aires in 2006, and by July 2008, he had fully retreated. Why? The fate of Dr. Ahorro might give us some insight. Given their similarities ("The same, but more economical!"), we might assume that Javier/Dr. Ahorro, too, would have failed. But there, we would be mistaken. Javier González Torres/Dr. Ahorro, with *his* robust commerce in cheaper brands of medicines, stayed. The chain remains a vibrant commercial force in Argentina, with a hefty presence in the city of Buenos Aires and outlets planted in cities across the country, including in Rosario, Mendoza, and Salta.

The pharmacies of Drs. Simi and Ahorro were not, in the end, interchangeable. Something differentiated them. It was not the drugs they sell, nor was it their message—the message of price. Indeed, Dr. Ahorro's staying power suggests that the niche for cheaper brands was not all that small, and it has certainly not become smaller in the intervening years. Many of the people I interviewed who were going to the pharmacies of both Drs. Simi and Ahorro told me, readily, that these pharmacies were "doing something important" in a context in which access and affordability of medicines remained a persistent issue, insurance and insurance-like infrastructures notwithstanding. People *do* buy copies/brands popularly known as genéricos. The Argentine chain Farmacity, alongside the pharmacies of Dr. Ahorro, has been a major intervention in this new dimension of pharmaceutical consumption. Price—and competition by price—is *not* irrelevant to the everyday itineraries of many people we might call pharmaceutical consumers, even or especially to those with an obra social. Just as generics pharmacies in Mexico count among their customers beneficiaries of the Seguro Social, so, too, do these pharmacies provide a potential alternative even for those with health insurance. Maru Gómez, whom I met in a Farmacias del Ahorro in San Telmo, told me pointedly, "I come to Ahorro to see what they have. If they don't have my medicine, I go with the obra social, but if they do, I'll buy it here. Yes, yes, people trust in these." She then pointed at the list of prices on the wall: "This is why people come here!"[40] Perhaps it is true that the leading laboratories do not compete with *each other* on price, but that very fact has created another story—a story of price and an opening, a "demand," for cheaper medicines. Filling that niche, a niche based on price, Javier the younger resolutely won the battle of the dueling Mexican brothers. The Argentine daily paper *La Nación* announced the denouement of the feud in August 2008: "La guerra entre las cadenas mexicanas de farmacias ya tuvo un claro ganador" (The war between the two Mexican pharmacy chains now has a clear winner) (Sainz 2008).

My interlocutors gave me some hints about what might have differentiated the two brothers' prospects early in the process of Dr. Simi's exit. There were grumblings, for example, that Dr. Simi was "too cheap"—not just in price but in aspect. Certainly, the Simi pharmacies I visited seemed hastily put-together, shabby, and none too solid compared to Dr. Ahorro's more expansive and fancy storefronts. But ultimately, the divergence landed at the nexus of distinction, uniqueness, and priority—the very pharmapolitical concerns that help organize the relation among copied medicines themselves in Argentina. Néstor Carbajal mused to me that Víctor/Dr. Simi was not, in the end, *distinctive enough*, as if Simi shared the same challenges faced by second- and third-tier medicines. In his words, "Despite favorable early conditions, Simi's problem was that *he lost his identity*, his uniqueness." On this point, I kept thinking of Edgar, the former ambulance driver who reflected on Simi's troubles, indignantly: "You can't sell drugs from a pharmacy with no name!"[41]

But Dr. Simi's problem was not merely that others (notably, his brother) were doing the same thing, nor that his pharmacies (temporarily) lost their name. His problem, in Argentina's regulatory context, was that Javier/Dr. Ahorro *got there first*. As we have seen throughout this chapter, priority can be a powerful force even when patent-mediated originality is taken out of the picture. Where the protectionist Argentine pharmaceutical market is concerned, the advantage, we have seen, can go to a copy that is allowed to enter the market first. If this is true of leading Argentine labs' productos copias, it has also held true for two Mexican pharmacy chains selling copies, no matter how similar one is to the other. ("It's all going into the same pocket, no?") Dr. Ahorro was first. Víctor/Dr. Simi, the "leader" in Mexico, became the "follower" in Argentina.

As with the very definition of generics, and as with the power of domestic copias, there are particular conditions of possibility shaping such relationships. They are the product of the contested regulatory, economic, and political arrangements that help set terms and structure relationships among versions of things, same and not the same. Dr. Ahorro, arriving first, could become the leader (at least vis-à-vis Dr. Simi) in part because of the regulatory structure of Argentina's commercial landscape. Very much *unlike* Mexican zoning laws, Argentine zoning codes do place some limits on the density and location of pharmacies. Regulations in the province of Buenos Aires prohibit the opening of a new pharmacy within three hundred meters (roughly 984 feet) of an existing outlet (Sainz 2008). In this context, arriving second very directly impeded Dr. Simi's habit of establishing a dominating, saturating, cheap commercial presence. With such zoning restrictions firmly in view, the Simi enterprise explained their exit from the scene by lamenting that the regulatory environment in Argentina was not friendly to them (and, hence, they accused the Argentine government of unfairly favoring Dr. Ahorro). "Argentina is a beautiful country to visit, but not to do business. There are many regulations that slowed our growth," said Vicente Monroy, director of the business group running the Simi pharmacy enterprise (Sainz 2008). Thus, he announced, they were picking up and shifting their energies to Chile, where things were already "going very well" for them (Sainz 2008).

Conclusion: Composing a Generic Problem Space

The divergent and ever-on-the-move trajectories of the brothers González Torres aside, there looms here a more consequential question: Where does a cheap consumer market fall within a larger set of debates over who, and what, shall have responsibility for ensuring access to medicines? That Dr. Ahorro continues to do business in Argentina, and that people do indeed buy "cheaper brands," tells us quite clearly that there is considerable space (need, demand?) between the options available to the very poor—eligibility for free medicines—and the coverage and discounts provided by the obras sociales.

The very existence of this space—the space of a low-cost consumer market for medicines—occasioned a robust debate at the time in Argentina about what it meant, politically and ethically, to turn to generics in the form of a *turn to the market* as an intervention into the problem of health. The impoverished idiom of "market competition" and the recourse to bare price were, to many on the Left, inadequate principles on which to base a response to deep inequality. By itself, lowering the price of medicines certainly could not be considered a sufficient guarantor of access. Patricia Silva generously shared her thoughts on the matter with me as we talked through the situation in which Argentina found itself in the years following the 2001 crisis: "The big theme for Latin America is serious inequality. The public health system [in Argentina] is free, but frankly there are huge numbers of people without any access to medicines at all. Below the poverty level, you simply can't buy drugs. You can lower the price all you want but people still can't afford them. You have to have ways to distribute medicines and primary care for free."[42]

I asked her, then, if she agreed with the critiques I had been reading and hearing, that generics were a neoliberal solution to the problem of pharmaceutical access. Though she identifies as a member of the Argentine Left, she was impatient with this argument and its implied demand for an either-or choice between public provision and the market. "You can't be nihilist vis-a-vis health! I think [generics] are among the solutions that form part of a larger vision we have to propose in Latin America, because in fact the question of access is much deeper than the price of medicines," Silva said. "Developed countries have generics policies and they have them for a reason. It's been proven a thousand times that they do actually have an impact on cost. . . . If it weren't the case, if generics didn't actually make a difference in costs, why would the multinationals, and the domestic industry here in Argentina, oppose them so strongly? . . . So this tells you that this is in fact one important route, one strategy, though it's not the only one."

With the introduction of a generics prescription policy in Argentina, multiple things and relations were, indeed, being de-composed and recomposed at once. The way that generics came into view *en la Argentina* tells us once again, in vivid and distinctive detail, that generics are not simply fungible pharmaceutical commodities for which there is now a (growing or shrinking, vibrant or chaotic) market in this or that country, region, or continent. Genericness is instead a pharmapolitical problem-space, a (partial) intervention into problems of access, problems that are in turn configured and arranged in specific ways. En la Argentina, this problem space is composed of many elements: a long-standing, protectionist politics of the domestic copia that has no simple or necessary relation to affordability or access; a tension between regulatory appeals to singularity (returning to the commodity drug its one true name) and the peculiar abundance of fantasy/brand names that only generates more excess; and a pointed reminder that generics travel *with* patent regimes, not against them. The generics that do not exist in Argentina are not an absence or a not-yet—they are a composition, a commodity arranged, as ever, pharmapolitically.

Access, Excess   4

What are the conditions of possibility for a consumer market in generic medicines to take root and to produce something that looks and feels like access? And what does affordability ("The same, but cheaper!") afford? If these questions reverberated in Argentina in particular ways, they were also very much alive in Mexico, where Dr. Simi had started and where he had found such fertile Simipolitical terrain. As Ramón Gutiérrez told me, "No, es que son bien baratooo! Ahora solo hay que ver si funcionan!" (The thing is, they're *really* cheap! Now we just have to see if they work!). For Gutiérrez, a taxi driver in Mexico City, the question of whether Dr. Simi's medicines actually worked was not a matter for idle speculation. It was an empirical question, and he had a strategy. As he explained to me on a summer day in 2005, he was routinely surveying his passengers (including me) about which of Simi's drugs he should feel confident about (antibiotics? What about cough medicines?) and which he should avoid. "They're educated," he said of his clientele. "They should know."[1] Gutiérrez was not alone in rolling up his sleeves to figure out *how to figure out* whether these new, cheap copied drugs work. That he and others have found it necessary or desirable to do so raises a series of questions about the role of the regulatory state (or, more to the point, the deregulatory state) in the constitution of Mexico's politics of access—and hence in the composition of generics as a commodity and of pharmacies as their delivery vehicles.

From the last days of the PRI's twentieth-century run, through two successive PAN administrations, and then into the return of the PRI from 2012 to 2018, Mexican federal administrations doubled down on cheap consumption as a solution to problems of pharmaceutical affordability and availability. They did so both by introducing new regulations for drug quality and generic equivalence and by effectively leaving quite a lot of room to maneuver around and through those regulations. To invoke *el estado desregulador* (the deregulatory state) in this context is not to unmask a hidden truth or even to draw a particularly controversial line in the sand. The sentiment that the state does not, will not, or cannot "regulate fully" is widely shared; it is a part of the air that one breathes in Mexico, and it powerfully marks the dynamics charted in this book thus far.

A (s)lightly regulated commercial topography is one of the enabling conditions for what I have described thus far as a peculiar abundance, a provisional excess that is lived by many people in Mexico as access—especially to cheaper medicines and to doctors' attention. The capaciousness of the state's regulatory categories is of course what helped usher a surfeit of generics into the market, adjacent to and in anticipation of the blanket requirement of generic bioequivalence. Generics pharmacies and their clinics feel ubiquitous in Mexico (somewhat unlike in Argentina, as we saw in the prior chapter), in large part because permissive zoning restrictions allow just about anyone to open a pharmacy anywhere.

These excesses have, without a doubt, produced new kinds of access, not just in terms of the availability of medicines and primary care but in terms of something like a very complicated, small-*d* democratization. Access to medicines and physicians' attention is no longer controlled by hard-to-reach experts and "inaccessible" institutions—whether measured in financial terms, the commitment of time, spatial proximity to everyday routes of circulation, the gatekeeping function of entitlement to state services, or the low inventories in the public sector. People who buy these medicines have their own classifications and ways of articulating quality that are not necessarily determined by a paternalistic state or by the transnationals. And, as many of my interlocutors emphasized—if emphasis can come in the form of a question—isn't the fact that "those with fewer resources" (a category that many used to describe themselves) can now afford medicines "a good thing"? *No será bueno?*

But this scenario of course generates other trailing, persistent questions that the people with whom I work and talk and to whom I listen don't always know how to answer for themselves or how to imagine on behalf of others. "Access" comes with a persistent asterisk, and as we've seen throughout this account, such questions have been particularly sticky when it comes to Dr. Simi's pharmacies, medicines, and clinics. When I first started this research, I spent a long, fascinating afternoon talking with Lety Velázquez, at the time a pharmacology professor and a consultant for the government on their new generics regulations. She had graciously invited me to her house in Mexico City to talk. When Víctor González Torres came up in the conversation, she laid out the content of this asterisk, quite baldly, as she meditated on the needs he was meeting, at least for *others* ("poor people"). Articulating what we might painfully call a "something is better than nothing" take on what's happening for those in a different class position than herself, Velázquez mused:

> He's not good for the country, overall. But maybe the social side of his work has its good sides: poor people who don't have access to resources or services at a low price, well, now they do. The quality of this service, well, hard to say. But it's cheaper, that's for sure. [Without Simi], if you have one hundred pesos, either you spend it on the medicine or you spend it on the [private] *consultorio*, so you go directly to the pharmacy and you self-medicate. The good thing about Similares is that there's a doctor who, no matter how badly he/she may have done in school, completed the training and is going to know a bit more than the patient. So the person leaves with both a *consulta* and some medicine![2]

Access to what? Is access in itself good enough? Are the drugs good? Are the doctors good, and are they even "real"? "They don't even have titles [medical school diplomas] hanging on the wall!" a friend of mine remarked indignantly after going to a Simi doctor in 2007. "Who the hell is credentialing them?"[3] How *can* we know? As Gutiérrez's approach suggests, many potential "consumers" are not just asking these questions for themselves or imagining them for others. They are finding ways to answer them too.

In this chapter, I will argue that such questions cannot be resolved solely with reference to the quality of medicines or of physicians working in generics clinics; the questions are not simply about drugs or doctors. Rather, they point to the broader implications of a politics of access based on a consumer market that has been, as several of my interlocutors observed, "left to regulate itself." This dynamic creates burdens and dilemmas, as well as pointed openings and opportunities. Accumulations of deregulatory force have given this market its shape. They have helped generate what we might call generic copies' multiplier effects, as analyzed thus far. We have seen these multiplier effects at work in the multiple definitions of generics and their many iterations of equivalence, same and not the same. We have seen them at work in the ways that Mexico's generics pharmacies, sprouting like mushrooms across cities and provinces, have come to serve as a proliferative double of the Seguro Social (and, in a different way, of the Seguro Popular) as health-care provider.

Here, I am interested in another set of multiplier effects including, prominently, those produced by the dispersal of regulatory work itself into popular, commercial practices. With the rise of Mexico's generics market, the project of regulatory qualification—Are the drugs good? Are the doctors good?—has been rearranged such that the commercial sphere comes to serve as a version of the state in this domain too. Thus, I will argue, it is not just drugs and health systems that generics-as-market copy and multiply. The state's regulatory functions—experiment, authorization, the stabilization of quality—are also being doubled, trebled, and troubled by other actors and other practices. The first half of the chapter explores some of these multiplications, including consumers' own practices of testing, as they engage in precisely the kind of "self-medication" (such as getting diagnostic and medication advice from friends or family or trying drugs out on their own hunches) that public health literatures have for so long denounced and discouraged. As M. Murphy (2016) has argued in a different context, the field of consumption has become, rather explicitly, experimental terrain.

What does this experimentalization produce? In the second half of the chapter, I will argue that one of the things it produces is yet another layer of openings and dilemmas, burdens and rearrangements. The question "Access to what?" will resurface somewhat transformed. A lightly regulated pharmaceutical market, a deregulatory state, and practices of experimental self-medication together have multiplied forms of access well beyond consumers' access to cheap drugs and primary care. This market provides access to wages for workers, access to training experience for young physicians, and access to modest forms of pharmaceutical capital for would-be entrepreneurs. This, too, is experimental terrain: the use of low-cost consumption to increase poor or poorer people's contact with medicines and (formalish) markets bears all the hallmarks of so-called base of the pyramid (BOP) experiments in health and development. There are in fact some pointed, direct entanglements between BOP orientations to medicines—which deemphasize public health infrastructures and public spending and highlight cheap consumption—and the way the Simipolitical generics market operates in

Mexico. The multiplier effects of copied drugs thus reverberate in the form of multiple agencies that the state in Mexico has long exercised, however problematically, from regulation (or, rather, deregulation), to brokering employment and providing medical training, to serving as a source of social(ish?) security in the form of postretirement income.

Taken together, these multiplying relations—the doublings and treblings enacted through a roiling, as-if regulated commercial market in generics—significantly complicate what we might mean by *access*. And they raise persistent questions about the kinds of openings that Mexico's generics market creates and for whom, as well as the distributed burdens and work it underscores.

Section 1: Trebling the State

The Magic Word

In contemporary policy debates and struggles over health, equity, and medicines, there are many avenues to, and hence many imaginations of, pharmaceutical access. A number of practices have attracted anthropological attention and critical analysis of late, including the rise of judicialization in which, in the context of a basic level of public provision and a constitutionally guaranteed right to health, individuals may petition the courts to demand that the state provide them particular (and often leading-brand) medicines, as has been the case in Brazil, Colombia, South Africa, Costa Rica, and elsewhere since the early 2000s (Lamprea 2017; Biehl and Petryna 2011). Or, there is the model in which philanthropic programs such as the Gates Foundation subsidize the transnational industry, buying antiretrovirals or antimalarial medicines from the major labs and then distributing them for free or at low cost to people in particularly hard-hit countries too poor to buy them otherwise (Pollack 2013; Tichenor 2017). There are national health care formularies, as in Canada, the United Kingdom, and Cuba. There is publicly funded drug development to help ease lower-cost and sometimes reverse-engineered drugs into the market, as in Brazil; there is the introduction of generic prescription laws (and hence the principle of market competition) alongside state-funded programs to distribute medicines for free to the poorest, as in Argentina. This is not an exhaustive list by any means. But the point is the following: to double down on low-cost private consumption as the avenue for improving access is a very specific, though certainly not arbitrary, response to widespread problems of pharmaceutical unavailability and unaffordabil-

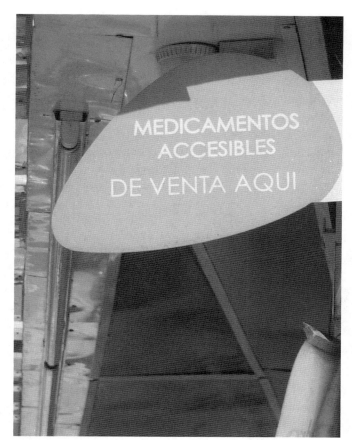

4.1 "Accessible (affordable) medicines for sale here," pharmacy sign, Avenida Miguel Angel de Quevedo, Mexico City, 2013. PHOTO BY AUTHOR.

ity. In Mexico, the state has committed to cheap markets as a key route to pharmaceutical access—even to the point where the expansion of a low-cost consumer market was effectively a condition of possibility for the expansion of the state's reach, in the form of the Seguro Popular. In this commitment to the market, the principle of access itself has come to mean something quite specific, perhaps even magical.

"Access is the magic word," declared Mikel Arriola, the head of the Federal Commission for the Protection against Health Risks (Comisión Federal para la Protección contra Riesgos Sanitarios; COFEPRIS), in his opening address to a conference for Mexican generic drug manufacturers gathered in the Hyatt in the tony Mexico City neighborhood of Polanco in June 2013, one year into

PRIista Enrique Peña Nieto's administration.[4] This means, he elaborated, "a pro-consumer politics, such that the market offers more competition, better prices, and the elimination of barriers to entry into the market" (Arriola 2013). Indeed, in the preceding ten months, 144 generic medicines had been, in COFEPRIS's language, "liberated" and released for sale, an unprecedented rate of approval in Mexico's still-young generic regulatory landscape. These approvals were celebrated by COFEPRIS and national and regional newspapers as they rolled out, bundle by bundle, *paquete* by *paquete*: "More generics liberated!," "COFEPRIS releases its ninth paquete of generics!," and, "Eighty-nine generics released!" (Comisión Federal de Competencia Económica 2017; Rodríguez 2017; *El Universal* 2018; Federación Mexicana de Diabetes 2015).

Arriola made sure to note at the June 2013 forum—around the corner from which the president of China was, that very day, meeting with Peña Nieto to discuss new trade openings between the two countries—that COFEPRIS had ushered all of these medicines onto the market without being sued for patent infringement "not even once!" Thus claiming for Mexico the mantle of the good copier, Arriola emphasized that generic liberation meant releasing onto the market drugs that can credibly be considered off-patent. It did not mean liberating active compounds from their still-active patents. That, as is the case (in some ways) in Argentina, would be a different pharmaceutical politics altogether.

This politics, instead, was premised firmly on making generic medicines available as commercial alternatives to expensive, leading-brand drugs. That much, we know: the very same sentence, or something like it, has already graced these pages countless times, to the point where it grows stranger to me each time I write it. The debates and politics of medicines in Argentina knocks that seemingly prosaic formulation off-center in some particularly pointed ways. Now, returning to the trajectory of generics in Mexico, I want to pick up the question again of what it means to democratize access to medicines as a process of democratizing access to markets. More competition, better prices, elimination of barriers to entry—if these are the ingredients of proconsumer politics, they can also be the ingredients for deregulatory dispersals and multiplications and for the popularization of regulation itself. A government commitment to reducing laboratories' barriers to entry into the market has raised big questions about what, precisely, is being approved and released onto this market.

A Self-Regulating Market

In his office at the heart of the UNAM campus in the southern end of Mexico City, senior pharmacology research scientist Antonio Salazar swatted away my question, in 2013, about whether the federal government's regulatory efforts over the prior decade had left Mexico's roiling generics market feeling more *settled* to him. The proposition was risible. To the contrary, he declared, "The state has declared itself unwilling or unable to regulate generics. This market has been left to regulate itself."[5] The notion of a self-regulating market is what Karl Polanyi, in *The Great Transformation* (1944), famously decried as the "stark utopia" of free marketeers: a fantasy in which consumer preferences and the laws of supply and demand all by themselves sort out questions of quality, price, and externalities. In such a vision, state regulation can only get in the way of profits, of corporate freedom, of consumers' right to choose. With Polanyi, many of my interlocutors in Mexico longed for a very different relationship among regulation, the state, and the market. To say that the generic pharmaceutical market in Mexico had been left to regulate itself, as I was told by several people in 2013—and hence with hindsight on a particularly complicated decade—was not a particularly good thing.

The complaint referred to several ways in which, as my interlocutors variously noted, the state was making itself "irrelevant" to the project of regulating this generics market. My interviews in spring 2013 with several regulatory officers in fact generated a steady stream of laments about the loosening or defanging of the very tools they were supposed to wield to monitor and affirm the quality of generic medicines. As a result, the sanctioned signature of "proper" generic equivalence (bioequivalence associated with the interchangeable generic, or GI) remained a question mark rather than a stamp of certainty. The accumulation of deregulatory force is certainly one way to produce a substrate for enhanced pharmaceutical access: "(No) será bueno?"

Let me be more specific. The lament or accusation that the state had effectively left this market to regulate itself first emerged on the same day in April 2013, in two different interviews I conducted in Mexico City: one in the morning, with the senior research scientist and laboratory director at UNAM mentioned previously, and another with a federal regulator later that day. The observation was sparked, in both instances, by my questions about the persistent tangle of multiple generic kinds—generics, bioequivalent interchangeables, and similars—that still populated Mexico's generics pharmacies in 2013. I had asked each of my interviewees that day whether they felt that the designation of the "GI" was holding steady or was having the state's intended effect. In other words, were new and existing generic drugs actually being certified as GI? Was the label GI working as a sign of bioequivalence, a sign of "quality?" In 2005, as we saw in chapter 1, the secretary of health had issued a decree that, within a five-year time period, all generic medicines would have to be deemed bioequivalent in order to be approved for sale on the market. Ultimately the dictate was meant to leave bioequivalent GIs as the only generic kind left standing in the eyes of the state, ruling (merely) chemically equivalent generics and *similares* out of order and hence out of the market.

My impression was that things were changing and that the GI seemed to be on the rise. The state's demand that all generics soon become interchangeable generics had certainly sparked some opportunistic acts of resignification (literally) in the commercial sphere. Starting around 2008 and continuing in earnest for the next five years and beyond, many smaller pharmacies started to change their names (or, wisely hedging, adding to them), supplementing their advertised genéricos, or similares, or simylares, with interchangeables and equivalentes. One chain went all-out and just named itself Farmacias GI (Interchangeable Generics Pharmacy). Moreover, in the time I had spent in generics labs, I had seen that major domestic manufacturers had very seriously adjusted their horizons, manufacturing equipment, and auditing processes with the new bioequivalence requirement in view. By 2010, a network of state-authorized public and private third-party bioequivalence testing laboratories, thirteen in all, was working around the clock (staffing three eight-hour shifts continuously) as the biggest generics companies in Mexico were facing the prospect of running their entire existing and approved product inventories through the bioequivalence testing regime necessary for COFEPRIS reapproval. These "authorized third-party" laboratories are a key part of the machinery through which generic drugs secure the status of GI in Mexico, and hence they are a key appendage of the regulatory state.

It was with these developments firmly in view that I asked my interlocutors that spring day in 2013 whether the regulatory process was making any dent in persistent questions over generic equivalencies and qualities. I was interested in their view on whether the GI was gaining traction as *the* sanctioned generic kind over chemically equivalent generics and the perennially unclassifiable similars. To these questions, each of my interviewees threw up their hands in frustration. With a force that surprised me, Salazar at UNAM pounded his desk: "The GI is irrelevant." And with its irrelevance, he declared, "We must also recognize the Mexican state's irrelevance" in the project of mediating drug quality.[6]

A few hours later, and a few miles up Avenida Insurgentes, a regulatory officer, speaking precisely (and very anonymously) as an agent of that Mexican state, effectively told me the same thing. "Mexican norms (regulations) haven't been very strong over the last decade," they said quietly, with a slightly pained look. "And the GI?" I asked. "The GI?" They sighed: "Well, in the best of all possible worlds, we would do another round of third-party validation, to authorize the results of the authorized third-party labs." In Spanish, the sentiment was conveyed much more concisely, even poetically: "Que hicieramos tercería" (If only we could do another round of thirdness). In other words, *if only there was a third party to validate the third-party bioequivalence-testing labs*. "Why?" I asked. "Some of those labs," they said, "were caught fixing data. We know because laboratory technicians came forth with complaints."[7] The current director of one of the testing laboratories in question confirmed the charge for me (this person also asked that their laboratory not be named): the prior director had indeed left under the cloud of being caught "adjusting the data" to show that the contracting lab's drug fit within the approved range for bioequivalence.

Alas. The compact phrase "Que hicieramos tercería" was a complicated lament that did not just point to two specific instances of something one might call corruption or, perhaps, cheating. "Que hicieramos tercería" seemed to me, in the context of the long series of laments and frustrations that constituted both of these conversations, a wistful and elusive hope that felt something like this: if only there could be a third party that could authorize the third party that had already been authorized by the state to validate the bioequivalence of one drug with another. In fact, someone with intimate knowledge of the regulatory environment, a former regulator who also asked that I not use their name, proposed at one point that I take some approved Mexican generics to an academic lab in the United States to verify their (bio) equivalence there. (The generics lab owners in Mexico whom I discussed in chapter 1 would likely have something to say, in turn, about how reliable *that* third-party evaluation would be.)

Signaling an elusive desire for a state that can regulate (itself), the lament certainly pointed to the complications plaguing this specific arena of evaluation. But it was also a fitting expression of the difficulties and politics of commensuration more broadly. The question "Será bueno?" insistently slips from invoking the equivalence of two ("Are they the same?") to the authorizing force of a third: "How can we know?" How *can* we know? This is of course a constitutive question for science studies and an anthropology of knowledge production, the elusive answer to which was so expertly anatomized by Néstor Carbajol in chapter 3, when he described just how impossible it is to evaluate the quality of a medicine if you do not trust the regulators, the companies, or even the clinical knowledge of prescribing doctors. It is also a central question for an analytics of state power that sits athwart another fantasy: that of the efficacious state, one that can provide, by virtue of its own potency, a particular kind of certainty, safety, reliability, and the stabilization of qualities and categories. In contemporary Mexico, such a fantasy is not sustained by anyone I know. The violence of the ongoing drug war, not to mention a widespread understanding that the Mexican state *is* in fact a deregulatory state, has fully worn through any idea of a state entity that can act effectively or reliably in its own name or that it can or should be trusted to do so. In this context, the lament "Que hicieramos tercería" seemed a wish not for a double but a *treble* of the state. It was a wish for an authorizing force that could stand "outside" and assert some kind of certainty at a moment in which the coordinates of state sovereignty—regulatory force, the monopoly over violence, even the state's self-identity—have been more violently rearranged and redistributed than ever.[8]

If the state, in this case in the form of COFEPRIS, had made itself "irrelevant," then who or what would perform this authorizing role? State functions have come to take on a particular distributed form through practices of consumption, as people seeking out cheaper medicines, physicians' attention, and even diagnostic tests have engaged in ad hoc processes of experimentation and evaluation. In so doing, they are not just "copying" the regulatory state—performing its roles in a different sphere—they are trebling it as they seek to answer the question "How can we know?" They are anchoring the questions of quality and equivalence in their own practices and assessments; they are triangulating their understandings with the impressions and knowledge of others. They are engaged in their own acts of tercería.

Popular Regulation
In Mexico, "trust" in authorizing regulatory institutions is certainly fragile and uneven, whether among those who regulate ("If only we could do another round of thirdness") or among those who are meant to be protected by such regulation ("Well," a weathered, middle-aged man working in construction in the city of Cuernavaca hedged in a conversation I had with him in 2008, "*supposedly* there is an agency that monitors [drug] quality, right? But . . . who knows."[9]) In a context in which such sentiments are commonplace, the au-

thorizing voice of generic drug regulation—the power to qualify or disqualify, to attribute quality or its lack—has been decentralized, doubled, and even, we might say (without celebrating), popularized.

Theorists of brand, consumption, and markets, including Celia Lury (2004), Rosemary Coombe (1998), Franck Cochoy (2005), and Michel Callon, Cécile Méadel, and Vololona Rabeharisoa (2002), have made seemingly analogous arguments for some time now vis-à-vis the matters of value, quality, and branding in North American and European contexts, arguing that the act of *qualifying* products should be seen as broadly dispersed and even performative. Quality is not an intrinsic property of commodities or branded goods themselves, they argue; rather, as Callon, Méadel, and Rabeharisoa have argued, the term is better thought of as a verb. In this analytic, the act of qualifying becomes an open, dynamic feedback loop in which consuming publics have a powerful role in shaping what shall count as both particular qualities or attributes of consumer goods or brands and of "quality" itself (see also Cochoy 2005).

Arguably, the analytic power of this move derives its force from an unstated assumption, perhaps reflecting its context in which certain kinds of normative arrangements (state regulation and standardization or the regulation of markets in the name of quality) are largely taken for granted. This is not to say that such classifications and relations are stable and actually reflect the world that they seek to name and control. But analytically, I would suggest many of these works proceed as if regulatory states do the work they say they do. To argue in those presumably "regularized" circumstances that the work of qualifying is actually performed by consumers (and not exclusively by corporate producers) has a certain "democratizing" power, both politically and analytically. The force of the argument, especially from a cultural studies point of view—emerging well before the idiom of crowdsourcing gained its currency—derived from an insistence that consumers, too, are authors and producers of value (see Coombe 1998).

But the popularizing work of qualification can and must be conceived in other registers. Anthropologists Kristin Peterson (2014) and Jane Guyer (2004), both working in Nigeria, lay the groundwork here, pointing to other conditions of possibility in which the work of qualifying products can migrate away from regulatory standardizations and into the popular sphere. They show that such migrations can be the result of the often-deliberate weakening of postcolonial states' regulatory power and authority—whether through radical structural adjustment programs (as in Nigeria) or, I would add, the equally radical but differently configured kind of structural adjustments produced by Mexico's market-friendly deregulatory state projects underway since the 1980s. In both scenarios, different in degree and in the political histories that give them form, the authority of state-sanctioned stabilizations—of categories and of quality—is radically unstable and dispersed. Peterson and Guyer both analyze highly refined Nigerian popular "discernments" (Peterson's felicitous term) of the differences among fake, authentic, copied, and real products, pharmaceutical and otherwise. In Mexico, as we have seen, official generic categories certainly do not answer or stabilize the questions of quality or kind. Instead, they generate still-more openings in which kinds and their qualities proliferate; even official regulatory categories help disperse the burden of discerning quality. This point, which occupied us in such detail in chapter 1, brings into view a larger observation. Deregulation (and its attendant dispersals) is not necessarily simply a question of lack, withdrawal, or state failure; it is also in many contexts what regulatory states do, allow, and enable, whether we are speaking of globalized pharmaceutical clinical trials (Sunder Rajan 2017) or environmental regulations and pollution (Murphy 2017; Liboiron 2021).[10]

More broadly, pharmaceuticals are products for which practices of consumption, and thus the bodies of consumers, explicitly serve to supplement state (de)regulatory functions. Consider postmarketing surveillance, an increasingly established feature of pharmaceutical regulatory regimes in the United States, Canada, the United Kingdom, Europe, Mexico, and elsewhere. The term refers to the ways that, once a drug is on the market, the experiences of patients/consumers—notably, side effects reported to physicians—are understood to be *continuations* of drug trials (Haque et al. 2017). Thus, even after a drug secures regulatory approval, the "testing" phase for both new and generic medicines (clinical trials, bioequivalence tests) is rarely considered complete. To the contrary, given the "small number of patients in clinical trials compared with the intended treatment population," the information on drug safety needed to approve drugs for the market is considered quite limited (Haque et al. 2017, 684). Consumption—the experience of consumers—is thus called on to refine or refute this data (Haque et al. 2017).[11] Most consumers of medicines are thus experimental subjects in this dispersed, informalized sense, though there is no good to come from homogenizing the effects of this point.[12]

In Mexico, the project of testing generic medicines, similars, and interchangeables has certainly been (pro)actively assumed by consumers themselves given a widespread understanding that the deregulatory state does not or cannot treble (itself). Mexican consumers have thus made their way through diverse pharmaceutical itineraries on their own terms. They have done so in conversation and consultation with others—friends, family, strangers, possibly a pharmacist or a doctor—all of whom may well be asking, too, Será bueno? If we might eventually choose to call these acts of deliberation and discernment popular, we can certainly also call them, again without celebrating, experimental.

How do you know if the drugs are good? If the doctors are good, or even real? You take on the state's authorizing function and, hence, you test. You test the doctors and the drugs by trying them. You ask others about their experiences. You conduct informal surveys, as did Ramón Gutiérrez from the driver's seat of his taxi. You develop your own accounts of efficacy based on your experiences and the experiences of people you know or trust. This active orientation to experimentation and evaluation was the approach taken by many people in the early days of generics' emergence in Mexico, especially in relation to Dr. Simi, whose similares and novel model of low-cost clinics generated an outsized degree of attention, scrutiny, interest, and skepticism. The very accessibility of the full suite of Dr. Simi's offerings—the medicines, the doctors, the diagnostic tests—seemed to invite such experimental treatment. Alberto Moriarty, an environmental researcher whom I have known since the mid-1990s, told me in 2005 that he had gone to a Dr. Simi clinic explicitly to "test the doctor." Moriarty knows the name, characteristics, and usual treatment of a skin condition that he gets with some regularity. Animated by something between skeptical curiosity and urgency (his private doctor's visits and medications were tremendously expensive relative to his salary), he made his way to a Simi consultorio when his rash next emerged and came out unimpressed: "The doctor diagnosed something totally different" and prescribed several medicines (to buy next door in Farmacias Similares) that, Alberto declared, had nothing to do with his psoriasis.[13]

But Simi didn't always emerge poorly in such consumer testing. An HIV/ AIDS advocate whom I met in 2004, whose organization the Simi enterprise was actively (though not successfully) courting for their political support, told me that their group was at the time sending their patients to Simi for various routine diagnostic tests (not HIV tests) "to test the quality of their labs." And? "Yes. They were good." Lety Velázquez, the pharmacology professor whom I quoted at the outset of this chapter about what Dr. Simi might be doing for "others," also had something to say about what Simi might offer to those like herself, routed through self-experimental practice. As we were talking about her role in the generic regulatory process, she veered from policy talk into an account of her own forays into personal generic pharmaceutical testing. Reminding us once again of how very powerfully the story of generics, and especially of Dr. Simi, was calibrated to questions of class and income, she paused at one point to emphasize the "possibilities" opened up by this new market "not just for lower income people," she said, "but also for professionals" such as herself. And then she told me about her own experiment. Against the (very strong) opinion of her doctor, a physician in private practice, she was determined to try a hypertension medicine sold by Dr. Simi. Lured by the radical price difference—Dr. Simi's enalapril cost a tenth of that of the brand-name version that had been prescribed to her (thirty pesos, or roughly three dollars, instead of the three hundred peso price tag of the brand-name drug)—and buoyed by confidence in her ability to monitor her own stats, she decided to try Simi's generic for three months, carefully tracking her blood pressure along the way. "Y fíjate," she told me with equal parts surprise and triumph, "se me controló!" (And wouldn't you know . . . it worked!).[14] If this experiment seems a small victory for Dr. Simi (not to mention the patient/consumer/experimenter), we must also note that Dr. Simi was resolutely not the only one being tested here. It was the regulatory state itself—an entity with which Dr. Velázquez herself was intimately involved—that was being supplemented, scaffolded, doubted, tested, and qualified.

Through such acts of ad hoc experimentation, the commercial sphere comes to both perform and reflect on the state's regulatory functions. Such doublings and treblings of drug regulation ricochet, in turn, into other domains, including generic manufacturing and sourcing. We might understand in this light yet another of Víctor González Torres's telling moves in the early 2000s when he began framing his Farmacias Similares enterprise not only as among the regulated but as a regulator too. That is, one of Similares' responses to early critiques of the quality of their drugs was to go on the offensive and assert their role as procurers of drugs in much the same way that the federal government is a procurer of drugs (and often at an analogous scale). Farmacias Similares, in other words, sells some drugs made by its own Laboratorios Best, but the majority of its products come from other laboratories. As I noted briefly in chapter 2, the Simi enterprise announced in 2005 that, alone among their competitors, their pharmacy chain would actively *surveil the laboratories from which it purchases drugs*, offering their own "certificate" of quality. Simi dramatically threatened to report and hence put out of business any source laboratory that did not meet their requirements (though they did not specify which thresholds were at stake) (see Chu and García-Cuellar 2007, 10). Simi was effectively announcing that there was space to be claimed here—the space and performative demand for a regulatory state. And in naming this space, González Torres also occupied it, in characteristically shouty fashion.

Generic pharmaceutical manufacturers have also, in some ways, taken matters into their own hands. They have done so not because they demand to have the privilege of regulating themselves, as an antiregulation industrial stance might have it. Rather, they have taken the matters of quality control into their own hands largely because securing a place in this well-populated pharmaceutical marketplace and finding their way into international markets, including the United States, depends on stabilizing a scaffolding of trust beyond what the Mexican state can guarantee—to find a convincing way to secure quality and to magnetize to it rather than letting it go skittering off into the receding horizon of elusive thirdness. Thus, the director of one of Mexico's biggest generics laboratories drew my attention to a consortium of generics manufacturers in Guadalajara (Mexico's major pharmaceutical hub) that has set up its own quality-control protocol for imports. This consortium tests the purity, quality, and stability of the imported chemical compounds its member laboratories use for their manufacturing. Let me emphasize that this move stands in addition to the quality-control mechanisms these laboratories already have in place to evaluate finished products within their own laboratories; it also stands in addition to the signature of the state conferred by a GI designation for their products. Here, they are making visible an extra layer of self-initiated regulatory oversight on imported raw material, most of which comes from China, and thus staking their own claims for thirdness on top of the state's approval of the quality of their drugs.

In still another zone of supplementation to the state, physicians and researchers have recounted to me how pharmacies in major commercial chains such as Walmart and Gigante tend to operate with their own rules for dispensing certain classes of drugs, particularly psychopharmaceuticals, in ways that are more restrictive than the federal regulations ostensibly guiding them. One of the researchers who told me about this tendency shared the story in the form of another complaint: although he had all of the required, elaborate paperwork demonstrating that he was purchasing medicines for research purposes, a pharmacist in Gigante still refused to sell him the antidepressants he was trying to buy and asked him to jump through several additional hoops required by the store: "I followed the rules, but they decided they had their own!"[15] Such a refusal is of course very directly about the role of pharmacies in the conversion of drugs from the "licit" to the "illicit" and back again. But it also points to the nontransparent merits of the "requisite paperwork" and the sense that the federal government's own guidelines require supplemental action to reach their full potency.

These trebling practices are among the multiplier effects of a (s)lightly regulated generics market. They are not just one more version of the state in similar form, not (just) a double (though there is nothing mere about the double). When the commercial sphere serves as experimental terrain and an authorizing domain, tercería—an authoritative thirdness—itself is being recomposed and redistributed. Consumers, merchants, and even producers have found ways to provide their own thirdness to the federal government's arbitration of drug quality and generic categories.

What are the implications of these more-than-doublings? Public health has long had a term for these kinds of experimental practices, and it is not a particularly celebratory one.

Medicating the Self

All that we have seen thus far trips a number of wires where public health discourse and practice have long been concerned. Beyond the crucial, unsettled questions of drug quality (and physician quality) to which the prior discussion directly refers, the practices of self-experimentation charted previously have long been red flags in public health, pointing directly to the much-criticized notion of self-medication. The acts of testing—conducting little experiments on oneself, sharing the results with friends and family, deliberating with others—make a mockery of the exhortation found at every turn in Mexico, and in broader contexts, to *say no to self-medication*. This warning was an insistent refrain accompanying the emergent market for low-cost generics and their pharmacies in Mexico. Even Dr. Simi's pharmacies posted abundant fliers to this effect: Dí no a la auto-medicación! (Say no to self-medication!) The phrase generally refers to taking drugs without a physician's supervision, prescription, or diagnosis. In this sense, Dr. Simi's exhortations against the practice were certainly in part an attempt to get people into the Simi medical clinics to consult their doctors; as many of Simi-loyal customers say quite readily of the Simi consultorios, "ahí me venden la receta" (there they sell me the prescription).[16] But prescriptions are not actually requested for most drugs sold in most pharmacies in Mexico. This simple transactional fact facilitates a wide range of practices that fall under the long-maligned category of medicating oneself.

To wit, well beyond the demand for a prescription, "self-medication" refers to exactly the kinds of deliberation and discernment discussed previously in the idiom of popular, experimental (de)regulatory practices. In colloquial terms, it can mean drinking or consuming all manner of substances to make yourself feel better or to "cope" with physical or emotional stress; it can also mean acting on the advice of your aunt, your friend, your passengers, or your spouse and seeking out drugs at pharmacies on this basis. In more specific terms, especially but not exclusively in Mexico, self-medication is closely associated with the overuse or misuse of antibiotics, which can lead to antibiotic resistance for a wide range of pathogens. The H1N1 flu outbreak in Mexico in 2009 prompted renewed attention to this effect of self-medication, engendering the specific criticism that cheaper generics pharmacies were enabling widespread, improper consumption of antibiotics that may well have worsened the outbreak's effects (Ellingwood and Sanchez 2010). More strict regulatory guidelines were subsequently placed on pharmacies by the federal Secretary of Health, including the requirement that pharmacists actually require prescriptions before they would sell antibiotics (Ellingwood and Ssnchez 2010; Dreser et al. 2012). It is in these many senses that medicating oneself has long been an accusation and a prohibition.

Veena Das and Ranendra K. Das (2006) have argued quite beautifully against the persistently punitive social-scientific and public health stance on such practices. They urge us to think of self-medication not as a misplaced surfeit of pharmaceutical desire on the part of the uneducated (another form of excess) but rather as a product of "particular formations of state and market, lived intimately." Again, we are in the terrain of experiment: self-medication emerges in their work in India as a situated "experiment with categories and medicines" (171) precisely when the "space surrounding therapy is crisscrossed by possibilities . . . [and you] do not know whom to trust" (201).

This analysis hits just the right note for me analytically, empirically, and ethically. But its implications have now come to feel slightly discordant and unsettled in light of the ways that self-medication has undergone a potent and market-ready rehabilitation over the last decade or so. As I will elaborate, in global health and public health circuits, self-medication has become less a compliance problem than a crucial lubricant for low-cost markets in medicines and primary care. It is in fact necessary for another kind of experiment—that which is known in global health and development as the "base-of-the-pyramid" approach to improving access to medicines and health care. As we'll see, self-medication in these circuits is not a failure but an opportunity—for pharmacies, pharmacists, the laboratories that produce and sell over-the-counter medicines, overstrained public health systems, and maybe even patients/consumers.

It would thus be a mistake to understand the multiplier effects, the doublings and treblings traced previously, exclusively as responses to a lack, as if they are only making do in the face of state failure or in the absence of something that should be there. They are this, to be sure, but they are also something more. The effective constitution of a consumer market as an experimental site that trebles the state isn't just an ad hoc response to a deficit in perceived regulatory force. This deregulatory excess also runs with the grain of broader trends in global health and development, which resonated quite powerfully in the early 2000s in Mexico and specifically with the Simipolitical entanglement of the new generics market and the Seguro Popular.

To explain, the next section will change scales or loci a bit in order to ask, Where and by whom are such experiments being run? Self-medication—and the central role of low-cost pharmacies therein—is central to broader experimental imaginations that seek to reorganize the delivery of health care and medicines through cheap consumption. This expansion in the terrain of experiment brings into view a broader set of the effects of Mexico's market liberation of copies and thus an expanded range of answers to the questions that opened the chapter: if this is a politics of access, to what and to whom are people gaining access?

Section 2: Health Effects as Market Effects

Self-Care at the Base of the Pyramid

Claudio Lomnitz has described the classic twentieth-century clientelist state in Mexico as a pyramid in which the machinery of local, municipal, and state-level patronage relations all ultimately fed the party bosses at the very top (Lomnitz-Adler 2001, 120–21). This was a mode of governance—the governance of social relations and labor—that many people hoped would break apart when the PRI's seventy-one-year hold on the presidency ended in 2000. I think we can safely say that, in the terrain of popular health, the clientelist pyramid has morphed since 2000. In its Simipolitical formation, it came to look uncannily like the base-of-the-pyramid approach that has become a new orthodoxy in the worlds of microenterprise (Roy 2010) and economic postdevelopment (Elyachar 2012)—an orientation that reframes the world's poorest people as an as-yet untapped market for global capital. This, at least, was the hope of economist C. K. Prahalad (2010), architect of the concept of the base of the pyramid, or BOP. With disconcerting cheer, Prahalad argued at the turn of the twenty-first century that "the very poor," who constitute the majority of the world's population, should not be written out of participating in global markets, nor should they simply be seen as passive potential recipients of development or state aid. Rather, they should be seen as a massive market for the goods produced by multinational corporations and as potential entrepreneurs themselves. This reframing aimed to provide poor people access to goods and hence to provide markets with access to "poor people." Experiment is a recurring theme here: Ananya Roy, in her influential critique of BOP approaches and in her subsequent work, has argued that "bottom billion" capitalism is itself a "conjunctural experiment" (Roy 2010; 2012, 132): "On the one hand, it is an experiment with the democratization of capital. . . . On the other hand, it is an experiment with strategies of capital accumulation, those that can mine 'the fortune at the bottom of the pyramid'" (2012, 132). Julia Elyachar (2012) notes the degree to which Prahalad himself saw the poor and the NGOs that work with them as "leading-edge experimenters"—in distinct contrast to the state or public infrastructure, which are the sites, for Prahalad, of mere stagnation. Experiment is the language of innovation; of try-and-fail-and-try-again; of nimble, infrastructure-free incubation; of the private sector and private-public partnerships; of NGOization. It is not the language of investment in the state, public health, or public infrastructure.[17]

Globally, the health sector (and prominently, within that, pharmaceutical provision) has been a lively site for trying out BOP principles, which notably include the double opportunity to "earn more while helping a lot," as Víctor González Torres himself likes to say. Indeed, if González Torres's Simipolitical interventions in Mexico activated a highly recognizable inventory of Mexican political tropes, tactics, and aesthetics, his projects have been legible in BOP terms as well. Notably, a 2007 Harvard Business School case study identified Farmacias Similares as a vivid example of "private health care for the base of the pyramid in Mexico" (Chu and García-Cuellar 2007). Reading across a number of reports and proposals for BOP interventions, it becomes clear why this Mexican generics pharmaceutical entrepreneur in particular might be held up as an instantiation of BOP operating principles.[18]

In Mexico, health at the base of the pyramid is constituted in and through Simipolitics, that particular arrangement of principles, practices, and conditions of possibility that have redounded in the Simi project, in the composition of Mexico's low-cost generics market more broadly, and in the related expansions-as-reconfigurations of the state discussed in chapter 2. The specific conditions that gave rise to Dr. Simi and to the Seguro Popular are precisely the conditions that BOP interventions target as ripe for, and as examples of, an experimentalized transformation in the delivery of health. These conditions include the disproportionate pharmaceutical cost burden borne by poorer, uninsured consumer-patients, the use of pharmacies as first points of access to health care, and the widespread practice of self-medication, which is precisely what brings people into enhanced contact with medicines and markets (see Hammond et al. 2007).

In base-of-the-pyramid discussions, such conditions serve as the paving stones for an innovative model for the delivery of health care for the poor, leading in many instances to the counters, the pharmacists, cashiers, and the consultorios of private-sector, low-cost pharmacies. Note, for example, how the 2007 report by the World Resources Institute (WRI), *The Next 4 Billion* (an extended discussion of BOP "experiments" in several arenas, from health to education), framed the problem: "The first response to illness in many BOP households, especially lower income segments that dominate bottom-heavy markets, tends to be self-medication" (Hammond et al. 2007, 38). Self-medication is in turn something to be cultivated and optimized because of the itineraries it produces: "For those at the base of the pyramid, pharmacies or other sources of medicines are often the first point of access to health care" (38). These itineraries produce optimal market opportunities. The WRI notes that, insofar as pharmaceutical costs at the base of the pyramid tend to be borne out of pocket, a disproportionate amount of pharmaceutical spending is generated by this population. They are, in other words, a significant market-in-waiting, and interventions that enable low-cost pharmacies and low-cost medications are the prescription (Hammond et al. 2007).

Pharmaceutical economists in Mexico have certainly made the point from the other side of the looking glass. Raúl Enrique Molina (2002), for example, has understood the maldistribution of pharmaceutical cost burdens as a major problem, not an opportunity: people in Mexico (still) incur a remarkably high percentage of medication costs out of pocket—70 to 80 percent (see also Wirtz et al. 2012). Nonetheless, reflecting the prior discussion of the delight and relief that Simi customers have expressed to me at the attention granted them by Simi pharmacists, spending *can* feel like care; it certainly is the same as care in BOP understandings of health delivery. That is, the idiom of access to health at the base of the pyramid is one in which health spending equals health services' utilization; this equivalence in turn is understood as if it were "health" itself (Hammond 2007).[19]

It is precisely in this context that the public health stance toward self-medication has undergone a marked transformation. The idea has been significantly rehabilitated since the late 1990s in international and global public health frameworks, coincident, I note, with the expansion of markets for low-cost generic medicines globally. In 1998, the World Health Organization (WHO) issued a report on the special role of pharmacists and pharmacies in health-care systems. Self-medication was highlighted as a central pillar of self-care; far from discouraging the practice, the WHO encouraged policy-makers, health professionals, and pharmacists to cultivate *responsible* self-medication (World Health Organization 1998, 3; Ruíz 2010)—a set of practices that can lead patients to "take charge" of their health and that can help reduce infectious disease burdens, among other things. The idiom of responsible self-medication has become widespread, promulgated not just by the WHO and pharmacist associations but also, quite prominently, by the manufacturers of over-the-counter (nonprescription) medications, brand name and otherwise—for it is their products that will be sold to those of us who self-medicate. In 2015, the Asociación de Fabricantes de Medicamentos de Libre Acceso (the Mexican Association of OTC Medicine Manufacturers, AFAMELA) and the World Self-Medication Industry trade group (WSMI) co-hosted a conference in Mexico City—in the fancy Hotel Camino Real where Dr. Simi often hosted elaborate breakfast banquets for business leaders in the early aughts—called Advancing Self-Care and Responsible Self-Medication for a Healthier Future. The opening salvo of the conference was the declaration that "self-care is increasingly recognized as the first step in healthcare" (Asociación de Fabricantes de Medicamentos de Libre Acceso 2015). The conference was also an invitation, featuring the head of COFEPRIS, Mikel Arriola, to discuss the regulatory moves that could most readily encourage responsible self-medication, including changing more medicines' status from "prescription" to "nonprescription." Prescription requirements are, after all, one more barrier to access between bodies and medicines, drug producers and their markets.

Responsible self-medication is a Simipolitical arrangement. Its potential benefits (to what and to whom?) are wide ranging, but above all, it promises to recompose the burdens and responsibilities of public- and private-sector actors. That is, when the self (or the low-cost private pharmacy and the low-cost private pharmacy's doctor) cares for and medicates the self, burdens are relieved for more than just the patient. In a 2010 article in the journal *Current Drug Safety* that teased out the differences between responsible (or "appropriate") self-medication and its irresponsible counterpart, María Ruíz wrote, "Several benefits have been linked to appropriate self-medication, among them: increased access to medication and relief for the patient, the active role of the patient in his or her own health care, better use of physicians and pharmacists [sic] skills and *reduced (or at least optimized) burden of governments* due to health expenditure linked to the treatment of minor health conditions" (2010, 315; emphasis added).

The 1998 WHO report was certainly frank about the relationship between self-medication and government burdens given the increasingly precarious state of health sectors worldwide: "In the midst of declining economic activity and resources, governments and other third party payers and individuals worldwide are grappling with escalating health care costs. Many countries are establishing mechanisms whereby these costs can be contained and health care made more cost effective. Worldwide, self-medication is being promoted as a means of reducing the health care burden on the public budget. *Structural changes including increased reliance on private sector delivery are also increasingly being put in place*" (World Health Organization 1998, 5; emphasis added).

Reducing or optimizing the burden of governments, structural changes that include increased reliance on private-sector delivery—these are certainly ways to frame the Simipolitical trajectory that came into relief in chapter 2, in which the private low-cost market for drug and primary health care both supplements and supplants Mexican public health insurance programs. Indeed, Eugenia González, whose musings on the welcome specificities of attention and care that both Simi doctors and Simi pharmacists grant her, captured this relationship in starkly hilarious terms. She noted with a big, knowing laugh that the Simi pharmacists are very helpful: they "self-medicate us!"[20]

Like so many of the twists and turns I discussed in chapter 2, this change in the valence of self-medication might sound, at heart, like a straightforward, privatizing move—yet another turn to private consumption. But there is, here too, a Simipolitical turn. Even the BOP became legible in Mexico as doubled—as multiple versions of itself, same and not the same. Where Dr. Simi grabbed the attention of the 2007 Harvard Business School case study as a prime example of "private health care delivery for the base of the pyramid," the government's Seguro Popular figures in the same study as Simi's "public" counterpart—that is, as a competing iteration of BOP health care provision in Mexico (Chu and García-Cuellar 2007). They are both, together, constituting and competing for the market of the uninsured, whether in the form of a Simi-state that cares for those who have the least or of an expanding, decentralized, coresponsible state experiment in universal coverage.

The resonances between base-of-the-pyramid approaches to health and Simipolitical reformattings of health care in Mexico bring into view some of the multiplier effects of Mexico's liberation of copies in and through the sphere and practice of consumption. The deregulatory excesses I have noted produce enhanced access with an asterisk—access to what? How can we know? The work of answering these questions sparks some radically dispersed practices of testing and authorization, as we have seen. But these practices of experimentalized consumption are not simply a response to a lack. The invocation of Dr. Simi and the Seguro Popular as competing versions of health care at the base of the pyramid tells us that experimentalized consumption—self-medication in its appropriate forms—is not a problem to be stamped out but a crucial condition for reimagining health care as private, low-cost consumption.

Consumption, in turn, is not the only story here. These recompositions of health care—in the form of consumption as testing, as self-medication, as private and public experimental rearrangements of health-care provision—deliver us to a broader set of questions about access in which we have to *rewrite* the question of access: For whom and to what?

Beyond Consumption

If base-of-the-pyramid approaches to health care see self-medication as key to the broader experimentalization of consumption, they do so in part because of what consumption can produce. At the heart of the BOP—and very much at work as an effect of Simipolitics—is the way that cheap consumption can bring ever more people into contact with formal(ish) markets, not just as consumers but also as workers and entrepreneurial subjects.

One of the things that BOP interventions make clear is that the project of improving consumers' or patients' access to medicines is rather difficult to distinguish from the project of ensuring that pharmapolitical actors (and markets themselves, as conceived in BOP idioms) can secure access to consumers. That much is stated explicitly in bottom billion articulations of problem-as-opportunity.

But as I came to see so vividly in Mexico, the question of *who* has access to *what* (or whom) is far more interesting and complicated than simply a story in which "the market" gains access to "the poor." Víctor Gonzáles Torres's Simipolitical interventions—in which his pharmacies provided him access to consumers as if they were a potential electorate—are an example of how this question must be expanded and transformed. Here, I want to continue to follow this thread. In Mexico, generics pharmacies selling low-cost generic medicines and offering cheaper health consultations rapidly became a source of livelihood—in the form of wage work, piece work, salaried work—for tens of thousands of people, from small vendors and franchise owners, to underemployed doctors and pharmacists in training, to retirees turned pharma entrepreneurs and low-wage cashiers. Far beyond the singularly spectacular entrepreneurial and pharma-political interventions of Dr. Simi, we must contemplate the more pervasive, more broadly distributed ways in which, with the liberation of generic copies, the equivalence of health effects with market effects generates still other forms of excess and other kinds of access.

Supplement
In 2008, the aunt and uncle of a friend of mine opened their second generics pharmacy. This new outlet had a small storefront, with an even smaller clinic and waiting room next door, in a working-class neighborhood far north of the city—a hefty traverse across this metropolis from where they lived in the southern zone of Coyoacán. Augusta and Fernando had turned to the business of generic pharmacy clinics as a source of retirement income to supplement the pensions earned from their careers as civil servants. These pensions, they recounted to me, were both meager and precarious—not enough to live off of and in any case, under constant threat, they worried about them evaporating altogether. (The generics economy shows up very visibly here as yet another kind of supplement to the state.) The idea of opening a pharmacy was initially not their own but their son's. As a medical student, he had taken sharp notice of the growth and popularity of generics around 2004 and 2005. "We hadn't thought about it before he brought it up, but it turned out to be a good idea," Augusta recounted to me. Their son was on to something. Their first outlet had done so well that they decided to open another one, employing a pharmacist in training, two physicians, and a custodian.

Their pharmacies were not the only generics outlets staking a presence in the neighborhood that they had carefully chosen for its demographics (a *barrio popular*), its relative quiet, and the availability of storefronts right on the path to the small but buzzing municipal market selling fruit, vegetables, cheap housewares, and other staples of daily consumption. I drove up with them one day in 2008, right when they had opened the second pharmacy; as we turned off the massive North-South thoroughfare (once again on Avenida Insurgentes) into a grid of small, quiet streets, I kept spotting what I thought must be their pharmacy. Farmacia de Genéricos y Equivalentes: was that it? "No, not ours." A smaller DIY Farmacia de Similares? "No, no; that's the señora around the corner." There it was, one right turn later, Farmaeconómica: Genéricos y Similares. Joining them in this neighborhood were not just the surfeit of neighbor competitors but, several blocks away on Insurgentes, a massive Walmart Supercenter and an actual Dr. Simi's Farmacias Similares.

In the car, Fernando made a dry observation about the crowded terrain in which they found themselves: "The thing is, there's no regulation—anyone can open a pharmacy, anywhere!" He was referring in part to the fact that Mexico does not impose zoning restrictions on the location and density of pharmacies, nor, crucially, are there restrictions on who can open or run one. The proprietor of a pharmacy, with or without an attached medical clinic, need not have any pharmacy or medicine-related experience or credentials. The federal health authority *does* require that a licensed pharmacist be on the premises during working hours. But this technicality was redescribed to me by multiple pharmacy proprietors with a wink and a smile and a slight modification: "Or, well, *near* the premises." Though such regulatory capaciousness was precisely what enabled his and Augusta's commercial incursions into that neighborhood, it was also a problem. "Too many pharmacies up here!" Fernando grumbled.[21]

There were, to be sure, very many pharmacies up there, and in many major cities across Mexico. In 2008, ten years after the emergence of generic medicines in the commercial sphere, there were over 20,000 private pharmacies in operation in Mexico, a significant number of which were new outlets (both chains and independent stores) dedicated exclusively to selling generic medicines. (To make a ridiculously incommensurate but perhaps evocative comparison, in 2018, there were 14,500 Starbucks in the United States and 10,000 McDonald's.) Dr. Simi's pharmacies, numbering around 3,500, accounted for a significant portion but obviously did not account for the sum total of this crowded field. They were joined by the kind of mom-and-pop (aunt-and-uncle?) generics pharmacies run by Augusta and Fernando or by *the señora around the corner* from them; by thousands of small, "traditional" pharmacies that have for decades sold perfumes, balloons, stationery, and a modest inventory of only brand-name medicines; and by a growing number of powerful chains, from Farmacias el Fénix and del Ahorro (both of which are González Torres family projects) or Farmacias de Deus and Farmacias San Pablo, to major supermarket chains such as Gigante and Superama (the latter now owned by Walmart). The number of pharmacies in Mexico continued to proliferate into the next decade: by 2013, there were an estimated 23,500 pharmacies, roughly 10,000 of which also had adjacent clinics, offering an estimated 250,000 *consultas* daily (Rodríguez 2013).

This deregulated excess produced nodes of access, opportunities, and openings well beyond the consumption of medicines and primary care. Around the same time I met Fernando and Augusta, I had started to take note of—and was frankly taken aback by—the frequency with which people whom I engaged in everyday conversation (friends, colleagues, copassengers on the Metrobus, or formal interviewees) would tell me that they, or a relative, or a friend owned or ran a pharmacy. Perhaps it was a small one-off, or a franchise of a larger chain, or a small one that did so well that they opened a second one in the same neighborhood. Or they worked as a cashier in a generics pharmacy. Or they had once worked for Simi, or had applied for a job with Dr. Simi, or worked as a doctor in a generics pharmacy-affiliated clinic, or had a cousin who worked for Dr. Simi's umbrella organization. A close friend of a friend told me in 2008, "I was working for the Foundation [Best] and in our monthly trips to Mexico City I noticed that all the upper-level people were opening pharmacies, so I thought I'd try it!"[22] Generics pharmacies in general—and the many tentacles of the Simi enterprise in particular—seemed to be proliferating in this sense too, figuring in a startling (to me) number of people's lives as sources of work, wages, revenue, and training. These forms of access started to become visible to me as a further dimension of the dizziness of Simipolitics, multiplying, as it were, its own multiplier effects.

Que Queden Bien/Make Sure They Come Out Well
Faced with the excesses that such regulatory permissiveness enables—too many pharmacies; too much competition; not enough barriers to entry—the proprietors of many of these pharmacies had come to understand that there was one kind of work in particular that could help them carve out a niche in this overcrowded field. Doctors are absolutely central to the competitive advantage of generics pharmacies in a context in which the lack of zoning regulations has meant that there is too much competition for the taste of some small-

scale pharmacy proprietors and larger ones as well ("Everyone's copying us," lamented Dr. Simi in 2005). The use value of these doctors was something that pharmacists and proprietors alike mentioned often to me, as did so many of the people frequenting these clinics. Tabatha, a pharmacist-in-training working at a tiny independent generics pharmacy on the outskirts of Mexico City, told me, "These new little pharmacies can become the *farmacias del barrio*" (neighborhood pharmacies, a place you know and trust), in large part "based on the quality and appeal of the doctors who work in your clinics." She elaborated, telling me that their comportment matters a lot, by which she meant not just how they treat people but their good "aspect" or "professional" appearance.[23]

Who are these doctors? They are retired physicians looking for supplemental income, recently graduated doctors waiting for their titles or to be admitted into residency programs, titled physicians who for one reason or another (a pregnancy or the cost and difficulty of gaining admission to highly competitive residencies) were never able to pursue a specialization or opted not to do so. The clinics in which I spent time across Mexico City tended to be staffed by young physicians relatively fresh out of medical school. These are not the kinds of jobs they expected to find themselves in. Dr. Bruno Treviso was blunt about his disappointment. My time with him at the clinic attached to Farmaecia Genéricos was punctuated by patient visits (I left the room) and the comings and goings of someone doing service as a plumber; the water was not working in the tiny bathroom in the consultorio, which was cut out from a space that might have once been a closet. The room in which he saw patients was about ten by twelve feet, with harsh light from a few bare bulbs, an examination table in the middle, a stool to sit on, and a rudimentary desk. Treviso told me at this desk, out of earshot of his employer who was in the pharmacy next door, that he had been working there for nine months.

He looked grim: "These things are not what you imagine after studying for six years. But they are an easy opportunity to get into the workforce, get experience at least in very basic primary care." He was also angry and frustrated with UNAM, his alma mater: he finished his medical degree nine months previously but was "still waiting for the fucking diploma." For some reason he could not fathom, UNAM was taking forever to send it to him: "I cannot get another kind of job without it."[24] Such delays are common for UNAM graduates, and this is one reason why a pharmacy-based clinician might not have a "title" displayed on the wall of the clinic: *Who is authorizing them? How can we know?*

To that point, we might note this project of popular private medicine also depends on and affects the absorption of another kind of excess: an overproduction of people who have graduated from medical school but who have not (yet) done their residencies or specializations, forming a surplus of unemployed doctors. There are roughly ten medical schools in Mexico City's greater metropolitan area alone, and the hospitals and clinics of the public sector no longer provide a reliable first entry point for general practitioners nor an adequate number of residencies for all of these medical school graduates to pursue specializations. Where are these students finding work?

Mexico City's major public university, UNAM, has glass information cases throughout its massive campus with job listings, event announcements, and student programming. By 2012 and 2013, the flyers cramming the cases at UNAM's Facultad de Medicina had become dominated by one particular kind of advertisement: "Solicito: médico para farmacia" (Seeking doctor for pharmacy) (see figure 4.2.). Treviso noted the conditions that were bringing people like him and his counterpart on the morning shift, Dr. Verónica López, to clinics like these, including the bottleneck that awaits recent medical school graduates: "UNAM now doesn't have space for all those who would like to do residencies. It's incredibly competitive to get into the residencies; to do well on the residency entrance exam, there are courses you can take but they cost ten to fifteen thousand pesos [$1,000 to $1,500 at the time]. The country has to open more universities, more hospitals, so the country can grow."[25]

But these tiny clinics have some advantages besides the sheer possibility of employment (something is better than nothing?). Treviso told me, "The Seguro Social itself doesn't really work with the level of resources [that they have here]." He meant resources both in terms of time and inventory: "Working at IMSS, doctors get a lot of experience, but it's crazy—they see twenty to thirty patients a day, between 9 a.m. and 3 p.m. Many would actually prefer to work in a place like this because you can actually take the time to review the patient's situation *con calma*. The quality of attention in IMSS is worse, much worse. And the public sector carries a much more limited quantity of pharmaceuticals—the *cuadro básico* is limited by a lack of resources." While the Seguro seems, at times, starved of resources, these little pharmacies are both bare bones—a picture of lack (including, that day, a lack of running water)—and a source of cheap "abundance" (pharmaceutical inventory, time to see patients).

Dr. Treviso had the afternoon shift at this tiny pharmacy down the street from the barrio's market. He staffed the clinic from 3 p.m. to 9 p.m., Monday

4.2 "High quality generics pharmacy seeks: Female doctor who presents well, is punctual. With title or professional credential. Half day salary $250 pesos (10:30–15:30 or [not visible]–21:30)," flyer posted outside of UNAM's School of Medicine, February 2013. PHOTO BY AUTHOR.

through Saturday. The morning shift—9 a.m. to 3 p.m.—was staffed by Dr. López, an alternation that Fernando and Augusta joked as having generated its own gendered patterns of customer loyalty: "Lots of old men come in the morning to see the beautiful *Doctora Verónica*; the señoras come in the afternoon to see handsome *Doctor Bruno*." It was a joke, for of course a lot of people simply come when they can or when they must, but there is something here too. Doctors are a crucial pull for bringing people to the pharmacies— and to ensuring that they come back. And hence they are crucial as well to keeping the pharmacists, clerks, and owners employed.

Dra. López, like Dr. Treviso, was biting her lip a bit about having ended up here, and she certainly did not intend for it to become permanent. She studied medicine at the Universidad Autónoma Metropolitana (UAM) and she had been working in this consultorio for about three months. She worked there Mondays through Saturdays, 9 a.m. to 3 p.m., and then on Sundays at a private (nongenerics pharmacy) clinic, where the treatments provided were distinct ("There are more emergencies there, and they have a surgery department," she said), and thus she gained a different kind of experience. And it is a supplement for her pay. At Farmaeconomica, she earned (as did Dr. Treviso) 5,200 pesos a month (roughly $520) at the little consultorio and lived at home with her parents on another edge of this vast city, almost two hours away by car, depending on the traffic. It was not at all a low entry-level professional wage for Mexico City. Like Dr. Treviso, she saw this post as a way in to future medical practice: "This job is like a step on a ladder—I mean really, you study for six years and here you are, giving consultations that are only worth twenty pesos? Working in these little clinics is hard. After all those years of studying, well this isn't really what you have in mind." She wanted to specialize in gynecology. Dr. Treviso wanted to do his residency in trauma medicine and imagined that he would have to do a stint in the *provincia* before he could work his way back to Mexico City.

Doctors Treviso and López both made clear that one source of their dismay was that the provision of cheap care directly cheapened their labor and knowledge: giving *consultas* that cost only twenty pesos seemed a radical devaluation of the investment of time and effort they had put into obtaining their degree. In many pharmacies, the equation between cheap care and cheap medical labor is even more direct. While Doctors Treviso and López and many doctors working at many other small pharmacies do in fact receive salaries, the doctors staffing the clinics at Farmacias Similares work on a different model altogether. They receive no salary at all. They simply keep the price of each consulta, which began at twenty to twenty-five pesos at Farmacias Similares ($2.50; it's up to thirty and thirty-five pesos now in many pharmacies). It is as bare a transaction as there can be, a one-to-one correspondence between low-cost access and low-paid doctors, a perfect "equivalence" that certainly leaves surplus accumulating elsewhere in other hands. Like all things associated with Similares, the labor demanded and offered is a both/and affair: this is regular, formal, and low-paid but still somewhat precarious work. It is a kind of piecework that is not "informal," but rather, in Guillermo de la Peña's (2000) apt formulation, informalized formal labor, without the benefits of other kinds of formal wage infrastructure, including pensions, a salary, and automatic entitlement to health insurance (regular work with a formal salary is what entitles one to membership in the Seguro Social).

Similares franchise owners are not naïve about the effects of this structure on their physicians (whom they need) and on their clientele (whom they also need). Even if they are not *supposed* to pay salaries, some recognize that a kind of baseline security is a form of social and economic contract, a kind of mutually beneficial decency to be meted out judiciously. Similares franchisee Katrina Martín decided to try her hand at running a pharmacy following the lead of senior employees at Fundación Best. On the generous introduction provided by a mutual friend, I met with her in the summer of 2008 in Guadalajara, where she lived and worked at the time. In a follow-up conversation on the phone, I asked her more about the physicians at her Simi franchise and how they get paid. On the latter point, she hesitated a second. Then she explained:

> Supposedly . . . the doctors are only supposed to earn the price of the consulta [at that time, twenty-five pesos each]. They keep that entirely, and no other salary. But, well . . . I have a doctor who's been working here for six years, and I give him a bit extra on my own account. It's not supposed to happen like that, but there are months when people just don't show up. I don't do this with the doctors who've been here less time. These are general practitioners, and some of them even have two of these jobs [they work at one pharmacy in the morning and another in the afternoon]. Some of them just never went on to specialize [do their residencies]. One, for example, got married and that was that; she didn't continue on with her studies.[26]

If the physicians who don't get a supplement from her under the table are unhappy about the wage structure, Martín has a strategy for them: *"Que queden bien, que vengan de vuelta!"* (Make sure they come out well, and they'll come back!).

We might recognize this phrase, or at least its form, from a prior chapter: *Que queden bien* (make sure they come out well, or happy) is the other side, the double, of *me atienden bien* (they take good care of me), the refrain we heard in chapter 2 to describe the sentiment and the experience Eugenia and Dolores, among others, invoked when they explained why they might forego the Seguro Social and go to generics pharmacies and clinics instead. *Que queden bien* (make sure they come out well) and *me atienden bien* (they take good care of me) travel together. And in Farmacias Similares, in particular, they are sutured together especially closely by the paired mechanisms of low wages and supplemental incentives for workers. This combination generates quite a bit of the attention given to customers at the pharmacy counter. It is important to note that Simi physicians, cashiers, and pharmacists do not receive commissions on medicines sold. (Though Simi pharmacy employees collectively get a bonus if the pharmacy moves a certain amount of product overall in a given month.) Simi pharmacists and cashiers are, by contrast, strongly "incentivized" with per-unit commissions to encourage customers to buy vitamins and natural products, which are often quite a bit more expensive per unit, box, or bottle than many of the pharmaceuticals sold in these pharmacies.

The vitamins, the supplements, the tailored choices just for her that helped Dolores feel cared for at Simi in chapter 2? These are among the most aggressively promoted products behind the Simi counters. Thus you can easily stop at a Simi pharmacy to buy a cheap bottle of pills for your headache (ibuprofeno, eight pesos) and emerge having purchased one hundred pesos' ($10) worth of "natural remedies"—maybe something for "women's problems" or your circulation. It has happened to me, and it happens to people who shop there routinely: *Fíjate, I went in for my medicine and came out with vitamins for this, and liquids for that, and I spent 125 pesos!*

To spend, to be cared for, to have things recommended just for you; to treat the patient well, to attend to their specificities so that they come back again—in these transactional relations are woven together the effects, both intimately experienced and broadly formatted, of a politics of access that multiplies far beyond the matter of ensuring that people can consume medicines at something like an affordable price. Access ramifies in wage labor, piecework, and salaried employment; in training and biding one's time until the next step; in an abundance of almost-titled physicians and an under supply of residencies for specialization; in a deregulatory zoning regime that allows pharmacies and consultorios to be the kind of business one might just try out to see what happens wherever a storefront, especially in a barrio popular, beckons.

Coda

With you, I want to know whether all of this has *really* had demonstrable effects where health is concerned. I want to know, with so many of my interlocutors in Mexico, if the medicines are good, if the doctors are good. And, with so many of my interlocutors, as with the state, I continue to find the answers somewhat elusive, slipping away toward an ever-receding horizon of *tercería*, thirdness. How can we know? But the answers are in fact tangible, reappearing in other forms, arenas, and relations. The effects of this market, the multiplier effects of generic copies, are not always what and where we think they will be.

Mexico's slightly regulated commercial sphere has, I have argued, generated a series of provisional abundances that have redounded for millions of people in Mexico over the last decade and a half as access. This access itself generates further excesses. Access to generics has redounded in the need that many consumers feel to conduct their own experiments and triangulations, to take on the state's authorizing functions, and thus to answer both the question of quality and the question of "How we can know?" themselves. More than just another multiplication, another copy, these experimental practices effectively treble the deregulatory state, dispersing and distributing the work of authorization in the act of consumption itself. The practices that lie at the heart of these treblings—self-medication, self-experiment, turning to pharmacies as first points of access for health care, and then testing their doctors to make sure they get it right—in turn radically expand the scope of the question "Access to what?" and its many answers. Seeing these experimentalizations of consumption precisely as the centerpiece of a broader orientation to medicines, pharmacies, and markets allows us to attend to the ways in which the de/regulated liberation of generic copies produces access to many things for many people: working- and middle-class consumers' access to affordable commodities and attention, pharmacists' access to wages and commissions, pharmacy franchisees' access to income, doctors' access to experience, and, to be sure, generic drug laboratories' access to a market.

These openings and opportunities lead us, finally, to another question. It is a question that was posed back to me by both the academic researcher Antonio Salazar and the regulator whose respective laments about the irrelevance of the Mexican state and the need for an extra round of thirdness helped set the terms for this chapter. The question was not "Are the drugs good? or "Access to what?" but rather "Who's winning?" Who benefits, in other words, from this accumulation of deregulatory force and from the many multiplier effects of a low-cost generics market? "Not the *nacionales*," Salazar answered his own question for me. "The transnationals are coming to sort it all out."

Supergeneric vs. Mere Commodity

5

A Rogue Escitalopram

Who *is* winning? What might it mean to say, as Antonio Salazar told me in his office at the Universidad Nacional Autónoma de México (UNAM) in the south of Mexico City in 2013, that "the transnationals" were "coming to sort it all out"? In July 2013, a generic version of the antidepressant escitalopram (also sold under the brand name Lexapro) made its way onto the shelves of Farmacias Similares in Mexico City. Featured prominently as one of its "new generics"—yet another differentiating designation Víctor González Torres adroitly summoned to tap into the Partido Revolucionario Institucional's (PRI) emphasis on "liberating" generics at breakneck pace—this escitalopram was bringing people in the door. "This one just came out!" the pharmacist behind the counter at the Similares on Avenida Miguel Ángel de Quevedo told me, excited to show me his new offering. I was taken aback by the price: 240 pesos (or $11.98 for fourteen tablets at ten milligrams each). It was only about a quarter of the price that the Lexapro brand commanded in Mexico City at the time, but it was still remarkably expensive for a drug sold in Farmacias Similares. Curious about this price, I walked down the street, six to eight long blocks in either direction, stopping in each of the six or seven pharmacies that clustered there to ask about their escitaloprams. The answer each and every time was, "No, no, we don't have it." Trying again, I asked for generic Lexapro: "No, we don't have it." I expected to be asked for a prescription, but that wasn't the obstacle. This drug was plenty "accessible" in one sense: a few of these other pharmacies only had the "patented" (name-brand) version and were happy enough to sell it to me without a prescription, at quadruple the price of Dr. Simi's escitalopram. What they did not have was *lo genérico*. And they did not have lo genérico because, they all insisted, "todavía no existe" (it did not exist yet).

And yet there it was on Simi's shelf (and then in my hands). I carried this little white box, marked simply "escitalopram," around with me for months afterward. It turned into a fairly generative object of conversation—yet another generic puzzle—in my subsequent interviews with researchers, physicians, and government officials. In the course of these conversations, the question that first suggested itself (How did Simi get its hands on this drug before the others?) quickly ceded ground to a bigger forensic concern: What was it? This escitalopram carried a registration number from the secretary of health, but it did not bear the signatures of *any* of the multiple established generic kinds recognized in Mexico. It was not marked as an interchangeable generic. But it didn't have a brand name either, the way a pharmacy's own chemically equivalent version of escitalopram would (e.g., something like "Simipram"). The identity of this manifold thing—the pills, the box, the labeling—flummoxed a number of people whose jobs demanded literacy in Mexico's regulatory and commercial pharmaceutical vernaculars, and even a few who were charged with actually policing those things in the first place. Juán Manuel Lazarate, a regulator who worked in the Federal Commission for the Protection against Health Risks' (COFEPRIS) enforcement office, suggested, without missing a beat, that it was probably counterfeit: "The registration number is easily available—all you have to do is take it off the government's website [where I, the intrepid ethnographer, had cleverly 'verified' it] and stamp it on the box."[1] Others with whom I deliberated were more willing to remain puzzled and less ready to punt to the specter of the fake. In the course of my interview with Antonio Salazar, I began to describe the scenario. Before I could bring out the evidence, he interrupted, musing, "Ah, it's probably their own brand? As in, it has a brand name, like Simipram, or something like that. . . . It doesn't actually just say escitalopram, does it?" Yes, it certainly did. Plain white box, nothing but the name of the active compound, escitalopram, ten milligrams, *caja con catorce (14) tabletas*. It was about as generic as it could be. And yet in this form, it shouldn't have existed. The only generics that were supposed to be sold exclusively by the compound's chemical name were those registered by the state as interchangeable generics and stamped with the GI logo, and there was at that time no GI escitalopram registered in Mexico. He was stumped. The other pharmacists were right, in this sense: *Escitalopram did not exist*.[2]

But as we have seen repeatedly, what happens in Simi, precisely for all of its unclassifiability, is deeply useful to understanding larger pharmapolitical horizons. What does this rogue escitalopram tell us? The box does not bear the state's insignia but it does bear another signature: "Manufactured in India by Sandoz (India). Distributed in Mexico by Sandoz (Mexico)." Sandoz, once a stand-alone Swiss drug company, became part of the Swiss-based transnational firm Novartis in 1996; Sandoz is now Novartis' generics division. The lab has subsidiaries across the world and is one of the world's largest generics companies. Sandoz/Novartis is not the original patent holder or developer of escitalopram (nor is the "original" escitalopram itself particularly original—it is a version of a predecessor compound called citalopram). Sandoz and its proliferating international versions of itself are, alongside many major "innovator" laboratories, increasingly asserting themselves within fast-growing markets for generic medicines in countries across Latin America, Eastern Europe, and South Asia. No longer ceding this ground to dedicated generics laboratories, major transnational drug companies have been busily setting up their own departments of "established products," as Pfizer calls them (i.e., generics), and entering into licensing agreements with, or just outright buying, existing generics laboratories across the world, from India, to the United States, to Mexico, and elsewhere (Shadlen 2007; Sunder Rajan 2017). Farmacias Similares had in fact announced in 2008 that Sandoz was interested in distributing its medicines through them (Anderson and López 2008).

Simi's not-fully regularized escitalopram, stamped with the (not-universally convincing) signature of Sandoz-India-Mexico, points to several key concerns for this chapter. It gestures, first and most obviously, to the growing role of transnational firms in global generics markets within and beyond Mexico. Here is how a *New York Times* article described the scenario, reflecting the transnational industry's framing: in "emerging markets" where "fear of counterfeit drugs or low-quality medicines runs high," major drug makers now see an opportunity to enter these generics markets with their "own differentiated generic kinds" (Singer 2010). These are not brand-name drugs per se but generics manufactured by a well-recognized laboratory (escitalopram, made by Sandoz), such that "the source" laboratory can function *as if* it were a brand or trademark. Pushing against the limits of the ever-fragile and expansive definition of the generic-as-commodity drug, the major labs' market analysts presume (and hope) that in contexts in which people do not quite know whom or what to trust—in situations that generate the kind of ad hoc normativity, self-medication, and trebling described in the previous chapter—"consumers who can afford it [will be] willing to pay a premium for generics from well-known makers" (Singer 2010).

The term of art for such medicines is "company-branded generics," or simply (and confusingly) "branded generics" (see also Greene 2011). And the entire point of company-branded generics is that they are not merely generic. Multinational labs hope that their generics—escitalopram by Sandoz—can become the top-tier copies in markets teeming with competing, confusing, and often stratified generic and similar copies. In other words: the generic proliferations, multiplications, and uncertainties or confusions discussed throughout this book are seen by multinational drug labs as an opportunity to assert themselves in the very generics markets that were supposed to challenge their dominance in the first place.

Introducing still another form of stratification and distinction into the domain of generic copies, the aspirational ascendance of company-branded generics in Mexico and elsewhere delivers a postpatent generic exuberance that both repeats and flips on its head much of what we have seen throughout this book. Mexico's and Argentina's generic and copy excesses *are* thus essential to my understanding of what's happening here but not because they provide the irregular, disharmonious confusion for which a "trusted source" (Pfizer, Novartis/Sandoz) can now come in and save the day (for a price). Rather, the preceding chapters provide a substrate for understanding how multinational companies too are, again and anew, turning generics into a site and source of distinction.

Company-branded generics are in fact only one example of the ways in which genericness is both being undermined and mined for its auratic possibilities by leading-brand drug laboratories as they seek ever more ways to stave off the *becoming-mere-commodity* of their products. There are many ways that patent-holding drug companies have attempted to do this over the last twenty to fifty years, from using trade agreements to enforce longer and stronger patent protection, to filing for new patents on minor modifications of the same molecule ("evergreening"), to demanding stronger restrictions on when the information contained in expiring patents can be released to other laboratories (data exclusivity provisions). In this chapter, I am interested in industry efforts to stave off mere commodification that reach into the very category of the generic and seek to radically transform, or even upend, it.

As I'll discuss in the second half of this chapter, this phenomenon reaches a peculiar apogee with the rise of new categories of copied *biological* pharmaceuticals, including "biosimilars," "biobetters," and the speculative "supergeneric." Dr. Simi is certainly not the only actor proliferating spectacular genericness.

By elaborating the act of copying as an engine and locus of valued distinction, drug and biotechnology companies are busily recomposing, while attempting to forestall, the very possibility of the fungible pharmaceutical commodity. From Sandoz's escitalopram to biobetters, much of what is at stake in these supergeneric articulations is a return to the distinctiveness of source—the manufacturing laboratory—in the (un)making of commodity drugs. If this return to source subverts and reconfigures a certain idea of genericness, it may also very well subvert access, in its many complex forms, by making the generic itself into new terrain for monopoly, valued uniqueness, and consolidation.

Bypass; or, The Return of the Source

Self-described innovator, pioneer, and leading-brand pharmaceutical laboratories routinely draw our attention to the distinctive imprint that their development and manufacturing processes—which we could call labor, but they do not—leave on the drugs they produce. They have long done so in the name of quality and in the form of the brand name. Branding and advertising are, of course, the companions to what Theodor Adorno and Max Horkheimer (2002) famously characterized as the numbing overwhelm that mass production and standardization visit upon "mass society." Trademarked brand names are tools through which companies invent and protect claims to distinction in such contexts of commodity saturation (Mazzarella 2003). Frederic Schwartz (1996), whose writing on early twentieth century German culture industry has spoken vividly to me, writes, "As manufacturers standardized their products, the effect on the market was, paradoxically, the need for visual signs of distinction, evocative and auratic, signs that would move the customer to choose one product over another. In the rationalized, disenchanted world of modernity, the market needed magical signs" (170). Trademark and brand were, Schwartz argued, a way to "concentrate capital" within "the semiotic explosion that accompanied the growth of a consumer economy" (70).

As we know from life in various consumer capitalisms, and as we saw so clearly in the context of Argentina's *copista* drug industry, the function of brand names is ostensibly to connect a particular product to its trusted source ("These are the big labs, the labs I trust," as pharmacist Norma Verastegui in Buenos Aires had told me),[3] especially in consumer markets awash with similarity or versions of versions of the "same." Leading-brand drug companies spend an enormous amount of money and effort surveilling and cultivating physicians' and consumers' attachments to their drugs and, hence, to the products made by *their* laboratories, to defend against actual or anticipated competition from other labs, generic or otherwise.

What, then, is happening when Pfizer or Sandoz manufacture and distribute a generic medicine stamped ("only") with their corporation's name? They are bypassing the brand while still doing its work by cutting straight to the source—the source of presumed distinction. That is one implication of company-branded generics. But trademarks or brand names aren't the only things being bypassed in this articulation of generic distinction. Retailers—pharmacy retailers in particular—are firmly part of the story here, as is the state. Historically, corporate brands have done much more than differentiate similar products from each other. They have mediated the relationships between producers and retailers in their competing efforts to reach consumers (Lury 2004). Schwartz (1996) argues that with its emergence in the nineteenth century in Europe, trademark law became a tool for manufacturers to reassert some control over a commercial environment in which it was merchants—not producers—who had direct access to consumers (162). Celia Lury (2004) similarly notes that the emergence of corporate brands as personalities in the late nineteenth century (in a North Atlantic context) functioned to supplant the "local shopkeeper as the interface between consumer and product" (19). Lury argues that producers' efforts to cut into the relationship between consumers and retailers soon generated their own countermove: "the emergence of retail outlets as brands themselves" (19).

Dr. Simi is of course front and center for me as I read such accounts of the work and histories of trademark and brand. For here is an outsized, more-than-corporate personality whose distinctive stamp on the goods his pharmacies sell—consumers insist that these generic medicines are *similares*—is not the mark of Simi as producer, even though Farmacias Similares sell some drugs made by Gonzalez Torres's own Laboratorios Best. It is the stamp of Simi as retailer that is imprinted on the drugs Similares sells. Attempting to interrupt this relationship—the considerable seepage or "influence" between charismatic retailers-as-brands and the kinds of drugs they sell—has been central to the Mexican state's complicated generic pharmapolitics.

The Asociación Mexicana de Genéricos Intercambiables (AMEGI; Mexican Association of Interchangeable Generic Medicines)—a private trade association promoting and representing the interests of manufacturers of bioequivalent interchangeable generics—made this point clear in an early informational page on their website, which has since disappeared from the site. In the course of explaining the then-new regulatory designation GI, the association noted, first, that the GI *is* a mark of distinction in a certain respect. Compared to other generic medicines, GIs are different and they are better. Just as importantly, the GI stamp is meant to take the merchant out of the equation as a mediator of pharmaceutical kind and quality: "Once a drug has received certification as a Generic medicine, this drug will have to include in its packaging the logo GI, so that the consumer will be able to identify it as such, no matter where s/he buys it" (Asociación Mexicana de Genéricos Intercambiables 2007).

That last, telling phrase—no matter where the consumer buys it—helps us understand why the Mexican government's insistence at that time on a near future in which all generics would become bioequivalent GIs was widely seen as a direct attack on Dr. Simi and his Farmacias Similares. But Simi wasn't the only pharmacy chain placing a high value on their retail outlet as a marker of generic kind or quality: pharmacies, after all, commonly sell their own brand of medicines. Dr. Simi's kin and competitor, Javier González Torres's Dr. Ahorro (of Farmacias del Ahorro), put out leaflets around 2008 encouraging consumers to "Fíjate en la marca" (Pay attention to the brand!), by which they meant, look closely to see who is *selling* your ampicilina.

It is this kind of retailer-specific marking that the GI was meant to interrupt. The GI logo or *logosímbolo* (mark) is neither brand nor trademark, of course. It is the opposite. Rather than pointing to a distinctive manufacturing or retailing source, it is an effort to stamp medicines with the trusted signature of the state, thus enabling (interchangeable) generics to circulate as pure commodities, untethered both from the original manufacturers and from charismatic generics retailers. Yet, we have seen that such a vision has not readily materialized in Mexico. From Dr. Simi's enduring similares to a pharmacy chain simply calling itself Genéricos Intercambiables, Mexico's commercial actors and consumers have made hay of the state's intention to interrupt this powerful mutual imprint of pharmacy names and pharmaceutical kinds. Into this space of continued generic differentiation, in which genéricos, intercambiables, and similares continue to materialize this contagious contact between drugs and the outlets that sell them, the transnational industry has joined the fray, adding company-branded generics to Mexico's jumble of copies and their stamps and signatures.

When Antonio Salazar asked me "Who's winning?" and then answered the question himself ("The transnationals are coming to sort it all out"), he was specifically lamenting the ineffectiveness of the state's signature (GI) in making a market for a true and trusted commodity. As the major transnational firms get into the Mexican generics market, he told me with frustration, "the interchangeable generic matters less and less. The GI is irrelevant." It (and thus the Mexican state itself) was being bypassed by the transnationals, for it is the companies, he lamented, who will be allowed "to regulate things for us." That is, "the transnationals set the quality [standards]" through their medicines, because they meet requirements that he characterized as more "strict" or "effective" than Mexico's. Thus, he speculated, whether or not a generic drug carries Mexico's GI logo will not ultimately matter, as Sandoz's escitalopram seemed to suggest. If you look on the box and see that your generic was made by Pfizer or Sandoz, *then* you can be confident of its "quality."[4]

The looming irrelevance of the GI, the return of the transnationals in more-than-generic form, and a state that allows itself to be bypassed by those same companies in the authorization of quality all added up, in Salazar's assessment, to a frustrating scenario for the politics of generic substitution and access in Mexico. For he had also noted, presciently, that Mexican drug laboratories, the *nacionales*, were not the ones winning in this scenario. Some Mexican laboratories were indeed finding it difficult to stay afloat in this new market;[5] at the same time, he was pointing to the growing presence of the transnational labs in Mexico's generics market. For example, the Israeli generics giant Teva bought the Mexican company Rimsa (albeit in an acquisition that Teva later regretted and from which they tried to squirm free), Sanofi-Aventis had bought Mexico's Laboratorios Kendrick several years prior, and Sandoz-México was further ramping up its generics efforts in the country (Coronel 2016; Silverman 2016; Singer 2010). The general manager of Sandoz-México, Mariano de Elizalde, noted in a published interview in 2016 that Mexico beckoned not just because of its still-rapidly growing generics market but because of the regulatory environment discussed at length in the prior chapter: that is, COFEPRIS's approach, starting in 2013 under the PRI to prioritize fast-track market access for generics, was especially attractive (Pharma Boardroom 2006). Access to what, and for whom? In a market that has been left to regulate itself, a concentration of capital emerges amid a semiotic explosion of sames and similars.

BioSimilarBetterSuperior

At roughly the same time that I started carrying the rogue escitalopram with me everywhere I went, I met an executive working for the Mexican pharmaceutical company Probiomed at a conference in Mexico City. We talked about his worries about the implications of looming US–Mexico trade and regulatory negotiations for his company's efforts in producing off-patent biological drugs. I was, alas, not particularly helpful to him; he was hoping for insight I did not have about the direction that these negotiations might take and whether things were about to go badly for his company (it turns out they were). Probiomed had been sued the year before by Roche, the Swiss pharmaceutical giant. Roche sued the Mexican company not for violating a patent but for making a copy of Roche's lymphoma drug rituximab that was not (yet?) a proper copy since Mexico did not yet have a fully operationalized regulatory framework governing *this* kind of generic.

Rituximab is a biological pharmaceutical, or "therapeutic protein product," and biologicals are different from the drugs I have discussed throughout this book, which are based merely (yet complexly) on single, active chemical compounds. Biopharmaceuticals are proteins made of and with living matter, and they have a much higher degree of molecular complexity than do "traditional" chemical drugs. Many cancer medicines are biological drugs, such as the breast cancer treatment herceptin; other well-known biopharmaceuticals are insulin (an older, more established biological), most vaccines, Humira (for rheumatoid arthritis), and various erythropoetins. Biopharmaceutical companies are heavily involved in the development of vaccines for SARS-Cov-2 (COVID-19).

The question of what might count as a proper copy of these medicines once they go off-patent was, at the time that Roche sued Probiomed (2013), a matter of heated and high-stakes transnational scientific debate and trade, regulatory, and access politics. If company-branded generics such as escitalopram (by Sandoz) draw our attention to the manufacturing laboratory as a source of generic distinction, ongoing debates around biological pharmaceuticals have amplified this (re)turn to the distinctive imprint of the source—the manufacturing laboratory—in an extreme form. In short, patent-holding biotechnology companies had been arguing that their proprietary drugs are *so singular* that it is technically and definitionally *impossible* for other laboratories to make substitutable generic versions of them, even after a patent expires. No patent, still no generic?

At the heart of this argument is the question of manufacturing process. Biopharmaceuticals are different from chemical drugs not just because they are made of larger and more complex molecules but also because of how they are made. Biotech-derived products are produced through what a Genentech executive characterizes as "intricate manufacturing processes that depend on living organisms (i.e., highly characterized cell lines)" (Garnick 2006, 269).

In the first decade of the 2000s, patent-holding biotechnology companies had started to insist that the biological manufacturing processes their labs use are so firmly sutured to the identity of the resulting medicine that it is essentially impossible for their original drugs to be turned into multisource, interchangeable commodities. A different process makes a different drug. They simply cannot be made biocommensurate, as Stefan Ecks might say (2022), to drugs manufactured by other labs.

In a 2006 forum published in *Nature Biotechnology*, Rob Garnick, then Genentech's senior vice president, made the case that the very idea of a "generic biological" was impossible: "Unlike [with] traditional pharmaceuticals, good scientific practice *does not allow the direct comparison* of one biotech product to another. This is because complex operational and proprietary details of the biotech manufacturing process are central to, and define the identity and unique structural characteristics of, each biotech-derived product" (Garnick 2006; emphasis added).

I will return to the not-incidental role of proprietary details later, but here let me just emphasize that in this argument, process doesn't just precede and hence stand in for the quality of product, as in ordinary quality control in drug manufacturing. More exuberantly, the manufacturing process determines the very identity of the product. In this argument, a different manufacturer using a different ribonucleic acid (RNA) vector will by definition produce a different drug, which therefore cannot be considered a generic version of the original lab's drug.

Such assertions surfaced in the early to mid-2000s when the laboratories producing biologicals were facing a first big wave of patent expirations. Given how many of these medicines are cancer drugs, there has been particular urgency in calls to ensure that more affordable biological drugs are made available in Europe, the United States, Latin America, and South Asia as cancer was coming into view as the new challenge for global health. I don't like to just throw market numbers around as if they speak for themselves, but here are some numbers that seem nontrivial: around 2006, when these arguments began to escalate, the total market for biologicals was estimated to be $30 billion while the value of the drugs on the verge of losing patent protection was nearly a third of that figure, on the order of $10 billion (Ben-Maimon and

Garnick 2006). A great deal of market share (i.e., revenue for patent-holding labs and cost to insurers, governments, and patients) was and remains at stake, as is a great deal of illness and potential treatment.

Genentech, Amgen, and other labs' argument that there could be no such thing as a generic biopharmaceutical was certainly a highly interested attempt to stave off the imminent loss of monopoly on several of their drugs.[6] But, as ever, there were and are some intriguing pharmacological (which is to say pharmapolitical) considerations in the midst. Advocates for approving multisource (generic, postpatent) biological drugs certainly acknowledge that biopharmaceuticals *can* be sensitive to changes in manufacturing processes, more so than conventional chemical medications (Generics and Biosimilars Initiative 2011; Anour 2014). In other words, they too note the imprint of the source (labor, laboratory, process, vector) on the drug. But is this imprint enough to completely forestall the commodification of biopharmaceuticals?

Taking a stand for public health, affordability, and access, the European Medicines Agency (EMA) declared in 2005 that it is, in fact, possible for other laboratories to make a same enough copy of a biological drug. Committing to a pathway for the evaluation and approval of these drugs, the EMA also had to commit to a name for them. The proposals in the trade press and in regulatory circles snowballed into a catalog of more-than-generic excess rivaling much of what we have seen in prior chapters: Generic biopharmaceutical? Biogeneric? Follow-on protein? Follow-on biologic? (Rader 2007).

The EMA eventually settled on what Dr. Simi might have considered the obvious solution: biosimilars (European Medicines Agency 2005). This move indeed gave new and official life to similarity just as some of those other similars were being ruled out of order in the governance and regulation of generic medicines in Mexico and Brazil. Despite much resistance from members of the US-based biotechnology industry (to paraphrase, *the EMA paved the way for mere similarity as a valid standard for copying our drugs!*), the US Food and Drug Administration (FDA) followed Europe's lead and in February 2012 released preliminary draft guidelines for biosimilar approval, noting that despite some minor differences, a (bio)similar can be same enough in the ways that matter—that is, in clinical effectiveness, safety, purity, and potency (US Food and Drug Administration 2012).[7]

Biosimilars thus are understood to produce the same effect as the original at a reduced price. Industry objections notwithstanding, there is now very little that is "mere" about this similarity. It has quickly become its own gold standard, engendering new apparatuses of testing, new sciences and techniques of evaluation, and the invention of methods for characterizing the activity of these molecules, in themselves and in relation to each other. Biosimilar status is difficult but not impossible to achieve. It is an aspiration; thus, makers of monoclonal antibodies started to debate whether they could aim to make a "true biosimilar" (Schneider and Kalinke 2008). Biosimilars have now been taken up as a regulatory category internationally, thus becoming a recognized kind and a significant market in Europe, the United States, Asia, and Latin America. The Mexican government issued guidelines on these drugs in 2013, though you will not be surprised to hear that Dr. Simi made his mark here too. For perhaps obvious reasons, regulators steered well clear of the term *biosimilares*. In Mexico, these drugs are now *biocomparables*.

Biocomparables are, in turn, among the generics sectors in which Mexican labs find themselves "not winning." In 2013, the Mexican Supreme Court sided with Roche in its legal action against Mexico's Probiomed, ordering Probiomed to withdraw its registration for its version of rituximab, even though the secretary of health had already approved the drug for distribution to the public sector, and even though Probiomed was getting ready to export it as well (Coronel 2012; Pallares 2017). Probiomed executives noted with dismay that this decision—premised on the argument that they had not conducted the clinical studies that had only *just* been written into the law—seemed an unfortunate example of the state and the Court siding with transnational pressure, perhaps not wanting to cause problems with the Swiss company or the Swiss government rather than protecting Mexican companies (Coronel 2016; see also Pallares 2017). As generics companies in Argentina and Mexico had already argued in other contexts, the harmonization of the proper copy does not always work out well for a domestic lab already making copies calibrated to other parameters. But the transnational firms with subsidiary manufacturing plants in Mexico see things otherwise: when the Sandoz executive mentioned prior spoke about his company's interest in Mexico's market, biocomparables were highest on his list of opportune niches (Pharma Boardroom 2006).

The "uptake" (and harmonization) of biosimilars regulation across regions, nations, and continents starting around 2012 has in fact turned biosimilars into a major, growing market—one that beckons a wide range of biopharmaceutical labs. Biosimilars have in turn become an important locus of savings for institutional buyers such as national- and public-health systems (notably, early on, in Italy and Germany [Anour 2014]). But the regulatory triumph of the very idea of biosimilarity has not actually resolved or somehow vanquished biotechnology companies' arguments that biological pharmaceuticals are utterly singular. To the contrary, this argument has mutated into a newly peculiar proliferation, one that undercuts the very access (i.e., a proliferation of more affordable biologicals) that the regulatory invention of biosimilars was meant to produce.

The complexity of these drugs, and their sensitivity to specific manufacturing processes, has become a major force in a new semiotic explosion akin to much of what we have seen in prior chapters: more-than-generic proliferations, multiplications of categories that do not exist but are nonetheless real, and assertions of distinction and differentiation in the form of the inventive copy. They are also fueling new articulations of monopoly against mere commodification. In other words, these developments have engendered a repetition of much of what we have seen throughout this book, with rather different implications: they are recomposing the spectacular generic.

To explain, let me return to the Genentech executive's assertion in 2006 that it is not just "operational complexities" that would make generic biologicals impossible. Proprietary complexities are in the mix as well. Elaborating on the role of intellectual property to this generic question, Garnick (2006) noted: "The proposed [biological] generic . . . would be manufactured using an entirely different cell line, plasmid, and process, [since] these materials and information belong to the biotech company and are closely guarded proprietary materials and trade secrets."

Such a scenario is of course not entirely unlike the situation that generics labs such as Label in Guadalajara, Mexico, confront when inactive ingredients and delivery mechanisms are kept under wraps as trade secrets, even after the patent on the active principal ingredient expires. But in the context of biopharmaceuticals, in which the manufacturing details arguably "determine" the identity of the drug, the implications of such secrecy can be all the more stark. Intellectual property is in this context folded effortlessly into the "materially necessary" nature of the singular drug. A new manufacturer *must* use a different process largely because the original process is often a protected trade secret. This pharmapolitical fact is a key starting point for some patent-holding companies' arguments that a different lab can only make a different drug, negating the very possibility of genericization.

Finding themselves thus in an as-if postcolonial predicament, those in the biosimilars business took note of how much work it is to copy while working around a patent. Stephen Charles, the vice president for business development at Nektar Therapeutics, argued in 2005 that bringing biosimilars to market is hard work, requiring a "full-fledged development program" precisely because manufacturers "must determine the availability of active ingredients via a non-patent-infringing route"(Charles 2005, 534). What followed from this assessment is a not-entirely-dissimilar version of the challenges faced, for example, by Indian pharmaceutical companies, Probiomed in Mexico, or Brazilian researchers working in pharmaceuticals (and microcomputing, for that matter) who have been contending with just such a predicament for several decades now. Copying in these circumstances is hardly a walk in the park: it takes quite a lot of ingenuity and a full-fledged development program to reverse-engineer an antiretroviral, a monoclonal antibody, or an Apple computer (Cassier and Correa 2007; da Costa Marques 2005). It takes so much ingenuity that the process may well result in improvements and even in new patents, such as when Brazilian drug researchers developed and patented a new pathway for synthesizing an antiretroviral that produced fewer impurities than Novartis' initial method (Cassier and Correa 2007).

This is the jouissance of the inventive copy that those of us working on invention and imitation in the Global South have so often been drawn to think with, precisely as a counter to a persistent, asymmetrical geopolitical and colonial imagination in which the North innovates and the South merely copies. Eden Medina, Ivan da Costa Marques, and Christina Holmes's edited volume *Beyond Imported Magic* (2014) does this critical work beautifully, as have so many others working on piracy (Liang 2014, Philip 2014; Larkin 2004), Latin American postcolonial nationalist "domestications" and hence transformations of European technoscience (Cházaro 2014), and, more broadly, critical analyses that toss the charge of (post)colonial mimetic imitation back into much more dynamic circulation (Taussig 1993). But what happens when the inventive copy becomes a means to foreclose access, to forestall commodification, to proliferate (singular drugs) in order to consolidate (capital)? To make a commodity drug so spectacular that it, too, becomes the opposite of generic?

I ask these questions because of what happened right alongside the regulatory invention of biosimilars in 2006. As I've elaborated elsewhere (Hayden 2013), Stephen Charles (2005), whom I quoted prior, was one of many biotechnology executives to argue that if you are going to go through the significant trouble of making a biosimilar, you might as well put that effort toward more lucrative ends. In 2005, he posed the question, "Why not [just go ahead and] bring a differentiated and better product to market with little to no increase in development cost?" (534). Substantially rewriting the very notion of the generic, he proposed calling these drugs "supergenerics." Most qualities conventionally defining the generic would not apply. Supergenerics would *not* be unpatentable. They would *not* be the site of indistinction or fungibility. Supergenerics, he proposed, "offer real product differentiation, patent protection, and branding opportunities for product manufacturers" (534). Why, we might ask, call it a generic at all?

The term *generic* in fact quickly dropped out of these discussions. The kind of drug Charles imagined has instead consolidated, rhetorically and materially, as a biobetter. Coined by the director of the leading Indian pharmaceutical firm Dr. Reddy's at a biopharmaceutical investor's conference in 2007 (Anour 2014), the term (and the drugs it names) has circulated with enormous enthusiasm in the globalized biotechnology industry despite the fact that it is *not a recognized regulatory category* anywhere in the world. Like Dr. Simi's similares, it is a name and hence a kind born of a market; it does not exist but is nevertheless very real. An Austrian regulator put the matter this way in 2014: "Biosimilars are in fierce competition with a different player which is, from the European regulatory perspective, no player at all—the 'biobetters'" (Anour 2014, 166).

Biobetters, in their stubborn actualization, do precisely what Charles's hypothetical supergenerics would have done: they improve upon existing biologicals. They also are *not* what the hypothetical supergenerics were not: "Biobetters are not copies and *will never be considered generics*. Biobetters are new molecular entities that are related to existing biologics by target or action, but they are deliberately altered to improve disposition, safety, efficacy, or manufacturing attributes" (Generics and Biosimilars Initiative 2011; emphasis added).

Thus, biobetters are newly patented versions of often still-patented biologicals—same and not the same. For example, a lab might make a biobetter version of an existing biopharmaceutical to which patients (or pathogens) have developed resistance. Biobetters are treated as novel enough in most regulatory contexts to require a full approval process, but they are marketed as close kin to existing biopharmaceuticals. *Neither mere copy nor mere original*, biobetters are high-cost, name-brand, patented, and thus monopoly-protected alternatives to original biologicals and cheaper biosimilars alike.

If you're not confused yet, there is, of course, still more. Befitting a pharmaceutical kind born of the market, biobetters continue to proliferate in name/kind as biotechnology laboratories, investors, and marketing executives invent more ways to distinguish betterness from and as itself. These proliferating terms range from the not-terribly imaginative "biosuperiors" to the grammatically challenging "me-betters," a gesture to the "me-too" drugs of the traditional, chemical kind that crowd the permissive US market (yet another statin, for example). Me-betters, a term that suggests a nearly Trumpian bludgeoning of (at least one) language, induces in me a not-insignificant despair. Me-betters feel like the *colmo*—a culmination that is surely not even "the end." It is just too much.

A Map as Big as the Territory: An IN of One

But the excess, of course, is the point; or, rather, it delivers me to my point. To bring this chapter to a close, let me step back and state the obvious. A market-driven shift of biotechnology industry investments in inventive copies (biobetters) over mere, same-enough copies negates the characteristic benefit—even the defining trait—of generics and biosimilars, which is that they are *lo mismo* but *más barato*. For this reason, regulators and advocates for pharmaceutical access see biobetters as a looming threat for the politics of affordable medicines globally (Anour 2014). That is, many biotechnology firms are turning away from producing what access advocates call "commodity bulk" biosimilars in favor of the stronger returns promised by differentiated, proprietary biobetters (Generics and Biosimilars Initiative 2011).

Generic pharmaceutical executives whom I know in Mexico City groaned at the (il)logical conclusion toward which these biopharmaceutical developments are straining and at the perverse relation they suggest between the singular and the general, the proprietary and the multisource, monopoly and access. We might recall that the term for a generic name is the *international nonproprietary name* (INN). When Argentina's health minister under Néstor Kirchner, Ginés González García, wanted to *return to drugs their one true name* (as discussed in chapter 3), it was the nonproprietary name to which he was referring. The implication of what's happening here, though, is that every biopharmaceutical will, can, or should *only* ever have its one true *proprietary* name. Contemplating the rise of biobetters, Alan Shepherd, speaking at a conference for generics manufacturers in Mexico City in 2013 (the same conference in which the then COFEPRIS director proclaimed *access* the magic word), said with equal parts bemusement and exasperation, "It's as if they imagine each entity is its own category!" (Shepherd 2013); that is ,as if there can only be an 'IN of 1,' a unique name for each unique thing. Such a fantasy—to each and every version of a biological drug its own patent and its own proper name—is one in which the generic, as genus or genre, is impossible. It is a nearly Borgesian formulation, as in Jorge Luís Borges's famous parable of the imperial cartographer whose map is precisely as big as the territory it describes—a one-to-one correspondence that is as grandiose in its will to specificity and representational power as it is absurd (Borges 1999). *This* absurdity, the fantasy of an IN of 1, sounds very much like a nontrivial aspiration to the fully spectacular world that Jean Baudrillard (1994) named in which there are no "kinds;" there are only proprietary brands (see also Haraway 2018).[8]

Where *does* this scenario lead? We need not assume that aspirations to the IN of one are being fully realized (they are not, of course—after all, "bulk" biosimilars and biocomparables both exist and are real in Mexico, Europe, the United States, and South and Southeast Asia) to get a sense of where the tensions discussed in this chapter lean. Taken together, they suggest how generic proliferation can become consolidation, and this shift in turn feels depressingly overdetermined, not just to many of my interlocutors but to me as well. The terrain of more affordable generics is being colonized by Big Pharma as transnational laboratories find ways to participate in the very markets that were meant to challenge their dominance in the first place. Sandoz's escitalopram shows, in interesting concert *with* Dr. Simi, yet again how genericness can be a locus for valued stratification and differentiation. Probiomed's travails point to scenarios in which some domestic generics laboratories find it challenging to stay viable in their own new, roiling market for postpatent copies even as well-capitalized transnational labs see this generics landscape, and its regulatory politics, as the locus of ever more opportunity. And with the rise of biobetters, we can see yet another arena in which an excess of more-than-copies of course(!) becomes instrumentalized in the form of new patents, forestalling the very possibility of cheaper commodity drugs through the multiplication of source-specific, proprietary versionings.

Such turns reflect many other forms of consolidation emerging out of the postpatent exuberance I have addressed throughout this book. Among these we might count consolidations in pharmacies: in Mexico, larger chains including megastores like Walmart, Comercial Mexicana, and Farmacias Similares and Ahorro have been devouring smaller outlets, prompting the pharmacy trade association ANAFARMEX (Asociación Nacional de Farmacias de México), representing smaller "farmacias del barrio," to file a complaint with the federal government on illegal anticompetitive practices (*El Universal* 2012). We could consider consolidations in interests—for example, when Argentine copistas and multinationals joined forces to lobby against new generics legislation in the early 2000s, as noted in chapter 3, or when

Teva, the Israeli generics giant, was granted membership in 2016 into the Pharmaceutical Manufacturers Association, the powerful lobbying group representing multinational innovator labs (Silverman 2016).

And we must consider a consolidation in prices. Moving very much against the grain of where this story started—with the proliferation of cheap copied medicines—generics prices in Mexico overall have now become among the *highest* in Latin America in relative terms; they are not 75 percent cheaper than the prices that leading-brand drugs command in Mexico but are closer to 28 percent cheaper, according to a recent federal commission report on economic competitiveness (Comisión Federal de Competencia Económica 2017). Not unrelated, by 2017, Mexico's pipeline for liberating off-patent generics had slowed down considerably, in part due to increases in tactics used by patent-holding firms to forestall generic competition, such as filing new evergreen patents (Comisión Federal de Competencia Económica 2017).

At this point, we have landed in a familiar story: ensuring that their drugs do not easily become mere commodities is central to the strategies of highly financialized innovator pharmaceutical companies. But I resolutely do not want to end on such a note, as if we have come all this way only to retell a teleological story about the consolidation of pharmaceutical capital and the return of the transnationals in supergeneric form. As with biopharmaceuticals themselves, there is nothing "materially necessary" about this trajectory, nor is the relationship between proliferation and consolidation a linear one. Rather, that relationship names an ongoing tension and pharmapolitical (Simipolitical) contest.

The tensions that have animated this book—the generic proliferations and excesses activated by Dr. Simi and in so many other forms—speak to histories and futures of the generic in which the samenesses that matter are sites and sources of potential and contradiction. We know very well that the commodity is a potent fiction; that the equivalence and interchangeability on which this fiction rests always dissolves into something *more than*; that indeed because of the ways that markets work, the liberation of generics into consumer markets cannot resolve on their own the problem of pharmaceutical access much less the infinitely larger question of health. For all of that, the developments in *this* chapter deliver me, somewhat disconcertingly given my intellectual upbringing, and quite counter to the opening moves of this book, to want to mount an impassioned plea for the merely equivalent pharmaceutical commodity. They deliver me to a commitment to access politics that insists that a copy can just be a copy. They lead me to want a politics of equivalence that is all the more potent precisely because it allows for the just same enough. To "mere" equivalence in this light is to redirect its charge, even if only for a moment and even as we note that this move is precisely what has generated the many ambivalent excesses laid out in the prior pages. These excesses and contradictions will surely continue to proliferate. What more could we expect of the precarious promise of the mere pharmaceutical commodity?

Coda

As I put this manuscript down, the novel coronavirus pandemic is doing in Mexico much of what it is doing in other places in the Americas, including in the United States: it is intensifying and laying bare existing contradictions and inequalities, not least where a politics of health and the state's defense of "those who have the least" are concerned. I cannot help but understand what's happening in Mexico in 2020, with the intersection of Andrés Manuel López Obrador's interventions as president and a global public health–sociopolitical disaster, without thinking about Simipolitics and the contours of populist political interventions on the question of health. Simipolitics—the echoes and rearticulations of a national(ist) pharmaceutical populism, forged around the excessive, contradictory politics of substitution—does not belong to Dr. Simi alone.

In Mexico, COVID-19 is disproportionately affecting (killing) poor and working-class people; it is taking a serious toll on health-care workers too, who have little protection and little infrastructural support. Several public hospitals were among the first documented hot spots in the country (Sheridan 2020). Distrust of the public sector hospitals (among others) has added to the catalog of reasons why some people are, according to investigative reporting in Mexico, not going to the Seguro Social, the Institute for Social Security and Services for State Workers (ISSSTE), or the secretary of health's (SSA) hospitals when they develop symptoms of COVID-19—instead heading to the clinics of Farmacias Similares and other low-cost private pharmacy-adjacent clinics (Estrada 2020). The general practice physicians working at these clinics, like doctors Hugo Treviso and Verónica López in chapter 4, are thus at particular risk themselves. After a number of *consultorio* physician deaths, many Similares and similar pharmacies have closed their clinics rather than expose their workers and other patients to such risk (Estrada 2020).

In the midst of all of this, the Simi jokes continue, though they don't feel quite as funny as they once might have. One making the rounds on Twitter went as follows: "If you use a Simi mask, you don't get coronavirus, you get something *similar*." To which another *tuitero* (tweeter) replied, "The problem is, that similar thing is atypical pneumonia, which is killing a lot of people" (Regio del Norte 2020). That Simi masks should be the setup for this exchange is fitting enough, for Farmacias Similares, alongside Walmart, has found itself again on the wrong end of a ruling by the Federal Consumer Protection Office (PROFECO), this time for price gouging on medical masks (Rojas 2020).

Mexico's health care system is, meanwhile, underfunded in a new and different way under López Obrador than it was in the decade and a half on which this book has focused, and the politics of medicines is just as contradictory, though ostensibly the political orientation has shifted dramatically to the left. Amlo, as López Obrador is called, has promised a popular and populist societal renewal under the banner of a fourth transformation (4T)—a successor moment to three hallmarks of Mexican national(ist) history: independence, the reform period, and the Mexican Revolution. This fourth transformation, he has declared, will be a revolution in the name of the poor, through an antielite, anti-institutionalist return to a properly populist state that "puts the poor first." Amlo's 4T and his expansive programs for *el pueblo mexicano* are largely to be funded from two sources. The first is oil, through revenue from the state petroleum company Pemex. That move certainly references Venezuela's petro-state heyday in the 1990s and early 2000s, but more importantly, it references the year 1937 in Mexico, when the postrevolutionary president Lázaro Cárdenas nationalized British Petroleum. Oil is a long-running theme in Mexican nationalism and in López Obrador's own political program ("El petroleo es nuestro" [the oil is ours], he had proclaimed during the 2006 presidential campaign, in which Dr. Simi tried to run against him). The second source of funding for his programs for the poor, Amlo has promised, will be savings generated from rooting out governmental and administrative corruption and "bloat." The latter commitment manifested in 2019 and 2020 as a highly contradictory populist politics of austerity—a "populist neoliberalism," as some of his disappointed critics on the Left have characterized it (Lemus 2019; see also Martínez 2020 and Alvarez 2019).

López Obrador's austerity measures have hit the public health systems particularly hard (Verdusco 2020). We might recall that he dismantled the Seguro Popular in January 2020 (just before the full arrival of the COVID-19 pandemic), citing the institution's failure to serve the poor and popular sectors (it is "neither *Seguro* nor *popular*!" he proclaimed [Masías 2020; Político MX 2018])—and bringing to fruition Dr. Simi's earlier declaration that "the Seguro Popular would fail" (Grupo Por Un Pais Mejor 2008). López Obrador's substitute for the Seguro Popular is his own highly centralized but not yet fully functioning national health-care system, INSABI (Instituto de Salud para el Bienestar; National Institute for Health and Well-being) (Gobierno de México 2020; CNN 2018). Indeed, López Obrador's promise, upon taking office, was to install a truly popular health system: one that would provide free medicines and care to all. By the end of his term, he announced, Mexico would have a health system "like that of Canada or the United Kingdom" (Belmont and López 2018). But in order to build such a future, it seems, one must first cut and cut. In 2019, as he argued the case for dismantling the Seguro Popular, he also reduced the budgets of IMSS and ISSSTE so severely that the director of IMSS resigned, issuing an unusually blunt public statement of frustration: "You cannot cut and cut, save and save, in the matter of health; it will only lead to disaster (Martínez Cázares 2019; *El Universal* 2019).

Much as Dr. Simi did in 2006 with his "national anti-corruption movement," López Obrador has specifically targeted corruption in the procurement of pharmaceuticals as a key problem and hence as a key locus of potential savings. With the amount of money that "disappears" into dodgy contracts and corrupt politicians' hands through the public sector procurement of medicines, López Obrador has argued repeatedly, the government could easily pay for free medicines for all (Morales 2019). Sounding not unlike Dr. Simi in 2006, who himself sounded resonantly familiar, Amlo has railed against the drug companies that have Mexicans by the throat, accusing these labs of running amoral monopolies, of price gouging, and of entering into collusion with each other and with the public health systems—in one highly publicized case, with a major pediatric hospital in Mexico City (Morales 2019; Morales and Villa Cañales 2020).[1] Indeed, faced with complaints about shortages of pediatric cancer medicines, and then with protests by the parents of sick children, López Obrador has insisted that it is not austerity but rather drug company hoarding and public sector corruption that are the culprits for these and other medication shortages (Morales 2019).

Significantly, much like Dr. Simi's attacks on IMSS, these pharmapolitics, too, have been aimed largely at *domestic* institutions: Amlo's Big Pharma fight around pediatric cancer medicines has in fact not been with "the transnationals" but rather with Mexican drug companies, specifically Pisa, the maker of two key pediatric oncology drugs. While López Obrador has declared that rooting out the "rot" at the heart of the domestic pharmaceutical–public sector nexus will enable a transformation in health care in Mexico, it also seems clear that such a transformation will not be instantaneous. There is, thus, a Simipolitical solution afoot—an act of substitution that once again scrambles the coordinates of a politics painted in the palette of populism and nationalism. Where Simi went all-in on the domestic copy to address the question of access, Amlo's administration announced that, to resolve the pediatric cancer drug shortage in 2020, they had been flying in planeloads of those same oncology medicines from France and Argentina, among other countries. In a subsequent agreement between López Obrador's administration and the UN, the UN made clear what the strategy would be going forward: streamlining the process of bringing medicines in from abroad (*Yucatan Times* 2020). The key to guaranteeing pharmaceutical supply and what Amlo described as "the right to health" is thus easing "legal obstacles for prestigious foreign pharmaceutical companies to introduce their medicines into the country" (*Yucatan Times* 2020). As López Obrador's secretary of health explained, "They are cheaper if you buy them abroad" (*El Universal* 2020b). *Lo mismo pero más barato!* Dr. Simi's famous formula takes another Simipolitical turn.

Notes

INTRODUCTION

1 Emilie Gomart (2002) and Anne Lovell (2006) have made this point beautifully in their works on opioid-substitution therapies.
2 Private health insurance has long played very little role in Mexico, accounting for only about 2 percent of insurance coverage (Martínez et al. 2009; World Bank 2012).
3 See, among many sources on the configuration of this market, the US Department of Commerce (2004).
4 For example, rather than offering cash assistance to the very poor, the Argentine government under Néstor Kirchner extended credit lines, thereby continuing what Verónica Gago (2014, 1–28, 164) calls a "neodevelopmental" form of a neoliberal project that entangled ever more people in debt and consumption. This is part of a dynamic that she calls the financialization of popular life.
5 Indeed, political scientists trying to get hold of the distinctive characters of Mexico's political formations have often pointed to the kind of unclassifiability that Dr. Simi, as we'll see throughout this book, personifies. Consider Stephen Morris's (1991, 21–22) take from the early 1990s: "Just as corruption tends to obscure the true nature of things, the Mexican political system supports a wide range of appearances. It is neither fully democratic nor blatantly authoritarian; public policies are neither wholly capitalistic nor decidedly socialistic; interest groups both mobilize and demobilize; and elections are neither honest nor 'completely fraudulent.'"
6 Gago's work in Argentina tracks such a dynamic—from scarcity to proliferation, "from below"—as does Angela Garcia's work on *anexos* in Mexico. These are clandestine drug treatment clinics that emerged in the context of Mexico's (neoliberal) reforms in the 1980s, which "exacerbated longstanding inequalities, severely affecting the lives of the poor and working classes, migrants, and indigenous communities. At the same time, [this inequality] has

been a crucial force in the production of new forms of survival and sociality. These two valences—depletion and production—characterize the expansion of Mexico's 'illegal' or 'informal' services and networks from the 1980s onward" (Garcia 2015, 460).

7   In many cases, as with India's Patent Law of 1970, drugs were subject to process patents but not product patents; thus, specific means of synthesizing or producing a molecule could be patented, but the "molecule itself" could not (see, among many others, Sunder Rajan 2017).

8   However, as we will see in chapter 3, there is nothing at all straightforward about this stance where price and access are concerned.

9   Legal scholar Amy Kapcyznski (2013, 1) has noted that in 2000, "when only patented anti-retroviral drugs for human immunodeficiency virus (HIV) infection were widely available, they cost approximately $10,000 per person per year, even in very poor countries. [In 2013], these same medicines cost $150 or less [when] purchased from Indian generics companies."

10 See, for example, the text of the Doha Declaration of the WTO, in which treatment activists and state negotiators succeeded in reaffirming the right to public health exemptions to patents in the case of public health emergencies (World Trade Organization 2001).

11 Brazil's efforts have been particularly famous and particularly complex. As Joao Biehl has shown so eloquently, this victory of the state, backed up by the leverage afforded by Brazilian public labs' capacity to reverse-engineer those medicines if the transnational laboratories did not lower their prices, also created a situation in which the Brazilian state effectively came to serve as a broker for the multinational pharmaceutical industry, guaranteeing its access to the Brazilian market (see Biehl 2004).

12 Martínez, personal communication with author, 2004. Víctor González Torres (Dr. Simi) also actually tried to organize a legislative push to limit the duration of pharmaceutical patents to ten years, in an unsuccessful effort to bring HIV/AIDS activists under the Simi political umbrella (see Hayden 2007 for a discussion).

13 Adriana Petryna and Arthur Kleinman use a similar phrase, "pharmaceutical nexus," in their introduction to *Global Pharmaceuticals* (Petryna and Kleinman 2006, 20–22). For them, as for me, the nexus points to the complex, multiscalar dimensions of globalized pharmaceuticals as empirical objects and sites of inquiry.

14 Anne Pollock (2011) and Susan Craddock (2017) have each argued persuasively that the arrangements and political economies of pharmaceutical research and development continue to change, marked by failure as much as dominance (Pollock) and organized around different kinds of partnerships (Craddock), such that the critical questions anthropology and science studies ask must, too, continue to shift.

15 Joseph Dumit (2012) has shown how drug companies "must" continue to grow their markets in the high-priced US market by finding ways to ensure that people in the United States are on multiple "drugs for life." Adriana Petryna (2009) argues that these same imperatives have driven the "innovator" drug industry to globalize their clinical trial apparatuses (setting up an entire new industry in outsourced experimental platforms), as the US population is "treatment saturated" enough that it is hard to find appropriate trial subjects.

16 As I'll discuss in greater detail in chapter 1, NAFTA required the Mexican state to set definitions for generic "bioequivalence" that are arguably more strict, and certainly more expensive for labs to prove, than the definitions on which its own public health system, and the public health systems of many countries across Latin America, had long relied.

17 In an apt reading of Debord and Baudrillard, Daryl Mendoza (2010, 51n28) observes that for Baudrillard, "there is no such thing as a generic loaf of bread; not even homemade bread is generic in a sense since the ingredients, the qualities, the brands, the labels, that it takes to create the bread, is loaded with Signs. . . . The raw object is nowhere to be found." As I note in the body of the chapter, this argument is not my destination but rather a point of departure for thinking about the unmaking and refashioning of the generic as the pharmaceutical's commodity form. It is also a point of return, as we will come back to this argument, seen anew, in chapter 5.

18 This erasure of the specificities of production, the concrete material conditions and the laboring relations that produce commodities, is of course precisely where Marx located the violence and power of the commodity form (Marx 1978, 302–29).

19 Thanks to Natalia Brizuela for pointing me to Monsiváis's essay in relation to this point.

20 Sánchez (2016, 6) writes, "Rather than the proverbial 'individuals' of liberal ideology, what initially filled these vast, flattened spaces were instead the newly formed crowds as a field of relentless differentiation and dispersion . . . : the dauntingly mimetic subjects of the Venezuelan postcolony. . . . These subjects were in principle free to adopt any and all identities that came their way, including, most disturbingly, that of their rulers."

21 Methodologically, this move keeps company (albeit somewhat perversely) with Isabelle Stengers's deployment of "the pharmakon" as a way to think about the political, pharmacologically. For Stengers (2010, 28–33), the pharmakon, that which can be poison or remedy depending on the dose or the context, demands a suspension of epistemological certainty or absolutism; it requires an embrace of ambiguity and a refusal to base radical politics (including the politics of knowledge) on the assignation of blame. As such, she finds it a productive model for inciting radical political action against the

paralysis that the demands for such purity of explanation can induce (see also Stengers and Pignarre 2011). The resonance with Dr. Simi is perverse only because Stengers would likely not tolerate casting Dr. Simi as a radical political actor (nor would I). But the suspension of the "really" that she demands is deeply resonant with the analytic work of chapters 1 and 2, and, in this, I am also trying to think of politics pharmacologically.

22 Not least among these shared conditions of possibility were the 1990s economic liberalizations that made regional and US-Mexico borders much more porous where goods and money were concerned (see Castañeda and Campos Garza 2009).

23 Angela Garcia's (2015) work on anexos, the informal drug treatment centers that have sprung up across the country, is an arresting example of this kind of doubling and troubling.

24 Fox's term was followed by a second PANista presidency, that of Felipe Calderón (2006–12), marked largely by the violence (often described as spectacular) of the intensified war between and among the cartels and the state. The end of the PRI's access to the presidency turned out to be temporary; the PRI returned to office in 2012, while left-leaning candidate Andres Manuel López Obrador won the office in 2018.

CHAPTER ONE. SAME AND NOT THE SAME

1 See Esther Leslie's *Synthetic Worlds* (2005) for an extensive discussion of the nonreductive chemical relations that suffused Marx's analysis. His famous passage on linens and coats (in which the two things of a "like substance" are in fact made of the substance of labor power) is surrounded by musings on chemicals, chemistry, and chemists. He writes of residues, crystallizations, and the chemists who, no matter what the economists say, have certainly not discovered exchange value "either in a diamond or a pearl." And it is the distinctive way in which chemical compounds themselves can be the same as but different from each other that helps him explain how capital's logic of equivalence can disrupt itself—in particular, how two things can be equivalent without being interchangeable. Marx illustrates this somewhat counterintuitive point with reference to two chemical compounds, which are by many measures the same—they are composed of the same molecules, in the same proportion even. And yet they are not interchangeable: their geometry is different and, thus, their identity is different. They have different names. They are, as I'll elaborate later in this chapter, same and not the same.

2 See Diane Nelson's (2015) exquisite thinking on the "beyond" of adequation and super-adequation for a potent way of approaching the beauty, abstraction, and violences of equivalence.

3 Dr. Simi employed dancing mascot versions of himself, men and women who were (and are) paid to don giant, padded Dr. Simi suits, take up positions outside Farmacias Similares, and dance to the music the pharmacy is blaring from its storefront.
4 See Isabelle Stengers (2010) on "culturing the pharmakon" regarding the urgency of reformulating the question of the "really."
5 This campaign was described to me in 2004 by María del Carmen Gutierrez, then the chief public relations officer at Grupo Por Un Pais Mejor, the umbrella organization under which Farmacias Similares is organized.
6 Peterson's work brilliantly reframes the "crisis" at work in the problem of adulterated medicines, away from the story that this is a "Nigerian" problem.
7 As mathematicians, linguists, and Marx, in his discussion of relative value, would also "remind" us, the arrangement of this equivalence, as a relation, is crucial. Try reversing the formula: "The original is the same as the generic!" calls forth a radically different relation, with radically different politics and a different charge, we might say (Marx 1978, 314).
8 In the science studies worlds in which I travel, this potent chemical turn has placed chemical compounds at the center of a lively, antireductive analytic, as with M. Murphy's (2017) powerful reconceptualization of the politics of accountability and exposure through the notion of alter-life, or of affinities rather than identification, as in Isabelle Stengers's (2005, 2010) understanding of the challenges of political coalition-building, reframed as a "cosmopolitical" recomposition.
9 Brazilian *similares* correspond roughly to what in Mexico have become known as regular genéricos: branded copied drugs, based on chemical equivalence, that have not been subject to bioequivalence testing. On their fate in Brazil, see Bourne Partners (2012).
10 Personal communication with author, 2008.
11 Javier Tolomayo (pseudonym), personal communication, July 7, 2005.
12 Personal communication with author, February 24, 2004. Unless otherwise noted, author's translation.
13 J. González, personal communication with author, 2002.
14 Personal communication with author, 2014.
15 "Descubre por qué decimos que IXE es lo mismo, pero no es igual," billboard on Avenida Insurgentes, Mexico City, March 2014.
16 As I have argued in an extended discussion of the relation between Dr. Simi and the tenets of trademark law and commercial distinction, Dr. Simi does not poach the aura of the original; rather, he invests similarity and even sameness (lo mismo!) with his own aura of distinction (Hayden 2013).
17 Of course, it also arguably misses the point that, "even" in the United States, for anyone for whom price is a serious obstacle or constraint, "as good but less expensive" can be plenty compelling.

18 Personal communication with author, July 2004.
19 Personal communication with author, April 2004.
20 Personal communication with author, April 2004.
21 Not incidentally, with Dr. Simi as a mediating rhetorical force, it is not difficult to weave generics and homeopathy into the same sentence, historically and conceptually speaking: homeopathy works through the generative principle of similarity, and in the late nineteenth and early twentieth centuries, homeopathic pharmacies, often with clinics alongside them (the original Similares?) were important, highly visible aspects of Mexico's therapeutic-commercial spheres (Hernández 2009).
22 "Las historias de un ente mexicano: Medicamentos en México, un mundo de oferta!!" (*Las historias de un ente mexicano* 2010).
23 Gutiérrez, personal communication with author, February 24, 2004.
24 Personal communication with author, 2005.
25 Personal communication with author, 2005.
26 Personal communication with author, 2008.
27 This shift had been implied in the 1997–98 law that introduced bioequivalence for the first time, but the corresponding "norms" (i.e., the actual details by which it was to be implemented) had not yet been specified. See "Decreto por el que se reforma el artículo 376 de la Ley General de Salud," Diario Oficial de la Federación, February 24, 2005, 13.
28 That debate itself unfolded in its own perfectly slippery set of word games. The government declared that this move would put an end to Similares, to which Similares proxies replied that it wouldn't, because Similares don't exist in the first place! What will really disappear, Similares officials countered, are interchangeable generics, because once all drugs meet the bioequivalence threshold, there will be no need to call drugs GIs—there will simply be patented medicines, on the one hand, and generics on the other.
29 As Joseph Dumit's (2012) work on contemporary pharmaceutical marketing shows, there is little point in trying to maintain a sharp distinction between innovator industry interests and scientific facts where pharmaceutical science is concerned. The pharma industry's interested facts, he argues, have *become* our facts.
30 Personal communication with author, May 22, 2006.
31 Personal communication with author, February 24, 2004.
32 As in the flyer they distributed around that time, "Why buy in Farmacias Similares?"
33 At the beginning of this chapter, I invoked Kristin Peterson's (2014) poignant phrase to evoke all that can ride on generic medicines and the promise of equivalence. Her articulation of a postcolonial, pharmaceutical "dream" of equivalence pointed specifically to the dream of bioequivalence as an anchor against the fluctuations produced by practices of chemical arbitrage.

34 Personal communication with author, 2010.
35 Personal communication with author, 2010.
36 For example, in their work producing a generic version of the antiretroviral drug efavirenz, a consortium of Brazilian labs developed a pathway for synthesis that was "cheaper, more efficient, more straightforward, and safer" than Merck's originally patented version—the quality of the copy in fact led the government to decline to renew a compulsory license on Merck's patent (Cassier and Correa 2013, 14). Similarly, chemists at the Brazilian lab Farmanguinhos made a version of didanosine that had "better bioavailability" than Bristol Myers Squibb's original, and that was two and a half times smaller to boot (24).
37 For one of many brilliant examples beyond the realm of pharmaceuticals, see da Costa Marques (2005).
38 Personal communication with author, June 2008.
39 These bioavailability data are then combined as averages: "If two averages are sufficiently close, then the two formulations are bioequivalent on average" (Hess 1998, 20).
40 To be more precise still, it is not the curves per se but the figure represented by the 90 percent confidence interval of comparison between the two curves that should fall between 80 percent and 125 percent. There are ever-more specific technicalities to attend to here, but the larger point remains that bioequivalent interchangeability is premised on the recognition that sameness is a form of difference that may **or** may not significantly change the therapeutic efficacy of the drug.
41 Personal communication with author, June 2013.
42 The year that Shewhart was working at the USDA was the same year that quality control itself was redefined within the Food, Drug, and Insecticide Agency, which was still within the USDA. A 1937 safety scandal involving the contamination of a sulfa drug (mixed with a poisonous solvent) became one of the sparks behind the 1938 Food, Drug, and Cosmetic Safety Act. The act explicitly took up Shewhart's redefinition of quality control: while the safety of drugs themselves had already been subject to regulation, the 1938 law noted for the first time that new drugs could not be approved if manufacturing methods, facilities, and controls were found to be inadequate (Cooper 2002, 17; Junod 2004; Daemmerich 2004).
43 See Callon, Méadel, and Rabeharisoa (2002) for a discussion from the point of view of STS on the implications of this shift from understanding "qualities" as particular things to measure (strength, stability, fuse blow time) to the formation of "quality" as a generalized statistical property.
44 Further, this intervention laid the groundwork for total quality management, which was directed to auditing "the firm" itself (Cochoy 2005).
45 Personal communication with author, June 2013.

46 For STS analyses of the rise of standardization and its implications, see, among many, Alder (1998), Bowker and Star (1999), and Slaton (2001).
47 Personal communication with author, June 2013.
48 Dominique Tobbell (2012) has shown that an early case for bioequivalence testing over chemical equivalence in the United States was based on differences in dissolution profiles (how the drug dissolved into the bloodstream) that resulted when an "innovator" company changed the formulation of one of its drugs from a capsule to a tablet.
49 Personal communication with author, June 5, 2013.
50 Sarah Franklin's analysis in *Dolly Mixtures* (2007) saturates my inquiry here into what is same, what is different, and how we might know the difference.

CHAPTER TWO. SIMIPOLITICS

1 See Poniatowska (1988) for a now-classic account of the emergence of a civil society from the ashes of the Mexico City earthquake in 1986.
2 As Tara Schwegler (2004), Cristina Puga (1993), and Roderic A. Camp (1989) have argued, the compromise (antagonism) that kept the private sector out of the political field marked Mexico as distinct from other Latin American and North American countries for much of the twentieth century.
3 As Tara Schwegler (2011, 132) writes, IMSS is much more than a provider of health care: "Among the benefits it provides are healthcare; retirement, death and accident pensions; nurseries for the children of working mothers; and social and cultural services such as self-service stores, theatres, sports complexes, funeral parlors and vacation centers."
4 Personal communication with author, June 2005.
5 Personal communication with author, 2005.
6 The Museo Evita (Evita Museum) in Buenos Aires memorializes this largesse; Argentine novelist Tomás Eloy Martínez's remarkable book *Santa Evita* (1997) also conveys in semifictional form the affective dimensions of this famous iteration of populist generosity, not to mention the potent relationship between populism and the copy.
7 Personal communication with author, June 2010.
8 Personal communication with author, June 2010.
9 Personal communication with author, June 2010.
10 Personal communication with author, June 2010.
11 Personal communication with author, July 2008.
12 Personal communication with author, 2008.
13 Personal communication with author, 2008.
14 Comaroff was indeed puzzling out how one might make such an evaluation in the context of, for example, the governments of Lula in Brazil, Evo Morales in Bolivia, and Hugo Chávez in Venezuela. In so doing, she confronts an elusive

and possibly ill-fated challenge: "We must attempt to distinguish what might be the real, redistributive gains achieved by these novel, populist regimes [Lula, Morales, and Chávez in Latin America] from the more repressive dimensions" (Comaroff 2011, 102–3).

15 The *Economist*'s report on Amlo's impending victory in 2018 is but one of many cases in point (*Economist* 2018).

16 I am referring specifically to the literal designations of Social Security (the Seguro Social) and its new counterpart Popular Security (the Seguro Popular). But these terms refer to broader political imaginations and vocabularies in which the social becomes an idiom of formal governance, while the popular points to much that escapes or exceeds the reach of such formality.

17 Raquel Pêgo, personal communication with author, 2004. Technically, those who are informally employed or not employed at all, and aren't dependents of Seguro beneficiaries, have access to *something*, but that something—the network of facilities gathered under the federal secretary of health (SSA) and run by individual states—has long been considered inadequate. Facilities for SSA are infamous for being underfunded and ill-equipped; they are described even by policy-makers as purveyors of "lower-quality services" (World Bank 2008, 2) and they charge a fee, no less. These facilities are thus a (hole-ridden) safety net of last resort rather than a provider of routine care (World Bank 2008). Finally, on the other end of the spectrum, there is private insurance for those with the means and desire to pay for it—a relatively tiny percentage (roughly 2 percent) of the population in Mexico (Bonilla-Chacín and Aguilera 2013, 2–3).

18 Personal communication with author, 2006.

19 For example, see Sophie Day (2015) on critiques of the United Kingdom's National Health Service, which have sought to gain traction for further privatization by attacking the inadequacy of a state-provided, "one size fits all" approach.

20 See also Holston (2008) for an extended analysis of this relationship.

21 Personal communication with author, 2008.

22 Personal communication with author, 2006.

23 "The size of premium payments for participation in the program . . . varies according to the participants' economic status. Families pay up to 5% of disposable income (defined as total spending after basic needs are covered). The size of the premium falls and size of government subsidy rises as one moves down the economic ladder, with people in the poorest 20 percent of the population paying nothing at all" (World Bank 2008, 2).

24 The Seguro Popular worked in many ways as a decentralizing financing reform, notably by channeling funds to individual states based on the number of enrollees rather than, say, the number of health providers—an incentive

for states to get people on the Seguro Popular's rolls. The federal government provided some of the funding for Seguro Popular services while the states were meant to pay a significant amount; a small portion of its funding comes from premiums (Pueblita 2013).
25 Gabriel Treviso, personal communication with author, April 2013.
26 Elly Yglesias, personal communication with author, 2013.
27 Elly Yglesias, personal communication with author, 2013.
28 For the Morena party's comments, see Aristegui Noticias Network (2015).
29 Grupo Por Un Pais Mejor (2005); see also Grupo Por un Pais Mejor's weekly newsletter, *SimInforma Por Un Pais Mejor: Semanario Latinamericano*, January 28, 2008.
30 Elly Yglesias, personal communication with author, 2013.
31 See also, among many other news accounts, PolíticoMX (2018).
32 Veronica Gago (2014, 5), for example, wonders why we would call the Kirchner regime(s) in Argentina a form of state populism when the kinds of provisions offered "the poor" come in the form of enhanced access to credit, financialization, and thus private debt.

CHAPTER THREE. NO PATENT, NO GENERIC

1 Personal communication with author, May 2006.
2 It bears keeping in mind that the relationship between the roiling crisis and medication shortages is not a straightforward one; it is not just that prices skyrocketed and therefore people could not afford them, though this certainly happened. Argentine human rights organizations and other chroniclers of the crisis have also documented acts of financial speculation and hording by the droguerías, the powerful distribution committees that act as intermediaries between laboratories and pharmacies. The accusation is that the droguerías fueled shortages by not releasing drugs to pharmacies unless each previous delivery was paid off in full. Given the devaluation(s), such payments became increasingly impossible for many pharmacies, leaving these commercial outlets without inventory. In particular, shortages of insulin led well-organized diabetes advocacy and patient groups to force the government to declare a medical emergency. I am grateful to Sylvia Brunoldi of the Liga Argentina de Protección al Diabético for her perspective on these questions (personal interview with author, May 22, 2006).
3 In this program, the government buys medicines at low cost from transnational firms. These medicines are distributed for free (and in packaging that does not display a commercial name) through primary care centers (CAPs) that are located throughout the country (Tobar 2004).
4 Raphael Bondi, personal communication with author, 2006.
5 Federico Tobar, personal communication with author, 2006.

6   It should be noted that in Brazil, state financing of the biomedical and pharmaceutical sectors has been accompanied, since 1996, by what João Biehl calls a dynamic relation to transnational firms who have remained highly involved in the Brazilian market for antiretrovirals (Biehl 2004).
7   Personal communication with author, 2006.
8   The US-based Pharmaceutical Research and Manufacturer's Association, PhRMA, in turn, led the charge against what it called "local pirate firms" in hard-edged trade disputes between the United States and Argentina throughout the 1990s. Argentina consistently featured in US State Department and US Trade Representative assessments as Latin America's most egregious pharmaceutical pirate, and the Clinton administration levied trade sanctions in 1997. For the extensive timeline of this dispute, see Mattson 2005.
9   Personal communication with author, 2006; my translation.
10 Néstor Carbajal, personal communication with author, 2006; my translation.
11 Maurice Cassier and Marilena Correa have also made an eloquent case on this point in much of their work in Brazil (see Cassier and Correa 2007) as have Lawrence Liang (2014) and Kavita Philip (2014) in their analyses of the figure of the pirate, especially but not only in South Asia.
12 Daniel Maceira, personal communication with author, 2006.
13 Personal communication with author, May 19, 2006; my emphasis.
14 Cohen writes evocatively of de-duplication in the context of the aspirational biometric database of the contemporary Indian state. AADHAAR, the database, has been proposed as a tool for weeding out corruption in state benefit distribution and more broadly for managing the population as one might manage a database: by trying to eliminate duplications and multiplicities and hence inscribing a fixed relation between one and only person and one and only one set of biometric markers. This aspiration, as Cohen notes, consistently produces its own excesses and its own violences (Cohen 2019).
15 Personal communication with author, 2004; my emphasis.
16 Personal communication with author, May 2006.
17 Mauro Ramírez, personal communication with author, May 31, 2006.
18 Federico Tobar, personal communication with author, May 2006.
19 Personal communication with author, May 2006.
20 Personal communication with author, May 2006.
21 Personal communication with author, May 2006.
22 Gonzalez García defends himself against this claim in a 2010 interview with the Mexican press, reprinted (or, rather, reposted) by an Argentine outlet. See *El Ojo Digital* 2010.
23 Personal communication with author, May 2006.
24 Personal communication with author, May 2006.
25 Alfonso Ferreira, personal communication with author, May 12, 2006.
26 Patricia Silva, personal communication with author, 2006.

27 Federico Tobar, personal communication with author, May 19, 2006.
28 Personal communication with author, May 2006.
29 Personal communication with author, 2006.
30 Personal communication with author, May 2006.
31 Guyer (2009) notes that from Marx we have long known that "the commodity and its price is a fetish (that conceals the social relationships on which it is based and confuses the analytical components of use and exchange value)" (204). And from Polanyi (1944), we have the argument that some commodities are almost self-evidently fictions. Land, labor, and capital are his iconic examples of the "fictitious commodity": commodities for which we know very well that price must be invented because no "market process" brought them into being. The contingency of their price is worn on their sleeve. But she notes that there is less and less point in maintaining a distinction between "real" and "fictitious" commodities in this sense: "In the twenty first century . . . an interesting phenomenon has begun to emerge, namely, an increasingly open recognition that prices are composites, across the board. People are actually reminded that all prices are fictions—literally the results of narratives of creation, addition, and subtraction—in ways that go far beyond Polanyi's discussion of 'fictitious commodities' in the mid-twentieth century or Marx's theory of commodity fetishism in the mid-nineteenth" (Guyer 2009, 204).
32 Joseph Dumit's work with pharmaceutical marketers in the United States illuminates clearly how corporate "obligation" has become sutured to the imperative to grow shareholder value, not to improving health outcomes (Dumit 2012). For one among many proposals for alternative research and development models that are not patent- and profit-driven, see Universities Allied for Essential Medicines (n.d.).
33 Personal communication with author, June 2006.
34 Personal communication with author, May 22, 2006.
35 Counterintuitively, perhaps, pharmaco-economists have also shown that once a leading-brand drug faces generic competition, the laboratory producing the "original" sometimes ***raises*** the price on the leading brand, hoping to bank on a solid core of brand loyalty and make up for any generic-driven sales losses (see Frank and Salkever 1997).
36 For an extended analysis of this dynamic, see Vasallo and Falbo (2007).
37 Personal communication with author, May 2006. See also Goldstein 2012, 221
38 Personal communication with author.
39 Personal communication with author, May 2006.
40 Personal communication with author, May 2006.
41 Personal communication with author, May 2006.
42 Personal communication with author, May 2006.

CHAPTER FOUR. ACCESS, EXCESS

1. Personal communication with author, June 2005.
2. Personal communication with author, June 2005.
3. Personal communication with author, June 2007.
4. Mikel Arriola, opening speech at the VECTOR PHARMA conference, Hyatt Regency, México City, Mexico, June 4, 2013.
5. Interview with author, 2013.
6. Interview with author, 2013.
7. Interview with author, 2013.
8. See also Julie Erfani's observations (1995) on the longer-term question of the "paradox of sovereignty" vis-à-vis the Mexican state.
9. Personal communication with author, 2008.
10. Feminist and Indigenous science studies scholars, including M. Murphy (2017) and Max Liboiron (2021), have been making this argument persuasively in the context of chemical pollution and settler colonialism.
11. As Arshadul Haque and colleagues write, "It is recognized that, at the time of marketing authorization, information on the safety of medicinal products is limited. Thus, PMS [postmarketing surveillance] studies—through data mining of patient records, for example—are [increasingly] being required for the identification and further characterization of the known risks, or for the identification of new risks, of a medicinal product in clinical practice" (2017, 684).
12. The rise of the self-tracking movement (which started in the United States but has since become an international phenomenon), speaks directly to this understanding of consumption and personal data-gathering as the locus of true knowledge ("I am an n of 1"), especially but not only where medicines and health are concerned (see Neff and Nafus 2016).
13. Personal communication with author, 2005.
14. Personal communication with author, 2005.
15. Marco Antonio Hernández, personal communication with author, April 6, 2013.
16. Thanks to Laura Cházaro for stimulating conversations on this point.
17. Paraphrasing Prahalad, Elyachar writes, "Poor people are solving problems of infrastructure on a daily basis at the BOP, Prahalad proposed. How can MNCs gain access to those incipient solutions? NGOs are crucial to that process. They are incubators for business models, 'the lead experimenters in BOP markets'" (Elyachar 2012, 114). The experimentalization of health as consumption is a broader and longer-running story, of course. It certainly builds on the substrate of social marketing and health development from the 1970s on (see Mahaffey 2012) and a longer story of public health access for all, which, in the 1970s, built on "the China model" to bring traditional medicine to underserved communities. Now, it is about another kind of "inundation,"

the kind that consumer markets can, if provided the right circumstances, produce.
18 Among many more and less incidental mentions, the website of the Child and Family Wellness Shops, one of the poster programs for bottom-billion health interventions, reposted an article about Farmacias Similares that initially appeared in the *Wall Street Journal* (Luhnow 2005) drawing attention to Simi and his SimiChicas as a salutary (and salacious) example of a pharmacy business that caters to the poor.
19 See also Erin Mahaffey's (2012) insightful analysis of social marketing.
20 Personal communication with author, 2008.
21 Personal communication with author, 2008.
22 Personal communication with author, 2008.
23 Personal communication with author, 2008.
24 Personal communication with author, 2008.
25 Personal communication with author, 2008.
26 Personal communication with author, 2008.

CHAPTER FIVE. SUPERGENERIC VS. MERE COMMODITY

1 Personal communication with author, 2013.
2 There were at that time several escitaloprams manufactured by diverse laboratories with approvals from the secretary of health and COFEPRIS for sale in Mexico. The approved versions all carried their own brand names; as such they were not certified by the state as bioequivalent GIs (interchangeable generics).
3 Personal communication with author, 2006.
4 Antonio Salazar, personal communication with author, 2013.
5 In 2016 alone, eighteen Mexican pharmaceutical laboratories closed down.
6 News coverage in the United States certainly made the same case. See Pollack (2013) for an example.
7 The FDA notes that approval for a biosimilar can be granted when "the biological product is highly similar to the reference product notwithstanding minor differences in clinically inactive components" and that "there are no clinically meaningful differences between the biological product and the reference product in terms of the safety, purity, and potency of the product" (US Food and Drug Administration 2012).
8 In her trenchant account of the implications of the intellectual property-fueled biotechnology boom in the 1990s, Donna Haraway (2018) argued that, with patented transgenic organisms, biological kinds (mouse) had become brands (OncoMouse). The scenarios I am talking about in this chapter certainly intensify that argument. Haraway's intervention extended into the realm of "the biological" extant critiques of capital and consumerism in which

the twentieth century had in fact already delivered us to this rather spectacularized extreme: a world so hypersaturated with signs and signification that there is nothing "real," prior, unmarked—just brands and signs all the way down (Baudrillard 1994; Mendoza 2010). The question for Haraway, and the question for Baudrillard and others, was, What kind of political subjectivities are possible in such a world? Here, I am interested in a slightly off-kilter question: What kind of politics might be possible or even necessary in defense of, and in the name of, the mere commodity?

CODA

1   See also the coverage of statements to this effect by López Obrador's secretary of health, who has blamed arrangements under the Seguro Popular for tying the hands of hospitals where pharmaceutical provisioning contracts are concerned. See *El Universal* (2020a); Morales and Villa y Cañales (2020).

References

Abbas, Akbar. 2008. "Faking Globalization." In *Other Cities, Other Worlds: Urban Imaginaries in a Globalizing Age*, edited by Andreas Huyssen, 243–66. Durham, NC: Duke University Press.

Abbott, Frederick. 2005. "The WTO Medicines Decision: World Pharmaceutical Trade and the Protection of Public Health." *American Journal of International Law* 99:317–58.

Agard-Jones, Vanessa. 2013. "Bodies in the System." *Small Axe* 17 (3): 182–92.

Alder, Ken. 1998. "Making Things the Same: Representation, Tolerance and the End of the Ancien Regime in France." *Social Studies of Science* 28 (4): 499–545.

Alvarez Texocotitla, Miguel. 2019. "¿Neoliberalismo populista en México?" Deuda, crisis financiera y desarrollo económico (Debt, financial crisis and economic development), Universidad Autonoma Metropolitana. http://doi.org.10.13140/RG.2.2.13463.73126.

Anderson, Bárbara, and Alma López. 2008. "La revancha del Doctor Simi en México." *CIPER*, December 15. http://ciperchile.cl/2008/12/15/la-revancha-del-doctor-simi-en-mexico/.

Anour, René. 2014. "Biosimilars versus 'Biobetters'—A Regulator's Perspective." *GaBI Journal* 3 (4): 166–67.

Aristegui Noticias Network. 2015. "Partido Verde favorece a los González Torres con los vales: Morena" (video). February. https://aristeguinoticias.com/undefined/mexico/partido-verde-favorece-a-los-gonzalez-torres-con-los-vales-morena/.

Arriola, Mikel. 2013. "Opening Remarks." VECTOR PHARMA conference, Hyatt Regency, Mexico City, Mexico, June 4.

Asociación de Fabricantes de Medicamentos de Libre Acceso (AFAMELA). 2015. Advancing Self-Care and Responsible Self-Medication conference, Mexico City, October 5–6. http://www.afamela.org/docs/AFAMELA-WSMI-Conference-Program.pdf.

Asociación Mexicana de Genéricos Intercambiables (AMEGI). 2007. Accessed February 12, 2014. http://www.amegi.com.mx/pages/medicamentos_genericos.html.

Auyero, Javier. 2001. *Poor People's Politics: Peronist Survival Networks and the Legacy of Evita*. Durham, NC: Duke University Press.

Banerjee, Dwaipayan. 2017. "Markets and Molecules: A Pharmaceutical Primer from the South." *Medical Anthropology* 36 (4): 363–80.

Barry, Andrew. 2005. "Pharmaceutical Matters: The Invention of Informed Materials." *Theory, Culture, and Society* 22 (1):51–69.

Baudrillard, Jean. 1994. *Simulacra and Simulation*. Translated by Sheila Faria Glaser. Ann Arbor: University of Michigan Press.

Belmont, José Antonio and Jannet López Ponce. 2018. "AMLO promete que sistema de salud como Europa." *Milenio*, October 12. http://www.milenio.com/politica/amlo-promete-sistema-de-salud-como-europa.

Ben-Maimon, Carole S., and Rob Garnick. 2006. "Biogenerics at the Crossroads." *Nature Biotechnology* 24 (3): 268–69. http://doi.org10.1038/nbt0306–268a.

Bensaude-Vincent, Bernadette, and Isabelle Stengers. 1996. *A History of Chemistry*. Cambridge, MA: Harvard University Press.

Bergallo, Paola, and Agustina Ramón Michel. 2014. *The Recursivity of Global Lawmaking in the Struggle for an Argentine Policy on Pharmaceutical Patents*. Oxford: Oxford University Press.

Biehl, João. 2004. "The Activist State: Global Pharmaceuticals, AIDS, and Citizenship in Brazil." *Social Text* 22 (3): 105–32. http://doi.org10.1215/01642472–22–3_80–105.

Biehl, João. 2005. *Vita: Life in a Zone of Social Abandonment*. Berkeley: University of California Press.

Biehl, João. 2006. "Pharmaceutical Governance." In Petryna, Lakoff, and Kleinman 2006: 206–39.

Biehl, João. 2009. *Will to Live: AIDS Therapies and the Politics of Survival*. Princeton, NJ: Princeton University Press.

Biehl, João, and Adriana Petryna. 2011. "Bodies of Rights and Therapeutic Markets." *Social Research* 78 (2): 359–94.

Blanchette, Alex. 2020. *Porkopolis: American Animality, Standardized Life, and the Factory Farm*. Durham, NC: Duke University Press.

Bonilla-Chacín, M. E., and N. Aguilera. 2013. *The Mexican Social Protection System in Health*. Washington, DC: World Bank.

Borges, Jorge Luís. 1999. "On Exactitude in Science." In *Collected Fictions*, translated by Andrew Hurley, 325. New York: Penguin Random House.

Bourne Partners. 2012. "Modernizing Pharma Markets in Brazil and Mexico." June 1. http://bournepartners.wordpress.com/2012/06/01/modernizing-pharma-markets-in-brazil-and-mexico/.

Bowker, Geoffrey C., and Susan Leigh Star. 1999. *Sorting Things Out: Classification and Its Consequences*. Cambridge, MA: MIT Press.

Callon, Michel, Cécile Méadel, and Vololona Rabeharisoa. 2002. "The Economy of Qualities." *Economy and Society* 31 (2): 194–217. http://doi.org10.1080/03085140220123126.

Camp, Roderic A. 1989. *Entrepreneurs and Politics in Twentieth-Century Mexico*. Oxford: Oxford University Press.

Carpenter, Daniel, and Dominique Tobbell. 2011. "Bioequivalence: The Regulatory Career of a Pharmaceutical Concept." *Bulletin of the History of Medicine* 85 (1): 93–131.

Cassier, Maurice, and Marilena Correa. 2007. "Intellectual Property and Public Health: Copying of HIV/Aids Drugs by Brazilian Public and Private Pharmaceutical Laboratories." *RECIIS Electronic Journal of Communication, Information & Innovation in Health* 1 (1): 83–90.

Cassier, Maurice, and Marilena Correa. 2009. "Éloge de la copie: Le *reverse engineering* des antirétrovireaux contre le VIH/sida dans les laboratoires pharmaceutiques brésiliens." *Sciences Sociales et Santé* 27 (3): 77–103.

Cassier, Maurice, and Marilena Correa. 2013. "Eulogy for Copying: Reverse Engineering, Generics, and Public Health in Brazil in the Age of HIV/AIDS." December. Unpublished paper, used with permission of the authors.

Castañeda, Rafael Rodriguez, and Luciano Campos Garza. 2009. *El México narco*. Mexico City: Planeta.

Célis, Fernanda. 2016. "El Doctor Simi domina mercado de farmacias en México." *Forbes México*, September 27. https://www.forbes.com.mx/el-doctor-simi-domina-el-mercado-de-farmacias-en-mexico/.

Charles, Stephen A. 2005. "SuperGenerics: A Better Alternative for Biogenerics." *Drug Discovery Today* 10 (8): 533–34.

Cházaro, Laura. 2013. "La fisiología de la respiración en las alturas, un debate por la patria: Mediciones y experimentos." In *México Francia: Memoria de una sensibilidad común; siglos XIX–XX. Tomo II*, edited by Javier Perez-Siller and Chantai Cramaussel, 317–39. Mexico City: Centro de Estudios Mexicanos y Centroamericanos.

Choy, Timothy. 2018. "Tending to Suspension: Abstraction and Apparatuses of Atmospheric Attunement in Matsutake Worlds." *Social Analysis* 62 (4): 54–77.

Chu, Michael, and Regina Garcia-Cuellar. 2007. *Farmacias Similares: Private and Public Health Care for the Base of the Pyramid in Mexico*. Cambridge, MA: Harvard Business School.

Clarín. 2004. "Llegó a la Argentina la guerra de las grandes farmacias mexicanas." June 10. http://www.clarin.com/diario/2004/06/10/elpais/p-02003.htm.

CNN. 2018. "AMLO sustituirá el Seguro Popular en México por un nuevo sistema de salud." December 15. https://www.cnn.com/videos/spanish/2018/12/15/desaparicion-seguro-popular-mexico-amlo-nuevo-plan-nacional-salud-pkg-rey-rodriguez.cnn.

Cochoy, Franck. 2005. "A Brief History of 'Customers,' or the Gradual Standardization of Markets and Organizations." *Sociologie du Travail* 47 (1): e36–56. http://doi.org10.1016/j.soctra.2005.08.001.

Cohen, Lawrence. 2019. "The 'Social' De-Duplicated: On the Aadhaar Platform and the Engineering of Service." *South Asia: Journal of South Asian Studies* 42 (3): 482–500. http://doi.org10.1080/00856401.2019.1593597.

Comaroff, Jean. 2011. "Populism and Late Liberalism: A Special Affinity?" *Annals of the American Academy of Political and Social Science* 637 (1): 99–111. http://doi.org.10.1177/0002716211406079.

Comisión Federal de Competencia Económica. 2017. *Estudio en materia de libre concurrencia y competencia sobre los mercados de medicamentos con patentes vencidas en México*. Mexico City, 2017. https://www.cofece.mx/wp-content/uploads/2017/11/estudio-de-medicamentos_vf-baja-1.pdf.

Comision Federal para la Protección contra Riesgo Sanitario (COFEPRIS), Secretaría de Salud (Secretary of Health), Mexico. 2013. "Genéricos intercambiables." http://www.salud.gob.mx/unidades/cofepris/bv/gi.htm.

Coombe, Rosemary. 1998. *The Cultural Life of Intellectual Properties: Authorship, Appropriation, and the Law*. Durham, NC: Duke University Press.

Cooper, Dale E. 2002. "Adequate Controls for New Drugs: Good Manufacturing Practice and the 1938 Federal Food, Drug, and Cosmetic Act." *Pharmacy in History* 44 (1): 12–23.

Coronel, Maribel R. 2012. "Dr. Simi, segunda fuerza en consulta externa en México." *El Economista*, July 29. https://www.eleconomista.com.mx/opinion/Dr.-Simi-segunda-fuerza-en-consulta-externa-en-Mexico-20120729-0007.html.

Coronel, Maribel R. 2016. "Sobre la situación de probiomed." *El Economista*, December 6. https://www.eleconomista.com.mx/opinion/Sobre-la-situacion-de-Probiomed-20161207-0009.html.

Correa, Carlos. 2000. "Implementing TRIPs in Developing Countries." Third World Network. Accessed July 15, 2010. http://www.twnside.org.sg/title/ment-cn.htm.

Craddock, Susan. 2017. *Compound Solutions: Pharmaceutical Alternatives for Global Health*. Minneapolis: University of Minnesota Press.

Cronista. 2004. "Farmacias del Dr. Ahorro Logra que le prohíban usar su marca a Dr. Simi." October 18. http://www.cronista.com/impresageneral/Farmacias-del-Dr.-Ahorro-logra-que-le-prohiban-usar-su-marca-a-Dr.-Simi-20041019-0058.html.

Cruz, Angeles. 2002a. "Farmacias similares apela demanda de impi y profeco." *La Jornada*, May 2. http://www.jornada.unam.mx/2002/05/30/049n2soc.php?origen=soc-jus.html.

Cruz, Angeles. 2002b. "Firmarán Amiif y Farmacias de Similares pacto de no agresión: Promoverán también el uso de medicamentos genéricos." *La Jornada*, July 2 http://www.jornada.unam.mx/2000/07/02/soc3.html.

da Costa Marques, Ivan. 2005. "Cloning Computers: From Rights of Possession to Rights of Creation." *Science as Culture* 14 (2): 139–60. http://doi.org10.1080/09505430500110887.

Daemmrich, Arthur A. 2004. *Pharmacopolitics: Drug Regulation in the United States and Germany*. Chapel Hill: University of North Carolina Press.

Das, Veena, and Ranendra K. Das. 2006. "Pharmaceuticals in Urban Ecologies: The Register of the Local." In Petryna, Lakoff, and Kleinman 2006: 171–205.

D'Avella, Nicholas. 2014. "Ecologies of Investment: Crisis Histories and Brick Futures in Argentina." *Cultural Anthropology* 29 (1): 173–99.

Day, Sophie. 2015. "Waiting and the Architecture of Care." In *Living and Dying in the Contemporary World: A Compendium*, edited by Clara Han and Veena Das, 167–84. Oakland: University of California Press.

Debord, Guy. 1994. *The Society of the Spectacle*. Translated by Donald Nicholson-Smith. New York: Zone.

de la Peña, Guillermo. 2000. "Corrupción e informalidad." In *Vicios públicos, virtudes privadas: La corrupción en México*, edited by Claudio Lomnitz, 118–23. Mexico City: Centro de Investigaciones y Estudios Superiores en Antropología Social.

Deleuze, Gilles. 1995. *Difference and Repetition*. Translated by Paul Patton. New York: Columbia University Press.

del Norte, Regio (@Gomaro Cruz). 2020. "La bronca es que algo 'similar' es Neumonía atípica y eso está matando mucha gente." Twitter, April 7. https://twitter.com/tuiteroregio/status/1247653630829707264.

Dirección General de Normas (DGN). 1998a. "Buenas prácticas de fabricación para fármacos." Norma Oficial Mexicana, NOM-164-SSA1-1998. http://www.salud.gob.mx/unidades/cdi/nom/164ssa18.html.

Dirección General de Normas (DGN). 1998b. "Que establece las pruebas y procedimientos para demostrar que un medicamento es intercambiable. Requisitos a que deben sujetarse los terceros autorizados que realicen las pruebas." Norma Oficial Mexicana, NOM-177-SSA1-1998. http://www.salud.gob.mx/unidades/cdi/nom/177ssa18.html.

Dreser, Anahí, Edna Vázquez-Vélez, Sandra Treviño, and Veronika J. Wirtz. 2012. "Regulation of Antibiotic Sales in Mexico: An Analysis of Printed Media Coverage and Stakeholder Participation." *BMC Public Health* 12:1051.

Dumit, Joseph. 2012. *Drugs for Life: How Pharmaceutical Companies Define Our Health*. Durham, NC: Duke University Press.

Ecks, Stefan. 2008. "Global Pharmaceutical Markets and Corporate Citizenship: The Case of Novartis' Anti-Cancer Drug Glivec." *BioSocieties* 3 (2): 165–81.

Ecks, Stefan. 2022. *Living Worth: Value and Values in Global Pharmaceutical Markets*. Durham, NC: Duke University Press.

Ecks, Stefan, and Soumiya Basu. 2009. "The Unlicensed Lives of Antidepressants in India: Generic Drugs, Unqualified Practitioners, and Floating Prescriptions." *Transcultural Psychiatry* 46 (1): 86–106.

Economist. 2018. "Tropical Messiah: How Andrés Manuel López Obrador Will Remake Mexico." June 23. https://www.economist.com/briefing/2018/06/21/how-andres-manuel-lopez-obrador-will-remake-mexico.

Ellingwood, Ken, and Cecilia Sanchez. 2010. "Mexico Cracks Down on Self-Prescribed Antibiotics." *Los Angeles Times*, June 14.

El Ojo Digital. 2010. "Ginés González García, en el negocio de las farmacias 'Dr Ahorro.'" July. https://www.elojodigital.com/contenido/8098-gines-gonzalez-garcia-en-el-negocio-de-las-farmacias-dr-ahorro.

Eloy Martínez, Tomás. 1997. *Santa Evita*. New York: Vintage.

El Senado y Cámara de Diputados de la Nación Argentina. 2002. Ley 25.649, "Promoción de la utilización de medicamentos por su nombre genérico." August 28.

El Universal. 2004. "Crece guerra en Argentina: Dr. Simi vs Dr. Ahorro." October 28. http://www.eluniversal.com.mx/notas/252644.html.

El Universal. 2012. "Farmacias de cadena devoran el mercado." September 24.

El Universal. 2018. "Se han liberado 15 paquetes de medicamentos genéricos en últimos 7 años: Cofepris." February 27. https://www.eluniversal.com.mx/nacion/sociedad/se-han-liberado-15-paquetes-de-medicamentos-genericos-en-ultimos-7-anos-coferpris.

El Universal. 2019. "Carta íntegra de la renuncia de Germán Martínez Cázares al IMSS." May 21. https://www.eluniversal.com.mx/nacion/politica/carta-integra-de-la-renuncia-de-german-martinez-cazares-al-imss.

El Universal. 2020a. "Hospitales están 'atados' a contratos monopólicos: Ssa." January 25. https://www.eluniversal.com.mx/nacion/hospitales-estan-atados-contratos-monopolicos-ssa.

El Universal. 2020b. "La mañanera de AMLO: Gobierno adquiere medicamentos más baratos en el extranjero." March 10. https://www.eluniversal.com.mx/nacion/la-mananera-de-amlo-gobierno-adquiere-medicamentos-mas-baratos-en-el-extranjero.

Elyachar, Julia. 2005. *Markets of Dispossession: NGOs, Economic Development, and the State in Cairo*. Durham, NC: Duke University Press.

Elyachar, Julia. 2012. "Next Practices: Knowledge, Infrastructure, and Public Goods at the Bottom of the Pyramid." *Public Culture* 24 (1): 109–29.

Emanuel, Ezekiel J. 2019. "Big Pharma's Go-To Defense of Soaring Drug Prices Doesn't Add Up." *Atlantic*, March 23. https://www.theatlantic.com/health/archive/2019/03/drug-prices-high-cost-research-and-development/585253/.

Emeequis. 2012. "Vales para medicinas: Un negocio auspiciado por peña nieto." June 10. http://www.m-x.com.mx/2012-06-10/vales-para-medicinas-un-negocio-auspiciado-por-pena-nieto/.

Erfani, Julie A. 1995. *The Paradox of the Mexican State: Rereading Sovereignty from Independence to NAFTA*. Boulder, CO: L. Rienner.

Estrada, Andrés M. 2020. "Miedo en la farmacia. La pandemia alcanza al Dr. Simi y similares." *Emeequis*, June 8. https://m-x.com.mx/al-dia/miedo-en-la-farmacia-la-pandemia-alcanza-al-dr-simi-y-similares.

European Medicines Agency. 2005. *Guideline on Similar Biological Medicinal Products*. Committee for Medicinal Products for Human Use (CHMP), October 23. https://www.ema.europa.eu/en/documents/scientific-guideline/guideline-similar-biological-medicinal-products-rev1_en.pdf.

Federación Mexicana de Diabetes. 2015. "Secretaría de Salud aprueba paquete de medicamentos genéricos." December 10. http://fmdiabetes.org/secretaria-de-salud-aprueba-paquete-de-medicamentos-genericos/.

Ferguson, James, and Tania Li. 2018. *Beyond the "Proper Job": Political-Economic Analysis after the Century of Labouring Man*. Cape Town: PLASS, UWC.

Frank, R. G., and D. S. Salkever. 1997. "Generic Entry and the Market for Pharmaceuticals." *Journal of Economics and Management Strategy* 6 (1): 75–90.

Franklin, Sarah. 2007. *Dolly Mixtures: The Remaking of Genealogy*. Durham, NC: Duke University Press.

Frenk, Julio. 2006. "Bridging the Divide: Global Lessons from Evidence-Based Health Policy in Mexico." *Lancet* 368 (9539): 954–61. http://doi.org.10.1016/S0140-6736(06)69376-8.

Frenk, Julio, O. Gómez-Dantés, and F. M. Marie Knaul. 2009. "The Democratization of Health in Mexico: Financial Innovations for Universal Coverage." *Bulletin of the World Health Organization* 87:542–48.

Gago, Verónica. 2014. *Neoliberalism from Below: Popular Pragmatics and Baroque Economies*. Translated by Liz Mason-Deese. Durham, NC: Duke University Press.

Galván Ochoa, Enríque. 2006. "Candidato genérico intercambiable." *La Jornada*, Jan 13.

Garcia, Angela. 2015. "Serenity: Violence, Inequality, and Recovery on the Edge of Mexico City." *Medical Anthropology Quarterly* 29 (4): 455–72. http://doi.org.10.1111/maq.12208.

García Canclini, Nestor. 1995. *Hybrid Cultures: Strategies for Entering and Leaving Modernity*. Translated by C. Chiappari and S. López. Minneapolis: University of Minnesota Press.

García Canclini, Nestor. 2001. *Consumers and Citizens: Globalization and Multicultural Conflicts*. Translated by G. Yúdice. Minneapolis: University of Minnesota Press.

Garnick, Rob. 2006. "Counterpoint: Why Biogenerics Are a Strawman." *Nature Biotechnology* 24 (3): 269.

Garzón Ortiz, Laura. 2006. "Farmacias: El aterrizaje del Doctor Simi." *Economía y Negocios*, January 8. http://www.economiaynegocios.cl/noticias/noticias.asp?id=14573.

Generics and Biosimilars Initiative (GABI). 2011. "Biobetters Rather Than Biosimilars." Accessed February 7, 2013. http://gabionline.net/Biosimilars/General/Biobetters-rather-than-biosimilars.

Gobierno de México. 2020. Insabi. https://www.gob.mx/insabi.

Goldstein, Donna. 2012. "How Corruption Kills: Pharmaceutical Crime, Mediated Representations, and Middle Class Anxiety in Neoliberal Anxiety." *City and Society* 24 (2): 218–39.

Gomart, Emilie. 2002. "Methadone: Six Effects in Search of a Substance." *Social Studies of Science* 32 (1): 93–135. http://doi.org.10.1177/0306312702032001005.

González, Jesús S. 2002. *Industry Sector Analysis: Drugs and Pharmaceuticals, Mexico 2*. Industry Sector Analysis. Washington, DC: US Department of Commerce.

González Amador, Roberto. 1997. "Empresario mexicano lanza al mercado serie de productos 'similares' para abatir precios." *La Jornada*, November 12.

González Garcia, Ginés. 2004. "Presentación de la política nacional de medicamentos en la República del Perú." Ministerio de Salud (Argentina), September 3.

Greene, Jeremy. 2011. "What's in a Name? Generics and the Persistence of the Pharmaceutical Brand in American Medicine." *Journal of the History of Medicine and Allied Sciences* 66 (4): 468–506. http://doi.org.10.1093/jhmas/jrq049.

Greene, Jeremy. 2014. *Generic: The Unbranding of Modern Medicine*. Baltimore, MD: Johns Hopkins University Press.

Grupo Por Un Pais Mejor. 2005. *El Universal*, December 22.

Guyer, Jane. 2004. *Marginal Gains: Monetary Transactions in Atlantic Africa*. Chicago: University of Chicago Press.

Guyer, Jane. 2007. "Prophecy and the Near Future: Thoughts on Macroeconomic, Evangelical, and Punctuated Time." *American Ethnologist* 34 (3): 409–21. http://doi.org.10.1525/ae.2007.34.3.409.

Guyer, Jane. 2009. "Composites, Fictions, and Risk: Toward an Ethnography of Price." In *Market and Society: The Great Transformation Today*, edited by Chris Hann and Keith Hart, 203–20. Cambridge, MA: Cambridge University Press.

Hammond, Allen, William J. Kramer, Julia Tran, Rob Katz, and Courtland Walker. 2007. *The Next 4 Billion: Market Size and Business Strategy at the Base of the Pyramid*. Washington, DC: World Resources Institute.

Haraway, Donna J. 2018. *Modest_Witness@Second_Millennium.FemaleMan©_Meets_OncoMouse™: Feminism and Technoscience*. New York: Routledge.

Haque, Arshadul, Sajjan Daniel, Tricia Maxwell, and Mariette Boerstoel. 2017. "Postmarketing Surveillance Studies: An Industry Perspective on Changing Global Requirements and Implications." *Clinical Therapeutics* 39 (4): 675–85. http://doi.org.10.1016/j.clinthera.2017.03.011.

Hayat, Zahra. 2021. "The Scandal of Access: Pharmaceutical Price, Quality, and Property in Pakistan." PhD diss., University of California, Berkeley.

Hayden, Cori. 2003. *When Nature Goes Public: The Making and Unmaking of Bioprospecting in Mexico*. Princeton, NJ: Princeton University Press.

Hayden, Cori. 2007. "A Generic Solution? Pharmaceuticals and the Politics of the Similar in Mexico." *Current Anthropology* 48 (4): 475–95.

Hayden, Cori. 2010. "The Proper Copy." *Journal of Cultural Economy* 3 (1): 85–102. http://doi.org.10.1080/17530351003617602.

Hayden, Cori. 2011. "No Patent, No Generic: Pharmaceutical Access and the Politics of the Copy." In *Making and Unmaking Intellectual Property: Creative Production in Legal and Cultural Perspective*, edited by Mario Biagioli, Peter Jaszi, and Martha Woodmansee, 285–304. Chicago: University of Chicago Press.

Hayden, Cori. 2012. "Rethinking Reductionism, or, the Transformative Work of Making the Same." *Anthropological Forum* 22 (3): 271–83. http://doi.org.10.1080/00664677.2012.711240.

Hayden, Cori. 2013. "Distinctively Similar: A Generic Problem." *UC Davis Law Review* 47 (2): 601–32.

Hernández, Jethro. 2009. "Revolutionary Medicine: Homeopathy and the Regulation of the Medical Profession in Mexico, 1853–1942." PhD diss., University of California, San Francisco.

Hess, María Luisa Benítez. 1998. "Evaluación de los criterios actuals de bioequivalencia con respecto al curso temporal del efecto farmacológico." MA thesis, Center for Research and Advanced Studies of the National Polytechnic Institute, San Pedro, Mexico.

Hoffmann, Roald. 1995. *The Same and Not the Same*. New York: Columbia University Press.

Holston, James. 2008. *Insurgent Citizenship: Disjunctions of Democracy and Modernity in Brazil*. Princeton, NJ: Princeton University Press.

Homedes, Núria, and Antonio Ugalde. 2005. "Multisource Drug Policies in Latin America: Survey of 10 Countries." *Bulletin of the World Health Organization* 83 (1): 64–70.

Horkheimer, Max, and Theodor W. Adorno. 2002. "The Culture Industry: Enlightenment as Mass Deception." In *Dialectic of Enlightenment: Philosophical Fragments*, edited by Gunzelin Schmid Noerr, translated by Edmund Jephcott, 94–136. Stanford, CA: Stanford University Press.

Hornberger, Julia. 2018. "From Drug Safety to Drug Security: A Contemporary Shift in the Policing of Health." *Medical Anthropology Quarterly* 32 (3): 365–83. http://doi.org.10.1111/maq.12432.

Hubbard, Tim, and James Love. 2004. "Paying for Public Goods." In *Code: Collaborative Ownership and the Digital Economy*, edited by Rishab Ghosh, 207–29. Cambridge, MA: MIT Press.

IntraMed. 2003. "Home." Centro de Atención IntraMed. http://www.intramed.net/contenidover.asp?contenidoID=24561&pagina=3.

Johnson, Tim. 2012. "For Mexico's Ecologist Green Party, 'Green' Mostly Means Money, Not Environment." McClatchy DC, June 18. http://www.mcclatchydc.com/2012/06/18/152479_for-mexicos-ecologist-green-party.html?rh=1.

Junod, Suzanne White. 2004. "'God, Motherhood, and the Flag': Implementing the First Pharmaceutical Current Good Manufacturing Practices (CGMP's) Regulations." US Food and Drug Administration. https://www.fda.gov/media/110460/download.

Kapczynski, Amy. 2009. "Harmonization and Its Discontents: A Case Study of TRIPS Implementation in India's Pharmaceutical Sector." *California Law Review* 97:1571–1650.

Kapczynski, Amy. 2013. "Engineered in India—Patent Law 2.0." *New England Journal of Medicine* 369:497–99. http://doi.org.10.1056/NEJMp1304400.

Karalis, Vangelis, and Panos Macheras. 2003. "Pharmacodynamic Considerations in Bioequivalence Assessment: Comparison of Novel and Existing Metrics." *European Journal of Pharmaceutical Sciences* 19 (1): 45–56. https://doi.org/10.1016/S0928-0987(03)00064-2.

Katz, Jorge, and Gustavo Burachik. 1997. *La industria farmacéutica y farmoquímica Argentina en los años 90*. Santiago: Naciones Unidas Comisión Económica para América Latina y el Caribe (CEPAL).

Kiddle, Amelia, and Maria Muñoz. 2010. *Populism in Twentieth Century Mexico: The Presidencies of Lázaro Cárdenas and Luis Echeverría*. Tucson: University of Arizona Press.

Knaul, Felicia Marie, Eduardo González-Pier, Octavio Gómez-Dantés, David García-Junco, Héctor Arreola-Ornelas, Mariana Barraza-Lloréns, Rosa Sandoval, et al. 2012. "The Quest for Universal Health Coverage: Achieving Social Protection for All in Mexico." *Lancet* 380 (9849): 1259–79. http://doi.org.10.1016/S0140-6736(12)61068-X.

Krikorian, Gaelle, and Amy Kapczynski. 2010. *Access to Knowledge in the Age of Intellectual Property*. New York: Zone.

Laclau, Ernesto. 2005. *On Populist Reason*. London: Verso.

Lakoff, Andrew. 2004. "The Private Life of Numbers: Audit Firms and the Government of Expertise in Post-Welfare Argentina." In *Global Assemblages: Governmentality, Technology, Ethics*, edited by Stephen Collier and Aihwa Ong, 194–213. New York: Blackwell.

Lakoff, Andrew. 2005. *Pharmaceutical Reason: Knowledge and Value in Global Psychiatry*. Cambridge: Cambridge University Press.

Lakoff, Andrew. 2006. "High Contact: Gifts and Surveillance in Argentina." In Petryna, Lakoff, and Kleinman 2006: 111–35.

Lamprea, Everaldo. 2017. "The Judicialization of Health Care: A Global South Perspective." *Annual Review of Law and Social Science* 13 (1): 431–49. http://doi.org.10.1146/annurev-lawsocsci-110316-113303.

Landecker, Hannah. 2013. "Postindustrial Metabolism: Fat Knowledge." *Public Culture* 25 (3): 495–522. http://doi.org.10.1215/08992363-2144625.

Lara, Gabriel, and Rocío Campos. 2003. "La inviabilidad del Seguro Popular." *Reforma*, December 7.

Larkin, Brian. 2004. "Degraded Images, Distorted Sounds: Nigerian Video and the Infrastructure of Piracy." *Public Culture* 16 (2): 289–314

Las historias de un Ente mexicano (blog). 2010. "Medicamentos en México un mundo de oferta!!" February 26. http://unentemexicano.blogspot.com/2010/02/medicamentos-en-mexico-un-mundo-de.html.

Lemus, Rafael. 2019. "AMLO en el laberinto neoliberal." *New York Times*, July 8. https://www.nytimes.com/es/2019/07/08/espanol/opinion/lopez-obrador-neoliberalismo.html.

Leslie, Esther. 2005. *Synthetic Worlds: Nature, Art, and the Chemical Industry*. Kings Lynn, UK: Reaktion.

Liang, Lawrence. 2014. "Beyond Representation: The Figure of the Pirate." In *Postcolonial Piracy: Media Distribution and Cultural Production in the Global South*, edited by Lars Eckstein and Anja Schwarz, 49–78. London: Bloomsbury Academic.

Liboiron, Max. 2021. *Pollution Is Colonialism*. Durham, NC: Duke University Press.

Lomnitz, Claudio, ed. 2000. *Vicios públicos, Virtudes privadas: La corrupción en México*. Mexico City: Miguel Ángel Porrúa.

Lomnitz, Claudio. 2001. *Deep Mexico, Silent Mexico: An Anthropology of Nationalism*. Minneapolis: University of Minnesota Press.

Lovell, Anne. 2006. "Addiction Markets: The Case of High-Dose Buprenorphine in France." In Petryna, Lakoff, and Kleinman 2006: 136–70.

Luhnow, David. 2005. "In Mexico, Maker of Generics Adds Spice to Drug Business." *Wall Street Journal*, February 14. http://online.wsj.com/article/SB110833733909653530.html.

Lury, Celia. 2004. *Brands: The Logos of the Global Economy*. New York: Routledge.

Macías, Misael. 2020. "El SP, no era seguro ni popular: AMLO." *Mundofarma*, January 8. https://mundofarma.com.mx/el-sp-no-era-seguro-ni-popular-amlo/.

Macroeconomia (Mexico). 2015. "Víctor González Torres partió plaza y llenó el Toreo de Cuatro Caminos." July 14.

Mahaffey, Erin. 2012. "Privatizing Public Health: Social Marketing for HIV Prevention in Tanzania, East Africa." PhD Diss., University of California, Berkeley.

Martínez, Fabiola. 2020. "Entra en vigor el plan de austeridad de AMLO." *La Jornada*, April 23. https://www.jornada.com.mx/ultimas/politica/2020/04/23/entra-en-vigor-el-plan-de-austeridad-de-amlo-8379.html.

Martínez, G., N. Aguilera, and D. Chernichovsky. 2009. *Reform of Mexican Health Care System*. Israel: Guilford Glazer School of Business and Management, Ben-Gurion University of the Negev.

Martínez Cázares, Germán. 2019. "Carta íntegra de la renuncia de Germán Martínez Cázares al IMSS." *El Universal*, May 21. https://www.eluniversal.com.mx/nacion/politica/carta-integra-de-la-renuncia-de-german-martinez-cazares-al-imss.

Marx, Karl. 1978. *Capital*, vol. 1. In *The Marx-Engels Reader*, 2nd ed., edited by Robert Tucker, 294–438. New York: W. W. Norton.

Mattson, Jennifer Ellen. 2005. "Timeline of US-Argentina Dispute on Pharmaceutical Patents." CP Tech, April 20. http://www.cptech.org/ip/health/c/argentina/argentinatimeline.html.

Mazzarella, William. 2003. *Shoveling Smoke: Advertising and Globalization in Contemporary India*. Durham, NC: Duke University Press.

Medina, Eden, Ivan da Costa Marques, and Christina Holmes, ed. 2014. *Beyond Imported Magic: Essays on Science, Technology, and Society in Latin America*. Cambridge, MA: MIT Press.

Mendoza, Daryl Y. 2010. "Commodity, Sign, and Spectacle." *Kritike* 4 (2): 45–59.

Mishori, Janit. 2011. "Why Are Generic Drugs Cheaper Than Brand-Name Ones?" *Washington Post*, July 5. https://www.washingtonpost.com/national/health-science/why-are-generic-drugs-cheaper-than-brand-name-ones/2011/07/05/gIQAwZdL9H_story.html.

Moise, Pierre, and Elizabeth Docteur. 2007. "Pharmaceutical Pricing and Reimbursement Policies in Mexico." Working paper, OECD Health, Paris.

Molina-Salazar, Raúl Enrique, Eloy González-Marín, and Carolina Carbajol-de Nova. 2008. "Competencia y precios en el mercado farmacéutico mexicano." *Salúd Pública de México* 50 (4): S496–S503.

Monsiváis, Carlos. 2000. *Aires de Familia: Cultura y Sociedad en América Latina*. Barcelona: Editorial Anagrama.

Morales, Alberto. 2019. "Desabasto en salud no es por austeridad: AMLO." *El Universal*, July 8.

Morales, Alberto, and Pedro Villa y Cañales. 2020. "La mañanera de AMLO: Gobierno adquiere medicamentos más baratos en el extranjero." *El Universal*, October 3. https://www.eluniversal.com.mx/nacion/la-mananera-de-amlo-gobierno-adquiere-medicamentos-mas-baratos-en-el-extranjero.

Morales, Juan José. 2012. "Política? . . . No, negociazo!! . . . El partido verde." *¡¡Exijamos Lo Imposible!!* (blog), May 3. http://exijamosloimposible.blogspot.com/2012/05/politicano-negociazoel-partido-verde.html.

Morris, Stephen D. 1991. *Corruption and Politics in Contemporary Mexico*. Tuscaloosa: University of Alabama Press.

Morris, Stephen D. 2009. *Political Corruption in Mexico: The Impact of Democratization*. Boulder, CO: Lynne Rienner.

Murillo-Godínez, Guillermo. 2006. "Sobre los medicamentos genéricos." *Revista Médica IMSS* 44 (4): 371–72.

Murphy, Michelle. 2016. *The Economization of Life*. Durham, NC: Duke University Press.

Murphy, Michelle. 2017. "Alterlife and Decolonial Chemical Relations." *Cultural Anthropology* 32 (4): 494–503. http://doi.org.10.14506/ca32.4.02.

Napolitano, Valentina. 2002. *Migration, Mujercitas, and Medicine Men: Living in Urban Mexico*. Berkeley: University of California Press.

Neff, Gina, and Dawn Nafus. 2016. *Self-Tracking*. Cambridge, MA: MIT Press.

Nelson, Diane. 2015. *Who Counts? The Mathematics of Death and Life after Genocide*. Durham, NC: Duke University Press.

Nguyen, Vinh-Kim. 2010. *The Republic of Therapy: Triage and Sovereignty in West Africa's Time of AIDS*. Durham, NC: Duke University Press.

Niazi, Sarfaraz K. 2014. *Handbook of Bioequivalence Testing*. 2nd ed. Boca Raton, FL: CRC Press.

Nigenda, G., E. Orozco, and G. Olaiz. 2003. "La importancia de los medicamentos en la operación del Seguro Popular de salud." In *Caleidoscopia de la Salud*, edited by F. Knaul and G. Nigenda, 263–73. Mexico City: Mexican Foundation for Health (FUNSALUD).

NotimexTV. 2018. "El Seguro Popular ni es seguro ni es popular será remplazado: AMLO." YouTube, December 14. https://www.youtube.com/watch?v=FlTI7pH5kbc.

Organización Editorial Mexicana. 2012. "Farmacias surtirán medicamentos del Seguro Popular." *La Prensa*, January 11. http://www.oem.com.mx/laprensa/notas/n2380974.htm.

Pallares, Miguel. 2017. "Probiomed, mexicana que hace frente a las grandes farmacéuticas." *El Universal*, October 7. https://www.eluniversal.com.mx/articulo/cartera/economia/2017/07/10/probiomed-mexicana-que-hace-frente-las-grandes-farmaceuticas.

Panizza, Francisco. 2005. "Introduction: Populism and the Mirror of Democracy." In *Populism and the Mirror of Democracy*, edited by Francisco Panizza, 1–32. New York: Verso.

Peterson, Kristin. 2014. *Speculative Markets: Drug Circuits and Derivative Life in Nigeria*. Durham, NC: Duke University Press.

Petryna, Adriana. 2009. *When Experiments Travel: Clinical Trials and the Global Search for Human Subjects*. Princeton, NJ: Princeton University Press.

Petryna, Adriana, and Arthur Kleinman. 2006. Introduction to Petryna, Lakoff, and Kleinman 2006: 1–32.

Petryna, Adriana, Andrew Lakoff, and Arthur Kleinman, eds. 2006. *Global Pharmaceuticals: Ethics, Markets, Practices*. Durham, NC: Duke University Press.

Pharma Boardroom. 2006. "Interview: Mariano de Elizalde—General Manager, Sandoz Mexico." July 28. https://pharmaboardroom.com/interviews/interview-mariano-de-elizalde-general-manager-sandoz-mexico/.

Philip, Kavita. 2014. "Keep On Copyin' in the Free World? Genealogies of the Postcolonial Pirate Figure." In *Postcolonial Piracy: Media Distribution and Cultural Production in the Global South*, edited by Lars Eckstein and Anja Schwarz, 149–78. London: Bloomsbury Academic.

Polanyi, Karl. 1944. *The Great Transformation: The Political and Economic Origins of Our Time*. New York: Farrar and Rinehart.

Político MX. 2018. "Ya no será Seguro Popular, ni es seguro ni es popular: AMLO." July 22. https://politico.mx//minuta-politica/minuta-politica-gobierno-federal/ya-no-ser%C3%A1-seguro-popular-ni-es-seguro-ni-es-popular-amlo/.

Pollack, Andrew. 2013. "Biotech Firms, Billions at Risk, Lobby States to Limit Generics." *New York Times*, January 28. http://www.nytimes.com/2013/01/29/business/battle-in-states-on-generic-copies-of-biotech-drugs.html?pagewanted=2.

Pollock, Anne. 2011. "Transforming the Critique of Big Pharma." *BioSocieties* 6:106–18. http://doi.org.10.1057/biosoc.2010.44.

Poniatowska, Elena. 1988. *Nada, nadie: Las voces del temblor*. Mexico City: Ediciones Era.

Prahalad, C. K. 2010. *The Fortune at the Bottom of the Pyramid: Eradicating Poverty through Profits*. Upper Saddle River, NJ: Pearson Education.

Pueblita, J. C. R. 2013. "Screening Seguro Popular: The Political Economy of Universal Health Coverage in Mexico." Working paper, Center for International Development, Harvard University, Cambridge, MA. http://www.hks.harvard.edu/var/ezp_site/storage/fckeditor/file/pdfs/centers-programs/centers/cid/publications/student-fellows/wp/61_Pueblita.pdf.

Puga, Cristina. 1993. *México: Empresarios y poder*. Colección Las Ciencias sociales. Mexico: M. A. Porrúa.

Quijano, Manuel. 2006. "En torno a 'Medicamentos genéricos y originales.'" *Revista Médica del IMSS* 44 (1): 79.

Rader, Ronald A. 2007. "What Is a Generic Biopharmaceutical? Biogeneric? Follow-On Protein? Biosimilar? Follow-On Biologic?" *BioProcess International* (March): 28–38. https://www.biopharma.com/Whatsabiogeneric_pt1.pdf.

Rangel, Raymundo. 2015. "(PVEM) pacto con IMSS e ISSSTE el 'Vales por medicinas.'" *Reforma*, February 13.

Rauhala, Emily. 2019. "As Price of Insulin Soars, Americans Caravan to Canada for Lifesaving Medicine." *Washington Post*, July 31. https://www.washingtonpost.com/world/the_americas/as-price-of-insulin-soars-americans-caravan-to-canada-for-lifesaving-medicine/2019/06/14/0a272fb6-8217-11e9-9a67-a687ca99fb3d_story.html.

Reich, Michael R., Joseph Harris, Naoki Ikegami, Akiko Maeda, Cheryl Cashin, Edson C. Araujo, Keizo Takemi, and Timothy G. Evans. 2016. "Moving towards Universal Health Coverage: Lessons from 11 Country Studies." *Lancet* 387 (10020): 811–16. http://doi.org.10.1016/S0140-6736(15)60002-2.

Ribbink, Kim. 2011. "Olá Brazil: Latin America's Biggest Market Accelerates." *PharmaVOICE* (IMS Health), 50.

Rodríguez, María Alejandra. 2017. "Liberan nuevo paquete de genéricos." *El Economista*, June 6. https://www.eleconomista.com.mx/empresas/Liberan-nuevo-paquete-de-genericos-20170607-0062.html.

Rodríguez, R. 2013. "Regulan consulta médica en farmacias." *El Universal*, August 8. http://www.eluniversal.com.mx/nacion-mexico/2013/regulan-consulta-medica-en-farmacias-941099.html.

Rojas, Rodrigo. 2020. "Profeco va contra 'Dr. Simi' por aumentar el precio de cubrebocas." *Saludiario*, March 3. https://www.saludiario.com/profeco-va-contra-dr-simi-por-aumentar-el-precio-de-cubrebocas/.

Rossi, Julieta, and Carolina Varsky. 2002. "La salud bajo la ley del mercado." In *Derechos humanos en la Argentina, informe 2002: Hechos 2001*. Buenos Aires: El Centro de Estudios Legales y Sociales (CELS).

Roy, Ananya. 2010. *Poverty Capital: Microfinance and the Making of Development*. New York: Routledge.

Roy, Ananya. 2012. "Subjects of Risk: Technologies of Gender in the Making of Millennial Modernity." *Public Culture* 24, no. 1 (66): 131–55.

Ruíz, María E. 2010. "Risks of Self-Medication Practices." *Current Drug Safety* 5 (4): 315–23. http://doi.org.10.2174/157488610792245966.

Sahuí, Alejandro, ed. 2009. *Gobernanza y sociedad civil: Retos democráticos*. Mexico City: Ediciones Coyoacán.

Sainz, Alfredo. 2008. "El negocio de los medicamentos genéricos: La cadena Dr. Simi Cerró Todas sus farmacias en la Argentina." *La Nación*, August 6. https://www.lanacion.com.ar/economia/la-cadena-dr-simi-cerro-todas-sus-farmacias-en-la-argentina-nid1036921/.

Salazar, Amílcar. 2000. "La guerra: El único que pierde es el enfermo." *El Universal*, March 11. http://archivo.eluniversal.com.mx/nacion/17440.html.

Sanabria, Emilia. 2010. "From Sub- to Super Citizenship: Sex Hormones and the Body Politic in Brazil." *Ethnos* 75 (4): 377–401. http://doi.org.10.1080/00141844.2010.544393.

Sanabria, Emilia. 2014. "'The Same Thing in a Different Box': Similarity and Difference in Pharmaceutical Sex Hormone Consumption and Marketing." *Medical Anthropology Quarterly* 28 (4): 537–55.

Sánchez, Rafael. 2016. *Dancing Jacobins: A Venezuelan Genealogy of Latin American Populism*. New York: Fordham University Press.

Sarlo, Beatriz. 2001. *Tiempo presente: Notas sobre el cambio de una cultura*. Buenos Aires: Siglo Veintiuno Editores Argentina.

Secretaría de Salud. 2005. *Hacía una política farmaceútica integral en México*. Mexico City: Secretaría de Salud, Sistema Federal Sanitario, and COFEPRIS.

Schneider, Christian K., and Ulrich Kalinke. 2008. "Toward Biosimilar Monoclonal Antibodies." *Nature Biotechnology* 26 (9): 985–90. http://doi.org10.1038/nbt0908-985.

Schwartz, Frederic J. 1996. "Commodity Signs: Peter Behrens, the AEG, and the Trademark." *Journal of Design History* 9 (3): 153–84.

Schwartz, Hillel. 1996. *The Culture of the Copy: Striking Likenesses, Unreasonable Facsimiles*. Cambridge, MA: MIT Press.

Schwegler, Tara A. 2004. "Economics in Action: Negotiating Authority and Building Markets in Mexico." PhD diss., University of Chicago.

Schwegler, Tara A. 2008. "Take It from the Top (Down)? Rethinking Neoliberalism and Political Hierarchy in Mexico." *American Ethnologist* 35 (4): 682–700. http://doi.org.10.1111/j.1548–1425.2008.00105.x.

Schwegler, Tara. 2011. "Intimate Knowledge and the Politics of Policy Convergence: The World Bank and Social Security Reform in Mexico." In *Policy Worlds: Anthropology and the Analysis of Contemporary Power*, edited by Cris Shore, Susan Wright, and Davide Pero, 130–50. New York: Berghahn Books.

Shadlen, Kenneth. 2007. "The Political Economy of AIDS Treatment: Intellectual Property and the Transformation of Generic Supply." *International Studies Quarterly* 51:559–81. http://doi.org.10.1111/j.1468–2478.2007.00464.x.

Shadlen, Kenneth C., and S. Guennif. 2011. *Intellectual Property, Pharmaceuticals and Public Health: Access to Drugs in Developing Countries*. Northampton, MA: Edward Elgar.

Shepherd, Alan. 2013. Discussion and commentary, "Vector Pharma." Conference, Mexico City, June 4.

Sheridan, Mary Beth. 2020. "Coronavirus Outbreaks at Mexico's Hospitals Raise Alarm, Protests." *Washington Post*, April 19. https://www.washingtonpost.com/world/the_americas/mexico-coronavirus-hospital-outbreaks-imss-amlo/2020/04/18/e3a4e48e-7f66-11ea-84c2-0792d8591911_story.html.

Sherwood, Robert. 1991. "Pharmaceuticals: U.S. Perspective." In *US-Mexican Industrial Integration: The Road to Free Trade*, edited by Sidney Weintraub, Luis Rubio F., and Alan D. Jones, 161–79. Boulder, CO: Westview.

Shewhart, Walter. 1931. *Economic Control of Quality of Manufactured Product*. New York: D. Van Nostrand.

Singer, Natasha. 2010. "Drug Firms Apply Brand to Generics." *New York Times*, February 16. http://www.nytimes.com/2010/02/16/business/16generic.html.

Silverman, Ed. 2016. "Teva, One of the Biggest Generic Makers, Joins the Brand-Name Club." *STAT*, July 18. https://www.statnews.com/pharmalot/2016/07/18/teva-generics-phrma/.

Slaton, Amy E. 2001. "'As Near as Practicable': Precision, Ambiguity, and the Social Features of Industrial Quality Control." *Technology and Culture* 42 (1): 51–80.

Soto Laveaga, Gabriela. 2003. "Steroid Hormones and Social Relations in Oaxaca." In *The Social Relations of Mexican Commodities: Power, Production, and Place*, edited by Casey Walsh, Elizabeth Emma Ferry, Gabriela

Soto Laveaga, Paola Sesia, and Sarah Hill, 81–126. San Diego: Center for US-Mexican Studies.

Soto Laveaga, Gabriela. 2009. *Jungle Laboratories: Mexican Peasants, National Projects, and the Making of the Pill*. Durham, NC: Duke University Press.

Soto Laveaga, Gabriela. 2010. "Searching for Molecules, Finding Rebellion: Echeverría's 'Arriba y Adelante' Populism in Southeastern Mexico." In *Populism in Twentieth Century Mexico: The Presidencies of Lázaro Cárdenas and Luis Echeverría*, edited by Amelia Kiddle and Maria Muñoz, 87–105. Tucson: University of Arizona Press

Steinijans, V. W., and D. Hauschke. 1993. "International Harmonization of Regulatory Bioequivalence Requirements." *Clinical Research and Regulatory Affairs* 10 (4): 203–20. http://doi.org.10.1177/009286159502900326.

Stengers, Isabelle. 2005. "A Cosmopolitical Proposal." In *Making Things Public: Atmospheres of Democracy*, edited by Bruno Latour and Peter Weibel, 994–1003. Cambridge, MA: MIT Press.

Stengers, Isabelle. 2010. *Cosmopolitics I*. Translated by Robert Bononno. Minneapolis: University of Minnesota Press.

Stengers, Isabelle, and Philippe Pignarre. 2011. *Capitalist Sorcery: Breaking the Spell*. Translated by Andrew Goffey. New York: Palgrave Macmillan.

Sunder Rajan, Kaushik. 2006. *Biocapital: The Constitution of Postgenomic Life*. Durham, NC: Duke University Press.

Sunder Rajan, Kaushik. 2011. "Property, Rights, and the Constitution of Contemporary Indian Biomedicine: Notes from the Gleevec Case." *Social Research* 78 (3): 975–98.

Sunder Rajan, Kaushik. 2017. *Pharmocracy: Value, Politics and Knowledge in Global Medicine*. Durham, NC: Duke University Press.

Sutter, Mary. 1998. "US Drugmakers Fear Generics Law in Mexico: Brand-Name Drugs Considered at Risk." *Journal of Commerce*, March 2. Archived at http://lists.healthnet.org/archive/html/e-drug/1998-03/msg00001.html.

Taussig, Michael. 1993. *Mimesis and Alterity: A Particular History of the Senses*. New York: Routledge.

Tichenor, Marlee. 2017. "Data Performativity, Performing Health Work: Malaria and Labor in Senegal." *Medical Anthropology* 36 (5): 436–48.

Tichenor, Marlee, and Devi Sridhar. 2017. "Universal Health Coverage, Health Systems Strengthening, and the World Bank." *British Medical Journal* 3347:358–70. http://doi.org.10.1136/bmj.j3347.

Tobar, Federico. 2004. "Políticas para promoción del acceso a medicamentos: El caso del programa remediar de Argentina." Technical paper 002/2004 presented to the Interamerican Development Bank, Washington, DC.

Tobar, Federico, and Lucas Godoy Garraza. 2003. "Políticas para mejorar el acceso a los medicamentos: Nota desde el caso argentino." In *Políticas farmaceuticas y estudios de actualizacion de medicamentos en Latinoamerica*, edited by José F. Rivas Vilchis and Raul Molina Salazar, 27–40. Mexico City: Organización Mundial de la Salud Fundación Oswaldo Cruz/Universidad Autónoma Metropolitana-Iztapalapa.

Tobbell, Dominique. 2012. *Pills, Power, and Policy: The Struggle for Drug Reform in Cold War America and Its Consequences*. Berkeley: University of California Press.

Tucker, Robert C., ed. 1978. *The Marx-Engels Reader*. New York: W. W. Norton.

Unite for Site. n.d. "Health Spending at the Base of the Pyramid." Accessed April 6, 2022. http://www.uniteforsight.org/global-health-university/health-spending#:~:text=The%20measured%20base%20of%20the,billion%20of%20the%20world's%20population.

Universities Allied for Essential Medicines. n.d. "Alternative R&D Model." Accessed April 3, 2022. https://www.uaem.org/alternative_rd.

US Department of Commerce. 2004. *Pharmaceutical Price Controls in OECD Countries: Implications for U.S. Consumers, Pricing, Research and Development, and Innovation*. Washington, DC: International Trade Administration.

US Food and Drug Administration. 2021. "Generic Drug Facts." October 22. https://www.fda.gov/drugs/generic-drugs/generic-drug-facts.

US Food and Drug Administration. 2012. "FDA Issues Draft Guidelines on Biosimilar Development." February 9. http://www.fda.gov/newsevents/newsroom/pressannouncements/ucm291232.htm.

van der Geest, Sjaak, and Susan Reynolds Whyte, eds. 1988. *The Context of Medicines in Developing Countries: Studies in Pharmaceutical Anthropology*. Amsterdam: Het Spinhuis.

van der Geest, Sjaak, Susan Reynolds Whyte, and Anita Hardon. 1996. "The Anthropology of Pharmaceuticals: A Biographical Approach." *Annual Review of Anthropology* 25:153–78. http://doi.org.10.1146/annurev.anthro.25.1.153.

Vargas, Eduardo Viana. 2010. "Tarde on Drugs, or Measures against Suicide." In *The Social after Gabriel Tarde: Debates and Assessments*, edited by Matei Candea, 208–29. New York: Routledge.

Varsky, Carlos. 2002. "No alcanza con recetar genéricos." *Ambiente Ecolígico* 85. http://www.ambiente-ecologico.com/ediciones/2002/085_09.2002/085_Opinion_AntonioBrailovsky.php3.

Vasallo, Carlos, and Rodrigo Falbo. 2007. "Estructura de la oferta y política de medicamentos." In *Política de medicamentos en Argentina*, edited by G. Ventura and L. Godoy Garraza, 49–82. Buenos Aires: Comisión Nacional de la Salud Investiga-Ministerio de Salud de la Nación.

Verdusco, Mario Alberto. 2020. "Da gobierno $18 mil 455 mdp menos los estados." *El Universal*, July 15. https://www.eluniversal.com.mx/nacion/recorta-la-4t-18-mil-millones-los-estados.

Wirtz, Veronika J., Yared Santa-Ana-Tellez, Edson Servan-Mori, and Leticia Avila-Burgos. 2012. "Heterogeneous Effects of Health Insurance on Out-of-Pocket Expenditure on Medicines in Mexico." *Value in Health* 15 (5): 593–603. http://doi.org10.1016/j.jva1.2012.01.006.

Wong, Winnie. 2014. *Van Gogh on Demand: China and the Readymade*. Chicago: University of Chicago Press.

World Bank. 2008. *Reaching the Poor with Health Services: Mexico*. Report 43057, World Bank and the World Health Organization. http://www-wds .worldbank.org/external/default/WDSContentServer/WDSP/IB/2008/03/25 /000333038_20080325055335/Rendered/PDF/430570BRI0ENGL10Box3273 44B01PUBLIC1.pdf.

World Bank. 2012. *Mexico's System for Social Protection in Health and the Formal Sector*. Report 76736, Human Development Department, Latin America and the Caribbean Regional Office. https://documents1.worldbank.org/curated/en /706101468287156360/pdf/767360ESW0whit000Labor0Market0final.pdf.

World Health Organization. 1998. *The Role of the Pharmacist in Self-Care and Self-Medication: Report of the 4th WHO Consultative Group on the Role of the Pharmacist*. The Hague: World Health Organization. https://apps.who .int/iris/handle/10665/65860.

World Health Organization. 2005. "Multisource (Generic) Pharmaceutical Products: Guidelines on Registration Requirements to Establish Interchangeability 7." Working Document, Qas/04.093/Rev. 4. Geneva, Switzerland: World Health Organization.

World Health Organization. n.d. "Health Products and Policy Standards." Accessed April 3, 2022. https://www.who.int/teams/health-product-and -policy-standards/inn/.

World Trade Organization. 2001. "Declaration on the TRIPS Agreement and Public Health." November 14. https://www.wto.org/english/thewto_e /minist_e/min01_e/mindecl_trips_e.htm.

Yates, Rob. 2009. "Universal Health Care and the Removal of User Fees." *Lancet* 373 (9680): 2078–81.

Yu, Nancy L., Zachary Helms, and Peter B. Bach. 2017. "R&D Costs for Pharmaceutical Companies Do Not Explain Elevated US Drug Prices." *Health Affairs*, March 7. https://www.healthaffairs.org/do/10.1377/hblog20170307 .059036/full/.

Yúdice, George. 2001. "From Hybridity to Policy: For a Purposeful Cultural Studies." In *Consumers and Citizens: Globalization and Multicultural Conflicts*, edited by N. García Canclini, ix–xxxviii. Minneapolis: University of Minnesota Press.

Zahl, Adrian. 2016. *International Pharmaceutical Law and Practice*. New York: LexisNexis.

Index

absorption, and bioequivalence (bioavailability), 48, 59–62
abundance, 5, 7; categorical, 14–15, 35–40; and deregulation, 145, 176–77
active ingredient (compound, substance): and chemical arbitrage, 47–48; and generic substitution, 8, 31; inactive ingredients, relation to, 56–59; and manufacturing copied medicines, 56–58, 190; in regulatory definitions of generic medicines, 54, 186. *See also* chemical equivalence; *paleta de limón*
Administración Nacional de Medicamentos, Alimentos y Tecnología Médica (Argentina). *See* ANMAT
Adorno, Theodor W., 182
Affordable Care Act (United States), 75
Amlo. *See* López Obrador, Andrés Manuel
ANMAT (Administración Nacional de Medicamentos, Alimentos y Tecnología Médica, or National Administration for Drugs, Foods and Medical Devices, Argentina), 132
antiretroviral medicines: bioequivalence requirement for (Argentina), 53, 127–28; Brazilian state policies for, 211n6; HIV/AIDS treatment activism and, 11, 202n9; reverse engineering and, 34, 57–58, 191, 207n36
Argentine economic crisis (2001–2002): and Farmacias del Dr. Simi and Dr. Ahorro, 107, 120; as health care crisis, 109, 210n2; and names that come and go, 124
austerity, 22, 198, 199

bad copy. *See* copy
Bagó, 122
base of the pyramid (BOP), 162–67; and experimentalization of health, 147, 213n17, 214n18

Baudrillard, Jean: and generic commodity as spectacular, 16–17, 194, 203n17; and political subjectivity, 215n8; and politics as spectacle, 85
Bayer, 122
Biehl, João, 73, 202n11, 211n6
Big Pharma. *See* transnational pharmaceutical industry
bioavailability: and bioequivalence, 59–63, 207n39; and inactive ingredients, 56; and reverse engineering, 207n36; variations within the same medicine, 67–68. *See also* bioequivalence
biobetters, 192–94. *See also* biosimilars
bioequivalence: in Argentina, 126–29; and Farmacias Similares, 53–54; and Interchangeable Generics (Mexico), 37, 40, 184, 214n2; and international harmonization, 49–56, 203n16; and Mexican regulations on, 8, 36–38, 145–54, 206nn27–28; and "postcolonial dreams of equivalence," 206n33; testing for, 59–68, 207nn39–40, 208n48
biological pharmaceuticals. *See* biosimilars
biosimilars (biosimilarity), 27, 182; versus biobetters, 192–94; as biocomparables (Mexico), 189; and biological pharmaceuticals, 186, 188–94; and Probiomed (Mexico), 186, 189, 191, 194; and regulatory definitions, 188–89, 214n7
biotechnology companies (biotech): Amgen, 188; and biological pharmaceuticals, 186–88, 190–93, 214n8; Genentech, 187–88, 190; Probiomed, 186, 189, 191, 194. *See also* biosimilars
BOP. *See* base of the pyramid
Borges, Jorge Luís, 193–94
bottom billion. *See* base of the pyramid

bottom of the pyramid. *See* base of the pyramid
brand (brand name): and Argentine *copias* (copies), 114, 117; and biobetters 192–94; and distinction in context of mass production, 42–44, 182–84; and generic prescription decree, Argentina, 109–10; and generic prescription decree, Mexico, 8, 29, 31; hierarchies of copied drugs (Argentina) and, 125–35; quality or "qualification" of products and, 155, 183–85; relation between kind and, 214–15n8; relation to drug patents (Argentina) and, 119; Similares as, 37–38, 69, 183–84; the spectacular and, 17, 203n17
branded (company-branded) generics, 181, 185
Brazil: and civic inequivalence, 94; generic market expansion in, 13; and HIV/AIDS medicines, 11, 211n6; and import substitution industrialization, 21; and judicialization, 73, 148; and public pharmaceutical laboratories, 113, 122; and reverse engineering, 58, 191, 202n11, 207n36, 211n11; and "similar" as regulatory category, 38, 52, 129, 205n9; "turn to the left," 7, 208n14

Calderón, Felix, 87, 91
cancer: and biological pharmaceuticals, 186–87, 199–200; and Gleevec case (India) 63; and shortage of pediatric cancer medicines (Mexico), 199–200
CANIFARMA (Cámara Nacional de la Industria Farmacéutica), 33
care: in generics pharmacies, 92–95, 177; and physicians' incentives ("*Que queden bien*"), 175–76; and self-medication, 164–67; as solidarity in Simipolitics, 22, 25, 73, 102–3
Cassier, Maurice, 56, 58, 207n36, 211n11
Catholic Church, 23, 31, 78–79
chemical arbitrage, 47–48, 206n33. *See also* Peterson, Kristin
chemical equivalence: and lime popsicle poster, 31; regulatory relation to bioequivalence, 49–57, 62, 90, 205n9, 208n48; as standard for generics in Mexican public sector, 36
chemistry: antireductionism in, 34, 47; biochemistry and bioequivalence, 56, 58; and chemical turn in STS, 34, 205n8; Marx and, 32, 204n1
China: and Chinese traditional medicine, 16, 213n17; global politics of the copy and, 115, 150; and informal vendors (Mexico), 42; as source of active pharmaceutical ingredients, 57, 159
clientelism: and Dr. Simi, 73, 77, 79–80; Farmacias Similares employment and, 86–87; twentieth-century PRIista state and, 162
clinic. *See consultorios*
clinical trials (drug trials): globalization of, 12, 203n15; patent protection duration and, 117; postmarketing surveillance and, 156, 213n11
COFEPRIS (Comisión Federal para la Protección contra Riesgos Sanitarios, or Federal Commission for Protection against Health Risks, Mexico): access politics of, 149–50, 165, 185; bioequivalence testing requirements of, 152; and definition of generic medicines, 54, 214n2; "irrelevance" of, 154
Cohen, Lawrence, 121, 211n14
Comaroff, Jean, 88, 208–9n14
Comisión Federal para la Protección contra Riesgos Sanitarios. *See* COFEPRIS
commodity (commodity form): equivalence and, 33, 37; fictitious, 212n31; forestalling of, 181–82, 188, 191, 194–96; generics as pharmaceutical's commodity form, 5, 16–18, 33, 35, 37, 55, 68–70, 109, 133, 143, 203n17; import substitution industrialization and, 21; Marx and, 32
company-branded generics. *See* branded generics
consultorios (generics clinics): consumer testing of, 157; physicians' employment in, 168, 170–71, 173–76, 197; versus private clinics, 146; and self-medication, 160, 166; Similares counseling center, 84; as substitutes for the state, 24–25, 72, 92
consumers, as citizens, 73, 86, 168. *See also* care; Simipolitics
consumption. *See* base of the pyramid; neoliberal; Simipolitics
copy (copies): Argentine *copias* (*copista* industry), 53, 113–14, 127–33, 141, 182; biological pharmaceuticals and, 186, 188–94; domestic, 20–22; generic proliferations and, 14–15, 36–38; good/bad or proper/improper, 15, 111, 118, 121, 128–29; harmonization and, 49–50, 52, 54–55; intellectual property regimes and, 113–19; inventive, 191; the political as, 73, 76; the spectacular and, 17–18; theories of populism and, 19–20, 76. *See also* reverse engineering
corn, 79

Correa, Marilena, 56, 58, 207n36, 211n11
counterfeit, 12, 118, 179–80. *See also* fake
COVID-19 (novel coronavirus), vii, 103, 186, 197–98
Craddock, Susan, 202n14
crowd: and the consumer market, 26; crowdsourcing, 155; and Simipolitics, 72–73, 81–82, 86–89; and theories of populism, 19–20, 76, 203n20

da Costa Marques, Ivan, 191, 207n37
Das, Ranendra K., 161
Das, Veena, 161
data exclusivity, 12, 51, 181
Debord, Guy, 16–17, 203n17
de la Peña, Guillermo, 80, 86–87, 174
diabetes, 93, 108, 210n2. *See also* insulin
doctor(s). *See* physician(s)
Dr. Ahorro. *See* González Torres, Javier
Dr. Simi. *See* González Torres, Víctor
droguerías (Argentina), 137, 210n2. See also *obras sociales*
drug trials. *See* clinical trials
Dumit, Joseph (Joe), 12, 203n15, 206n29, 212n32
Duncan, 122

Echeverría, Luís, 21–22
Ecks, Stefan, 12, 63, 187
Ecological Green Party of Mexico (PVEM), 77, 100–101
Elyachar, Julia, 163, 213n17
employment: clientelism and, 84, 86, 90, 98; generics pharmacies as sources of, 167–76; social insurance and, 6, 74, 130. *See also* labor
enalapril: *copias* of (Argentina), 114; and Dr. Simi's version of, 158
equivalence, puzzle of, 29–34, 55, 57. *See also* bioequivalence; chemical equivalence; commodity; fungibility
escitalopram, 178–82, 185–86, 214n2
expansions of state and market, 7
experiment (experimentalization): and base of the pyramid, 147, 213n17, 214n18; and experimental subjects, 12, 156–57; of health as consumption, 213–14n17
evergreen(ing), 63, 181, 195

fake, 115, 156, 179. *See also* counterfeit
Farmacias del Ahorro, 77, 101; in Argentina, 106–8, 123–25, 134, 139–42, 170. *See also* González Torres, Javier
Farmanguinhos, 58, 207n36

FDA (Food and Drug Administration), United States: and bioequivalence definition, 54, 60–62; and biosimilars approval, 188, 214n7; statistical understanding of quality control, 65, 207n42
Federal Commission for Protection against Health Risk (Mexico). *See* COFEPRIS
Foundation Best. *See* Fundación BEST
Fox, Vicente, 8, 23, 49, 74, 76, 96, 204n24. *See also* Seguro Popular
Franklin, Sarah, 208n50
franchise: and Farmacias Similares, 2, 80, 169, 174–75, 177; and proliferation of generics pharmacies, 16, 170
Frenk, Julio, 8, 74–75, 81–82, 96, 98, 102
Fundación BEST (Foundation Best), 79–80, 175. *See also* González Torres, Víctor
fungibility: of names, 119, 124; and the pharmaceutical's commodity form, 15, 7, 33, 56, 69–70, 182, 192; in pharmapolitics, 105, 109, 143

Gago, Verónica, 7, 201n4, 201–2n6, 210n32
GATT (General Agreement on Tariffs and Trade), 115–16
General Agreement on Tariffs and Trade. *See* GATT
generic substitution: in Argentina, 108–13, 133–34; and biosimilars, 188–94; decree in Mexico, 8; as foundation for access, 7; as market principle, 30–31, 69. *See also* substitute (substitution)
GI (*genérico intercambiable*, or interchangeable generic): and doubts about, 151–53, 179–80, 206n28; and Dr. Simi, 82; GI symbol (*logosímbolo*), 180, 184–85; as pharmacy name, 41; as regulatory category, 14, 35–37, 46, 49, 214n2. *See also* bioequivalence
GMP (good manufacturing practice), 58, 128; and chemical equivalence, 36; and statistical quality control, 65–66, 207n42. *See also* regulation, of manufacturing and quality control
González García, Ginés (Argentina), 109, 114–15, 120–21, 124–26, 193
González Torres, Javier (Dr. Ahorro, Farmacias del Ahorro), 41, 77, 101, 184; in Argentina, 106–10, 125, 134, 139–42
González Torres, Víctor (Dr. Simi): in Argentina, 106–8, 124–25, 134, 136, 139–42; attacks on Mexican public health institutions by, 24, 81–82, 102; background, 77–78;

González Torres, Víctor (*continued*) and base of the pyramid (BOP), 163; as candidate for president, 82–87; critiques of, 2, 47, 146; and the Ecological Green Party of Mexico (PVEM), 77–78, 100–101; emergence of, 1–5; and health clinics, 24–25; and pharmapolitics (Simipolitics), 19–22, 24, 71–73, 77–81, 90–92, 102–5, 168; as regulator, 158–59; and *similares* as kind, 38–44; and the Simi Seguro, 24, 95–96; and theories of populism, 87–92. *See also* Simipolitics

good copy. *See* copy

Good Manufacturing Practice. *See* GMP

Guevara, Che, 71, 90

Guyer, Jane, 69, 134–35, 137, 155–56, 212n31

Haraway, Donna, 194, 214–15n8

health insurance. *See* IMSS; INSABI; ISSSTE; *obras sociales*; Programa Remediar; Seguro Popular Simipolitics; Sistema Similar de Seguros

HIV/AIDS, 10–11, 157, 202n9, 202n12

Hoffmann, Roald, 25, 34

Homedes, Núria, 15

homeopathic medicine, 46, 206n21

Horkheimer, Max, 182

hypertension, 65, 158. *See also* enalapril

import substitution industrialization (ISI), 20–21, 23, 72. *See also* substitute; protectionism

improper copy. *See* copy

IMSS (Instituto Mexicano de Seguridad Social, or Seguro Social): Andrés Manuel López Obrador and, 199, and inclusions/exclusions, 6, 74–75, 209n16; and medication shortages, 74, 92; and physician training and employment, 172; as purchaser of generic medicines, 37–38, 50, 52, 77, 78; and relation to generics pharmacies, 24–25, 72, 79, 81–82, 92–95, 100–102, 147, 197; scope of services, 208n3

inactive ingredient, 56–58, 65, 190, 214n7. *See also* active ingredient

India: and company-branded generics, 180; and de-duplication, 211n14; and Dr. Reddy's, 192; and Gleevec case 63; and global pharmaceutical politics, 11–12, 63, 202n9; and self-medication, 161

INSABI (Institute for Health and Well-being). *See* López Obrador, Andrés Manuel

Instituto Mexicano de Seguridad y Servicios Sociales de los Trabajadores del Estado (Mexico). *See* ISSSTE

insulin, vii, 5; and Argentine economic crisis of 2001–2002, 109, 210n2; and biological pharmaceuticals, 186. *See also* diabetes

intellectual property (IP): and biological pharmaceuticals, 190–91; and brand distinction, 44, 133, 214n8; generic medicines as product of, 112, 113–19, 129; and 1990s trade agreements, 10–12; and postpatent markets, 15, 51, 69. *See also* data exclusivity; patent; reverse engineering; trademark

intercambiables (interchangeables). *See* GI

interchangeability: bioequivalence and, 60, 207n40; and biological pharmaceuticals, 187; in chemistry, 34, 204n1; in definition of generic as commodity, 17–20, 69, 195; as distinction, 40–41, 55; and liberal citizenship, 89–90, 94; in mass production, 65–66; and nation-state 134. *See also* commodity

interchangeable generic. *See* GI

international nonproprietary name (INN), 121, 193

ISSSTE (Instituto Mexicano de Seguridad y Servicios Sociales de los Trabajadores del Estado): Andres Manuel López Obrador and, 103, 199; and González Torres family, 77; and inclusion/exclusion, 6, 74; as purchaser of generic medicines, 50; and relation to generics pharmacies, 24–25, 95–96, 197. *See also* IMSS

Johnson and Johnson, on rationale for high drug costs, 135

judicialization, 73, 148

Kapczynski, Amy, 63

Kirchner, Néstor, 7, 201n4, 210n32; as "Dr. K.," 125. *See also* Ginés González, García

Kleinman, Arthur, 202n13

labor: informalization of, 6, 36. *See also* IMSS; Simipolitics

Laboratorios Best, 37, 158, 183. *See also* González Torres, Víctor

Laclau, Ernesto, 87–90

Leslie, Esther, 204n1

Lexapro, 178

lime popsicle. See *paleta de limón*

Lomnitz, Claudio (Lomnitz-Adler, Claudio), 82, 162
lo nuestro ("what is ours"). See *nuestro, lo*
López Obrador, Andrés Manuel (AMLO, or Amlo): and the Fourth Transformation (4T), 22, 198–99; and "populism" 209n15, 215n1; and presidential elections, 87, 91, 204n24; and the Seguro Popular, 103, 197–200
Lury, Celia, 155, 183

Mahaffey, Erin, 214n19
manufacturing: and interchangeability, 65–66; relation to brand and trademark, 182; as source of distinction, 35–36, 182, 186–188. *See also* biosimilars; GMP (Good Manufacturing Practice)
Marx, Karl, 4, 16, 32, 134, 203n18, 204n1, 205n7
medicinal plants, 46
Mendoza, Daryl, 203n17, 215n8
Menem, Carlos, 112, 116, 130
Merck (Merck Sharp & Dohme), 65, 114, 122, 207n36
Mexican Revolution, 23, 198
molecule (therapeutic molecule): biological, 187, 189; not self-identical, 34, 204n1; and pharmaceutical patents, 11, 56, 117–18, 181, 202n7. *See also* active ingredient; chemistry; evergreen(ing)
Molina Salazar, Raúl Enrique, 8, 101, 164
monopoly. *See* patent
Movimiento Nacional contra la Corrupción. *See* National Movement against Corruption
Murphy, M., 147, 205n8, 213n10

NAFTA (North American Free Trade Agreement): and harmonization of generic regulations, 37, 50–55, 64, 203n16; and intellectual property regimes, 10, 15; "opening" of protected markets, 22–23, 76, 79, 104; and pharmaceutical prices in Mexico, 6–7
National Administration of Drugs, Foods and Medical Devices. *See* ANMAT
nationalism, viii, 20–21, 88, 134, 198
National Movement against Corruption (Movimiento Nacional contra la Corrupción, MNA), 24, 81. *See also* Víctor González Torres
neoliberal (neoliberalism): decentralization and, 101; generics as, 108–10, 133, 142; peculiar abundances and, 201n6; state responses to, 7, 22, 72–73, 105, 113, 198, 201n4

Novartis: and Brazilian reverse-engineering, 191; and Indian Gleevec case, 63; Sandoz as generics division of, 180–83. *See also* Sandoz
nuestro, lo, 21–22, 198. *See also* López Obrador, Andres Manuel

obras sociales, 124, 130, 137–39, 142
off-patent. *See* patent(s)
original(s): copy and, 26, 110–11, 117, 127; copies without, 17–18; irrelevance of, 119; variability within, 35, 48. *See also* intellectual property; patents

paleta de limón (lime popsicle), 14, 30–32, 36, 38, 44, 46–47, 54, 56, 110
PAN (Partido Acción Nacional), 23, 74, 76, 79–80, 87, 91, 96, 145. *See also* Fox, Vicente
Panizza, Francisco, 89
Partido Nacional Revolucionario (Institutional Revolutionary Party). *See* PRI
Partido Revolucionario Democrático (PRD). *See* Andrés Manuel López Obrador
patent (patents): and biological pharmaceuticals, 193, 198; decoupled from brand name, 119; and generics as "off-patent" medicines, 2, 119, 150, 195; postpatent analytic, 12–13, 49–50; and reverse engineering, 58, 119. *See also* intellectual property
Pemex (Petróleos Mexicanos), 6, 74, 198
Peña Nieto, Enrique, 100, 150
Perón, Eva, 80, 134, 208n6
Peronism, 89, 112, 113, 130
Peterson, Kristin (Kris), 205n6; on chemical arbitrage, 47; on discernment of quality, 155–56; on permanent monopoly, 13; on "postcolonial dreams of equivalence," 31, 55, 206n33
Petryna, Adriana, 12, 73, 202n13, 203n15
Pfizer, vi, 180
pharmaceutical clinical trials. *See* clinical trials
Pharmaceutical Manufacturers Association. *See* PhRMA
pharmakon, 71–72, 91, 105, 203–4n21, 205n4. *See also* Stengers, Isabelle
pharmapolitics (pharmapolitical), Andres Manuel López Obrador, and, 199–200; defined, 3–5, 11–13, 18–20; and generics in Argentina, 133, 143; as Simipolitics, 73, 75–76, 82, 104–5

PhRMA (Pharmaceutical Research and Manufacturers of America; formerly the Pharmaceutical Manufacturers Association), 51, 195, 211n8
physicians (doctors): authorization/testing of, 146, 157, 177; and generics pharmacy clinics, 24–25, 92–95, 104, 147, 170–76, 197, 102; and prescription practice, 8, 110, 113, 117, 121–23, 136; in public sector, 26, 72, 92–95; and self-medication, 160, 176; and trust in generics, 29, 44–46, 48, 61, 158
piracy, 12, 16, 112, 115, 118, 127, 191, 211n8
Pisa, 199
Polanyi, Karl, 151, 212n31
Pollock, Anne, 202n14
populism (populist), 4–5, 19–20, 87–91, 197–200, 203n20. See also *nuestro*, *lo*
postmarketing surveillance. See clinical trials
postpatent. See patent
Prahalad, C. K., 163, 213n17
PRD (Partido Revolucionario Democrático). See López Obrador, Andrés Manuel
prescription: and antibiotics, 161; generic decree in Mexico, 8; law for prescription of drugs by generic name, Argentina, 109–10, 117, 120–21, 133, 143; versus nonprescription (over-the-counter) medicines, 162, 165; and self-medication, 160–61; and similars, 38, 44, 81; and *vales por medicinas* (Mexico), 99–100. See also physicians (doctors)
PRI (Partido Nacional Revolucionario, or Institutional Revolutionary Party), 7–8, 22–23, 73, 76, 79–80, 84, 87, 100, 145, 162, 178, 204n14. See also clientelism; neoliberalism
privatization: and commodity, 17; and neoliberalism, 22, 130; and public health systems, 74, 92, 101, 209n19
Probiomed, 186, 189, 191, 194
proper copy. See copy
Programa Remediar (Argentina), 109–10, 120, 139
protectionism: pharmaceutical "public good" (Argentina), 112, 114, 128, 141; and pharmaceuticals in the Global South, 10, 21–22; Simipolitics and, 104
puzzle of equivalence. See equivalence
pyramid. See base of the pyramid

quality: and brand names, 126, 130, 182, 184; debates over generic, 45, 61, 127–29, 180; as equivalence, 15, 33, 50, 53; and Farmacias Similares, 40, 48, 81, 146; of physicians, 160, 171; of public health care (Mexico), 97–99, 172, 209n17; and the regulatory (deregulatory) state, 147, 152–60, 177, 185; as statistical property, 207n43; and trust in institutions, 132–33, 145
quality control. See GMP; manufacturing

regulation: of biosimilars, 188–89; and deregulatory state, 22, 116, 150–60, 176–77; Dr. Simi as agent of, 84; efficacy of, 131–32, 154, 184–86; generic medicines, Mexican regulations on, 8, 35–37; and harmonization of bioequivalence, 13, 49–55, 118, 128–29; of manufacturing and quality control (GMP), 64–66, 159; of pharmacies, 93, 141; and the right to copy (Argentina), 114
Renitec, 114
"return of the state" (Latin America), 7, 13, 104
reverse engineering: bioavailability and, 207n36; in generics manufacturing, 57; patents and, 58, 119; as "unlicensed" copying, 112, 119, 148, 191
rituximab, 186, 189. See also biosimilars
Rivera, Diego, 4, 83
Roemmers, 114, 122
Roy, Ananya, 163

safety. See GMP
"same and not the same": as chemical principle, 34, 204n1; in consumer markets, 15–16, 119; in Simipolitics, 73
samenesses that matter, 15, 35, 69, 195
Sanabria, Emilia, 94
Sánchez, Rafael, 19, 87, 89, 203n20
Sandoz: and biosimilars, 185–86, 189; and branded generics (Mexico), 194. See also Novartis
scarcity, 5, 13, 99, 105, 201n6
Schwartz, Frederic, 42–43, 182–83
Schwartz, Hillel, 43
Schwegler, Tara, 7, 74, 76, 208nn2–3
science studies. See STS
Seguro Popular, 96–101, 209n16; and base of the pyramid, 167; creation of, 8–9, 23, 74; dismantling of, 103, 198–99; and Simipolitics, 75–76, 102–3, 139, 162
Seguro Social. See IMSS
self-medication, 160–76; as consumer experiment, 146–47; and trust in brands, 181. See also base of the pyramid
Shewhart, Walter, 65–66, 207n42

Simicondón (Simi condom), 78–79, 84
similarity: and biosimilars, 188; as Dr. Simi's mark of distinction, 38, 69, 78, 205n16; in homeopathy, 206n21; and sameness, 48, 55; and theories of populism, 19–20, 89–90
similars (*similares*): as diminished copy, 46–48; as generic category associated with Farmacias Similares, 4, 14, 16, 37–44, 72, 183–84, 192; versus generics, 129, 152; as regulatory category in Brazil, 38, 52, 129, 205n9; versus *simylares*, 16, 38, 41, 152. *See also* biosimilars
Simipolitics (Simipolitical): and base of the pyramid, 167; and consumers as citizens, 73, 86, 168; and consumption as experimental terrain, 144, 147–48, 162; defined, 13, 25–26, 73–77, 197–200; and expansion of health care state, 102–5; and populism, 87–92. *See also* González Torres, Víctor; pharmapolitics
simulation, 4, 19, 82, 85, 91. *See also* Baudrillard, Jean
Sistema Similar de Seguros (el SimiSeguro, or SSS), 95. *See also* González Torres, Víctor
social contract, 6, 87
Soto Laveaga, Gabriela, 21
spectacular: as analytic, 16–19, 25, 68–70, 214–15n8; biological pharmaceuticals as, 182, 190–94; and commercial sphere, 40–44; and pharmapolitics (Simipolitics), 73, 78, 82, 89–90, 104; and violence, 204n24. *See also* brands; commodity
Stengers, Isabelle, 20, 32, 34, 68, 71, 91, 203–4n21, 205n4, 205n8. *See also* pharmakon
structural adjustment, 22, 155–56
STS (science and technology studies, or science studies), on authorization of quality, 129, 153, 207n43; chemical turn in, 34, 205n8; on deregulatory state, 213n10; on equivalence and standardization, 15, 60, 68, 208n46; the inventive copy and postcolonial/Latin American STS, 58, 191, 207n37
substitute (substitution), as analytic, 4, 7–13, 34–35, 78; and popular politics, 21–22; and Simipolitics, 82, 104, 197, 199–200; state as target of, 4, 25, 71–74. *See also* generic substitution
Sunder Rajan, Kaushik, 12, 63
supergenerics, 182, 191–92

Tarde, Gabriel, 61, 88
tercería (thirdness, or authorized third-party testing): bioequivalence testing, 59; deregulatory excess and, 177; dispersal of state regulatory functions and, 147, 154, 157, 159–60; insufficiency of (*que hicieramos tercería*), 153–54. *See also* experiment
Teva, 185, 194
Tobbell, Dominique, 208n48
trademark (trademark law), and manufacturing source as distinction, 180–84, 205n16. *See also* brand
trade secret, 56, 190. *See also* inactive ingredient; reverse engineering
transnational pharmaceutical industry (transnational laboratories): anthropology of, 11–12, 202n14; and bioequivalence, 50–55, 64, 67–68; Dr. Simi versus, 1–2; dominance in Mexico, 4–6; and global trade and access politics, 10–11, 115–16; HIV/AIDS medicines in Brazil, 211n6; opposition to new generics markets, 29, 33, 131–33; as purveyors of generic medicines, 177–91, 194; and rationale for high prices, 135–16. *See also specific companies*
Treble (trebling). *See* tercería
TRIPS (trade-related intellectual property provisions of NAFTA and the WTO), 10–12, 112, 116; TRIPS-plus provisions, 12. *See also* intellectual property

Ugalde, Antonio, 15
universal coverage (universal access, universal health care): and access to medicines, Brazil, 11; and access to medicines, Mexico, 100; competing models of, 103, 199, 213n17; Seguro Popular as example of, 9, 75, 95–99; and United States Affordable Care Act, 75. *See also* experiment; Frenk, Julio; Seguro Popular
Universidad Autónoma Metropolitana (Metropolitan Autonomous University, UAM), 173
Universidad Iberoamericana (Ibero-American University), 77
Universidad Nacional Autónoma de México (National Autonomous University of Mexico, UNAM), 63, 97, 171–72

vales (coupons) for medicines ("vales por medicinas"), 100–101

Venezuela: and Dr. Simi's expansion, 5; as petrostate, 198; and theories of populism, 19, 89, 203n20. *See also* Sánchez, Rafael

vitamins: as care, 93–94, 176

WHO (World Health Organization): and definition of generic medicine, 17, 69, 121, 128; and Julio Frenk, 81, 96; on responsible self-medication, 165–66

WTO (World Trade Organization): and bioequivalence requirement, 37, 64; and Doha Declaration exemption for public health, 202n10; and patent enforcement in the Global South, 10, 15, 112–13. *See also* intellectual property; NAFTA